anglistik & englischunterricht

British Drama of the 1990s

Annelie Knapp · Erwin Otto
Gerd Stratmann · Merle Tönnies (Hg.)

anglistik & englischunterricht

Band 64

British Drama of the 1990s

UNIVERSITÄTSVERLAG C. WINTER
HEIDELBERG

British Drama of the 1990s

Verantwortliche Herausgeber
für den thematischen Teil des Bandes:
Bernhard Reitz und Mark Berninger

UNIVERSITÄTSVERLAG C. WINTER
HEIDELBERG

Die Deutsche Bibliothek – CIP-Einheitsaufnahme

Ein Titeldatensatz für diese Publikation
ist bei der Deutschen Bibliothek erhältlich.

Herausgeber:
Prof. Dr. Annelie Knapp
Dr. Erwin Otto · Prof. Dr. Gerd Stratmann
Dr. Merle Tönnies

ISBN 3-8253-1375-1
ISSN 0344-8266

Imprimé en Allemagne · Printed in Germany
Satz: Fotosatz Behrens, 68723 Oftersheim
Druck: Strauss Offsetdruck GmbH, 69509 Mörlenbach

Gedruckt auf umweltfreundlichem, chlorfrei gebleichtem und alterungsbeständigem Papier

Den Verlag erreichen Sie im Internet unter: www.winter-verlag-hd.de

Contents

Bernhard Reitz / Mark Berninger, Mainz

Introduction

In the seventies, British theatre experienced a surge of enthusiasm. An expanding fringe generated a wealth of new talent, and at that time young playwrights such as David Hare declared self-confidently, "We can now command the standards we want, the style of presentation that we want".[1] The competitive eighties which were to follow not only put an early end to lunchtime theatres but eroded the fringe as a whole. Moreover, the decade was marked by the deep antagonism between Mrs Thatcher and the arts, an antagonism, however, which allowed politically committed playwrights to establish themselves as the conscience of the nation.

What then distinguishes the nineties? Of course, the forced resignation of the Iron Lady bereaved the political playwrights of their favourite target. However, in spite of Conservative cut-backs there is still a fringe, and although *Time Out* does not list fringe productions before the West End shows any longer, as it once did in the seventies, the fringe seems to have found a permanent niche in the theatrical set-up. Some of the playwrights who had emerged in the sixties and seventies, such as Edward Bond, greatly reduced if not ceased their output in the nineties, while other old hands such as Alan Bennett moved somewhat unexpectedly into the limelight or, like Howard Barker, continued to struggle on. Moreover, due to the enduring encouragement of the grant-aided theatres, most notably the Royal Court, as well as of private companies such as Max Stafford-Clark's Out of Joint, no less than previous decades the nineties had a reservoir of young dramatic talents, always ready to fill any gap in the playbill. During this decade, more than twenty new writers made a successful debut (cf. the paper by Aleks Sierz).

At first glance, the overall impression of continuity seems to be supported by statistics as well. In 1988, West End theatres[2] had a total attendance of 10.9 million; for 1998 the figures rose to 11.9 million. There was a slight decrease from 43 to 41 in the number of theatres open during that year, a larger decrease in the number of productions (from 228 down to 207), and a substantial reduction in the number of performances (16,018 in 1999 compared to 16,970 in 1988).[3] In view of the increase in attendance, which resulted in overall box-office takings of £ 257.9 million (an increase of £ 11.8 million compared to the previous year), the figures seem to give no cause for alarm. However, statistics not only underscore developments; they are also prone to levelling them as well, regardless of whether for good or bad.

During the nineties, the theatres received most welcome additional support from the National Lottery, the net earnings of which are to be spent on sponsorship. In 1995, the Arts Council of England distributed the first capital grant from the National Lottery Fund. Among the theatres which have received extra funding since then are the Royal Court, which underwent substantial renovations, provincial reps such as the Empire Theatre in Liverpool, which received money for the restoration of its neo-baroque ceiling, or the Royal Exchange Theatre in Manchester, which had been damaged severely by a bomb in 1996, and last but certainly not least the once famous Cambridge Arts Theatre. Even if most of the money which comes to the theatres from the National Lottery Fund is reserved for 'hardware improvements', the release of strain on the theatres' budgets should not be underestimated. Already in the days of Sir Peter Hall, the running costs of the National Theatre complex exceeded the annual Arts Council grant, and thereafter, the pressure of maintenance expenses has further increased all over theatreland.

Both the Royal Shakespeare Company and the now equally 'Royal' National Theatre are expected to cover more than half their budgets by box-office takings or by sponsorship. The Royal National manages an average of 36 per cent at the box office, a figure which would make any German city councillor for the arts weep for joy, because average box-office takings in Germany hover between meagre 10–15 per cent. However, as there are no city councils in Britain which, albeit grudgingly, cover deficits out of the community's tax-bill, the pressure on British theatres to meet the demands of the budget is much higher and enforces artistic compromises. If the successful RSC transfer of *Les Miserables* to the West End ensured the company an additional revenue of £ 1.000.000 *per annum*,[4] why should the Royal National not follow up and produce *My Fair Lady*, as it did to the chagrin of many critics in 2001?

While German directors still would presumably tar and feather Trevor Nunn for his claim "Surely the only thing that is not permissible these days is to lose the audience",[5] a remarkable statement from a director of the Royal National Theatre (Nunn was succeeded by Nicholas Hytner in 2001), their British colleagues seem to have accepted the notion that theatres have to earn the greater part of the money they spend. However, this is not a triumph of the West End over the grant-aided theatres, but a belated victory of Mrs Thatcher's monetaristic convictions. After Mrs Thatcher had been elected to government in 1979, the Trade Unions and the deregulation of British economy were of more immediate concern than the arts. Moreover, in view of the enmity between the Prime Minister and Britain's leading artists, most notably among these the playwrights, and in spite of the occasional outbreaks of individual conservative MPs against the public funding of "agitation", Mrs Thatcher's successive governments were very wary about giving the impression that they would use their grants-policy as a means of censorship. The subsidies for fringe companies were cut back heavily, but the large grant-aided theatres were left more or less unscathed. It was as late as 1987 that the Conservatives decided to apply their economic convictions to the public funding of the arts as well. The Conservative manifesto *The Arts: The Next Move Forward. A Plurality of Riches: A Plurality of Funding* defined "arts organisations" as "businesses" in a competitive market and demanded that these "businesses" should "increase their turnover by 'getting out there and selling'".[6]

Everyone in the arts, including the critics, denounced the manifesto as an attempt to cut the jugular of culture in Britain, but it also allowed the theatres, including the grant-aided ones, to make the unpopular move of raising their ticket-prices and to excuse this by pointing to the government. More morally scrupulous theatres such as the Royal Court tried to provide some compensation. The Royal Court now offers a preview night of its new productions for students at which all tickets are sold for 50p. However, such fig-leaves cannot cover the fact that ticket prices have risen considerably during the nineties. For students there are still affordable stand-by tickets and senior citizens can rely on a considerable reduction as well. Against the background of lower-middle-class incomes, a much bleaker scenario does emerge however. 'A good night out' for two in stall seats can easily exceed £ 50 for tickets only, and this drastically reduces the number of those who can afford such expenses regularly. In the light of this it is important to know that much of the statistical increase in ticket sales mentioned above is due to tourism, a taste the West End has catered for by producing more and more musicals. In the summer of 2001, 24 of the 51 theatres which belong to The Society of London Theatre showed musicals, with the standard Lloyd-Webber-fare of *Cats*, *Starlight Express* and *The Phantom of the Opera* being replenished by revivals of old favourites such as Rodgers' and Hammerstein's *The King and I*.

There are indications however that the price-spiral may have come to a stop. Even for the musicals, which for years boasted that they were sold out for months beforehand if not longer, an increasing amount of tickets has become available at London's half-price ticket-booths. However, it seems that the damage has already been done. Although Arnold Wesker's dream of the working classes crowding the theatres has never been realistic, during the sixties, the seventies, and even in the eighties, theatres attracted a considerable number of younger people. Now, however, any interval at one of London's theatres, whether grant-aided or not, underscores the impression that the educated, comparatively well-to-do middle class is back in what it has always believed to be its rightful place. The playbills could not remain unaffected by this. The successful revival of plays as dated as Priestley's *An Inspector Calls* is evidence for Aunt Edna's, Terence Rattigan's archetypal incarnation of the middle-class theatregoer, triumphant return to the stalls. In the nineties, neither the centennial of Oscar Wilde's rise to the top of popularity with audiences, nor his subsequent fall, could be neglected. With few notable exceptions such as Nicholas Hytner's production of *The Importance of Being Earnest* at the National Theatre in 1993, not only the West End welcomed this occasion to present Wilde once more as the playwright who seemingly invented 'Ibsen Light' to be consumed by audiences who, like Aunt Edna, expected 'a little moral uplift' from their evening at the theatre.

In view of these developments, the statistical evidence for the decade between 1988 and 1998 could be interpreted as a consolidation at a high level, or even as stagnation. However, the new writing is evidence that there was a countermovement as well. This volume attempts to show that statistics alone cannot do justice to British theatre in the nineties, and that in spite of the commercialisation described, decisive changes took place.

When Margaret Thatcher won her third consecutive election in 1987, the *Sun* showed her picture under the headline '1997', implying that she would remain in power for the decade to come. Though by no means unexpected, her victory was another blow to the political playwrights who, supported by the subsidised theatres, had since 1979 exposed her politics and philosophy at home and abroad as inhuman and as outrightly 'evil'.[7] However, instead of surrendering, the political playwrights increased their scrutiny of Thatcherism. David Hare began his trilogy *Racing Demon* (1990), *Murmuring Judges* (1991) and *Absence of War* (1993); unquestionably the most ambitious project within his own work as well as among contemporary playwriting, inspired by the will to resist the ongoing Conservative roll-back. However, rather than attacking Mrs Thatcher directly once again, portraying her as a monster, Hare pointed to the dominantly conservative mentality of the Anglican church, the Law and the political system, of which the Iron Lady in all her limitations was shown to be rather an emanation than the mastermind.

When the trilogy was well under way, the Prime Minister resigned. Hare completed his project, but in retrospect his further work during the nineties is indicative of the limbo in which the political playwrights suddenly felt themselves cast. John Major was also a Conservative, but should his efforts to give Thatcherism a human face be criticised just as relentlessly? The notion that the resistance against Thatcherism had achieved its purpose became even more widespread when, in March 1997, Rupert Murdoch's most influential paper declared in a blazing headline, 'THE SUN BACKS BLAIR'. Even if some of the political playwrights distrusted Blair from the very beginning, recognising in his 'New Labour' and 'the Third Way' the 'Feel-Good-Thatcherism' which Blair was going to practise after his election, there was a tacit understanding that after nearly 18 years of Conservative rule Labour should be given the benefit of the doubt.

Blair's landslide victory left the political playwrights in a dead end. In *Skylight* (1995), Hare relinquished politics in favour of the 'gentler matters of life, love and circumstance' as advertised on the cover. *Amy's View*, which premièred in 1997, wove the then topical issue of Lloyds underwriters facing ruin into the plot, but – not only in the star role it provided for Dame Judi Dench – the mother-daughter conflict which is central to the play is well-made play and brilliant only in its conventionality. *The Blue Room* (1998), Hare's adaptation of Schnitzler's *Der Reigen*, advertised as 'sheer theatrical viagra' became a box-office hit, not because of its merits as a play, but because it allowed all of London's punters a brief glimpse of Nicole Kidman in her birthday suit. By contrast, Hare's more ambitious *The Judas Kiss* of the same year, flopped. His attempt to blame an immature and egoistical young Lord Alfred Douglas for Wilde's downfall convinced neither audiences nor critics.

Hare's plays after 'New Labour' expose a constitutive element of his playwriting, which, in the reviews of his earlier plays, more often than not receded behind the topicality of the issues he dealt with. With the exception of his more experimental plays from the seventies, such as *Teeth'n'Smiles*, Hare is structurally a predominantly conservative playwright, who is likewise obliged to the post-experimental, condition-of-England plays of John Osborne and the Shavian play of ideas.

The self-imposed restriction not to criticise 'New Labour' right from its beginnings had a cramping effect on other writers as well, or it encouraged them, as was the case with Louise Page, to turn to writing for the small screen instead of theatre. Caryl Churchill, who had spear-headed the protest of women playwrights against the Victorian role-models advocated for women by Mrs Thatcher, abandoned politics as well and wrote *Blue Heart* (1997); a double-bill of two one-act plays which intelligently and entertainingly explored the representational and linguistic possibilities of theatre. Not to comment on the changes which Britain was or was not undergoing was even harder for Howard Brenton, who had not only been the most fervent of Mrs Thatcher's critics, but who had also never relinquished the utopian dream of a socialist Britain, to which, perhaps with Stephen Poliakoff as the only exception, the political playwrights had aspired in the seventies. From 1992 onwards, in plays such as *Berlin Bertie*, and in *Ugly Rumours* and *Collateral Damage* (written together with Tariq Ali in 1998 and 1999 respectively), Brenton turned away from domestic issues and explored the consequences of the breakdown of socialism.

However, that Howard Brenton would abstain for long from commenting on contemporary Britain was deemed unlikely not only by those who are privileged to know him personally. Together with Tariq Ali and Andy de la Tour, Brenton founded Stigma, a company which has as its motto, 'we're political, and we're proud'. Their first production was *Snogging Ken* in April 2000, a satire on the efforts of the Blair administration to prevent Ken Livingstone from becoming elected as Mayor of London. This 40-minute-piece heralded the end of the close season for 'New Labour', but structurally it is a long stride backwards as far as Brenton's most accomplished playwriting is concerned. Brenton has a tradition of lampooning politicos which dates back to *A Short Sharp Shock* (1980) and beyond, and *Snogging Ken* was accurately described by a critic as 'mainly a piece for people who like the warm glow that comes from the confirmation of their prejudices'.[8] A more challenging play, Alistair Beaton's *Feelgood*, was produced by Max Stafford-Clark early in 2001, albeit at a time when there was no doubt that Blair's re-election was safe and that 'New Labour's' rule would continue. *Feelgood* cleverly exploits the possibilities of both comedy and satire. Located at a Labour convention in Brighton which is streamlined to sell Tony Blair at his best, the play shows the Prime Minister, who is referred to by his staff as 'DL' ('Divine Light'), as the puppet-on-a-string of Labour's true leader Eddie, a spin-doctor who is 'a nightmarish cross between Alistair Campbell and Peter Mandelson'.[9] The play culminates in the Prime Minister's speech to the convention, which is delivered by a Tony Blair-look-alike actor. Against the background of the play's twisted plot, the speech is irresistibly funny, but at the same time it is a devastating exposure of political rhetoric attempting to camouflage opportunism.

Both *Snogging Ken* and *Feelgood* justify the assumption that committed political drama in Britain has not ceased for good with 'New Labour's' victory. Klaus Peter Müller's essay underlines that no less than five different groups and types of political plays can be identified for the nineties. Moreover, the impression that stagnation is the predominant feature of this decade needs to be modified in the light of the achievements of the new playwrights who emerged during this period. In spite of unfavourable conditions, new voices established themselves. The scope of this development is analysed in the present volume in the case studies of Mark Ravenhill, of the short but brilliant career of Sarah Kane, and of Patrick Marber, who succeeded in establishing himself with West-End and grant-aided theatre audiences as successfully as Tom Stoppard had three decades earlier.

In the second part of this volume, which is devoted to individual case studies, their work is balanced against the achievement of established playwrights such as Stoppard himself and Harold Pinter, whose increasing political commitment during the nineties sparked off controversies, and against the – because of its radical aesthetics – always controversial work of Howard Barker. The case studies are preceded by surveys of political drama, and of the history play, as well as of the achievement of women playwrights during the nineties (with special attention given to Black women playwrights), and by Christopher Innes' analysis of science as a theatrical *sujet* in that decade.

We are grateful to the editors of *anglistik & englischunterricht* for commissioning this volume, to the contributors, and to Fiona Campbell, Esther Dewes, Gideon Haberkorn, Kirsten Kearney, Martin Schupp, Katrin Thomas, and Julia Touché for their invaluable support during the successive stages of the preparation of the manuscript for publication.

Notes

1 "Commanding the Style of Presentation. David Hare Interviewed by Catherine Itzin and Simon Trussler". – In Simon Trussler (Ed.): *New Theatre Voices of the Seventies*, London, 1981, p. 117.
2 The 51 theatres which are members of The Society of London Theatre include grant-aided and commercial venues.
3 For the statistics cf. *Britain 2000*, published with the permission of the Office for National Statistics by The Stationery Office, London, 1999, p. 254.
4 Cf. Michael Raab: *Erfahrungsräume. Das englische Drama der neunziger Jahre*, CDE Studies 4, Trier, 1999, p. 11.
5 Trevor Nunn quoted in Richard Eyre & Nicholas Wright: *Changing Stages. A View of British Theatre in the Twentieth Century*, London, 2001, p. 320.
6 *The Arts: The Next Move Forward. A Plurality of Riches: A Plurality of Funding*, London, 1987, p. 10 (published by The Conservative Political Centre).
7 Cf. "Selbstzweifel als Tugend. *Spiegel*-Interview mit dem britischen Dramatiker David Hare", *Der Spiegel* 49, 1985, 221.
8 For the reviews of *Snogging Ken* cf. *Theatre Record* 8, vol. 20, 2000, 488–490.
9 For the reviews of *Feelgood* cf. *Theatre Record* 9, vol. 21, 2001, 543–546.

Klaus Peter Müller, Stuttgart

Political Plays in England in the 1990s

1. Cultural Contexts and Critical Categories for Political Plays in the 1990s

The 1990s in England began with many complaints about the lack of new plays and new playwrights and ended with an enormous increase in new writing. There was a new play boom, but on the other hand seat prices in the English theatre rose by 50 per cent while attendances fell by 30 per cent between 1991 and 1998. I completely agree with David Edgar's conclusion when he provided these facts: "Now and for the foreseeable future, the health of the British theatre is and will be inextricably bound up with the health of new writing".[1] This article on political plays in the 1990s can investigate the health of the new plays of that decade only by referring to some typical examples, and it must limit itself to English plays (so that the very strong political playwriting of Ireland cannot be dealt with), but through its perspective it addresses some of the essential characteristics of this playwriting, especially as political elements are nowadays not as prominently presented as they often were in the past. It has become conspicuously more difficult to define political plays, because of the strong effects of both postmodernism and political reality. That is why it is necessary to briefly point out important cultural contexts and then define useful critical categories for political plays in the 1990s.

The most striking characteristic of the new plays written by young, unknown playwrights is their outspoken depiction of a remarkably rude, violent, and destructive world and their lack of suggesting alternatives or ways of changing such a world and of stopping the destruction of human life. There is a strong element of pessimism often mixed with a strange sense of relish in the destructive and dehumanising worlds depicted. The amount of direct political statements is accordingly rather small in these plays, even though they can easily be interpreted as reflecting a specific cultural and thus also political climate. The texts in this way also reveal another characteristic of the 1990s, namely a much greater emphasis on individual lives than on social worlds. The fact that the personal is political, which needed emphasising in the 1960s and 1970s (even though it had been plainly evident for earlier playwrights, such as Shakespeare, for instance), became almost a truism in the 1990s, and everything personal was regarded as worth presenting on stage, with or without political intentions. Ian Rickson, artistic director of the Royal Court Theatre, said that whereas "many seventies and eighties plays came from a left-wing point of view, nineties plays were based in a more 'privatised dissent'".[2] This was connected with another kind of freedom, bluntly expressed by the artistic director of the Bush Theatre from 1990 to 1996, Dominic Dromgoole: "In the eighties, most theatres wanted well-meaning, well-reasoned, victim-based plays. But in the nineties, [...] there were nor ideologies, no rules, no 'taste' – writers were free to follow their imaginations."[3] What many writers imagined resulted in the "dirty writing" also described by Dromgoole, "the flip side of the New Age thing: the big spiritual smile that characterised new writing in the early nineties".[4]

The scope of the writers' imagination varied substantially, and there was not only dirty writing in that decade, but the new freedom of the nineties in connection with other aspects of the cultural climate (as diverse as, e.g., the end of the Eastern bloc, the influence of Tarantino-like violence in film and on TV, 'pulp fiction' in plays, frustration with politics, and a sense of helplessness with regard to overpowering structures, such as society, globalism, and language) led to new combinations of form and content in plays and affected political plays in significant ways, especially by inhibiting too direct political statements. The nineties also brought a new confrontational aesthetic favouring experiential drama, plays addressing emotions much more than thought and sometimes seemingly celebrating violence, even when they perhaps just wanted to show how violent contemporary society was. Violence was often presented as torture, with people torturing not only others, but even more often themselves. Violence and violations of people's freedom and private lives appear as the worst fears and threats of the decade most directly presented on stage.

Violence and its social as well as personal effects are strongly connected with the questioning of masculinity, another important topic in the nineties. The entire range of men's positions in society is discussed in this context: in families, the workplace, among friends, in their leisure time. David Edgar has called this tremendous cultural conflict the biggest issue of the last thirty years in Western countries.[5] Mark Ravenhill gives an equally appropriate, but slightly different reason for the same phenomenon, relating it to an even more comprehensive topic and expanding the questioning of masculinity to the encompassing problem of gender relations: "I would suggest that the all-male and the gay play or the all-male gay play have been popular because there is a crisis in heterosexuality. So deep are the suspicions and tensions between heterosexual men and women that it is almost impossible to stage their relationships".[6] Typical plays of this kind are Nick Grosso's *Real Classy Affair* (1998)[7], or Jez Butterworth's *Mojo* (1995), and Patrick Marber neatly describes the situation in connection with his great success, *Closer* (1997), as being concerned with "what is happening after feminist politics and the age of the New Man, when no one knows what's going on any more".[8] Because of this extreme lack of knowledge and of a sense of direction, the political outcome of these plays is frustratingly weak: there is no exploration of how a new masculinity or new heterosexual relationships might be created, and – to make things even more difficult – the plays often suggest that depraved behaviour is "much more attractive than mature ways of relating to men and women. [...] The evidence of the plays seems to be that men not only can't grow up but don't even want to".[9] This conclusion needs to be qualified with reminders of the fact that drama basically portrays negative situations and crucial problems in a society and usually does not provide answers or predominantly positive characters. But negative behaviour seemed to be particularly marketable in the 1990s, when it was indeed often regarded as especially entertaining.

There were, however, also different kinds of plays in that decade that revealed the need for change in more direct ways, and some of them will be mentioned later. But hardly anywhere in plays of the 1990s can one find the attitude expressed by Edward Bond in 1978 – "we have to rewrite human consciousness" – and then voiced by one of his characters: "To judge rightly what is good – to choose between good and evil – that is all that it is to be human."[10] The later decade did not favour such attitudes, and claims that one knew the difference between good and evil were looked upon suspiciously, especially among young writers and those who believed with Francis Fukuyama that the end of history as such had been reached.[11] Whereas history was an outstanding topic in British novel writing in the 1990s, it was significantly neglected in those numerous plays which emphasised present situations, experiences and feelings, without any references to origins or causes, and in this way left out important elements of traditional political drama.[12] At the same time an old political hand like David Hare could successfully write three plays about the state of the nation at the beginning of the decade and demand substantial changes in its important institutions, because they were evidently not good enough and needed to be adapted to a permanently changing human history.[13]

Plays by younger writers did not share Bond's (already beleaguered) confidence that the answer to the fundamental question "Who Can Choose?", and who, therefore, determines human history and politics, was "He can choose",[14] and voices like David Greig's, who clearly states that political plays must show that it is possible to change human lives, were in the minority.[15] Andy de la Tour, who has written the only successful play on New Labour so far, *Landslide* (1997), relates this minority position to the general political situation in the country, where "there is less and less real political debate in our political life", so that he wants this debate to take place in the theatre.[16] He also feels that people have no objections to political plays at all, they are rather very interested in them and in political issues, but that the theatre managements have a too narrow agenda and should widen their limited and very personal perspectives, in order to include issues that affect all people. Greig also contradicts the idea that political theatre does not sell, and the two authors correctly describe the strong influence of both the theatre managements and what's thought to be fashionable and marketable on the production of plays in the 1990s.

Any celebration of violence and viciousness in plays produces serious doubts about their political implications and raises the question to what extent people really enjoy violence rather than avoid it. The problem is quite evident in Tarantino films, and Ian Herbert's comment on the audience's response to Butterworth's play *Mojo* is clearly not everybody's reaction: "We have been dehumanised, and we're loving it."[17] A play that supports this view cannot be called political, even though it may perhaps claim to represent an important attitude in contemporary society. Political plays present negative situations in order to elicit social and political changes. Where change is not desired, there is no space for political theatre. The desire for change may also arise in the spectators, though, who are, therefore, greatly involved in defining a particular play as political or not. The implication of the audience that has repeatedly been described with regard to contemporary plays and which gives spectators much responsibility as well as the obligation to participate actively in the plays they are watching, to think about them, try to make sense of them, etc.,[18] has clearly increased again and is particularly evident not only in the new experiential plays of the 1990s, but also in the problematic definition of political plays of that period.

Against this cultural backdrop, I think it is useful to distinguish five different groups and types of political plays in the 1990s for a critical analysis:

a) The traditional kind and authors, who sometimes write in not so traditional forms any more, with David Hare and David Edgar as the most prominent playwrights with a substantial output of texts and vivid response from both critics and spectators. Howard Brenton, on the other hand, is an example of a political writer who has not found attractive topics and appropriate theatrical forms in this new cultural climate after his endeavours to address the great changes in Europe with *Moscow Gold* (1990, written with Tariq Ali) and *Berlin Bertie* (1992), two clearly political plays, but too topical and too closely connected with the events of the period to claim lasting significance. Howard Barker's plays, which have been given political interpretations, even though the author emphasises that they do not really serve such servile functions, have not shown any significant changes in form or content either.[19]

b) Plays and writers where ethnicity is significant. The best example of this group was formerly Mustapha Matura, but he was without influence in England in the 1990s and his former topics are no longer dealt with in plays. Hanif Kureishi is another example of how ethnic and political questions lost relevance in the 1990s: his play *Sleep With Me* (1999) is concerned with the emotional problem expressed in the title and disregards the central political questions of his work in the 1980s. This emphasis on private worlds is also visible in Winsome Pinnock, but in her as in Kureishi it does not often elicit favourable responses. Pinnock's most recent play *Water* (2001) has been described as her weakest so far, and both playwrights are good examples of the lack of appeal that ethnic questions now have for many writers of that group themselves. Ayub Khan-Din's successful play and film *East is East* (1997 and 1999) is, therefore, probably the best example of this group in the decade and will briefly be discussed later.

c) The women's group with extremely different kinds of writing and various forms of political theatre: Caryl Churchill clearly belongs into this group, although she could also be placed in group a), and her work again reveals important aspects of playwriting in the 1990s. Sarah Kane must be mentioned here, but will not be discussed, as her work has been dealt with elsewhere,[20] and, therefore, Sierz' comprehensive remark must suffice here: "[A]lthough her work is not explicitly political [...,] it does implicitly criticise a society built on violence and denial".[21] I will briefly look at Churchill's latest plays and compare them with work by April de Angelis and Judy Upton. Deborah Levy is another important writer in this group, addressing among other things the loss of cultural identity among young adult females in post modernist Europe in her play *The B File* (2000). Bryony Lavery could be mentioned with her intriguing transferral of Kate Atkinson's novel *Behind the Scenes at the Museum* (1995) into a play with the same title (2000) and the same emphasis on history and human constructions of (political) reality. Rebecca Prichard is a young playwright using theatre in new social contexts, as, for instance, in *Yard Gal* (1997), written for a theatre group of female prisoners. The play is a good example of 1990s poor theatre, just two actors presenting the story of female friendship.

d) The group of new writers (in addition to the new women writers just mentioned and Patrick Marber, whom I prefer to put into the next group), such as Nick Grosso, Joe Penhall, and Mark Ravenhill, whose first success, *Shopping and Fucking* (1996), is usually looked upon as one of the 'in-yer-face' plays of the nineties that generally criticise the values of the throwaway culture. As his work is discussed in Aleks Sierz' article in this volume, I will concentrate on Grosso, Anthony Neilson, and Nick Stafford (even though he already began writing plays at the end of the 1980s).

e) The vast group of plays dealing with political issues in individual guises, but showing that the personal still is indeed very political. Many names could be mentioned here, such as Peter Barnes, Peter Whelan, Patrick Marber, Harold Pinter, Simon Gray, or Michael Frayn, but I can take up briefly only Barnes, Gray, Whelan, and Hugh Whitemore.

2. *Traditional Political Playwrights in the 1990s: David Hare and David Edgar*

After his three state-of-the-nation plays, David Hare openly addressed political issues again in *Via Dolorosa* (1998) about the problems in the Middle East. The way in which the text is written is already a strong indication of how it differs from his other political plays: it is a monologue, perhaps better called a meditation, and as such it was presented by the author in London and New York. The text itself says that it is "*ideally to be performed by its author*",[22] which is a rather strange statement and another indication that this is not really a play at all. It is a personal view on the fightings between the Israeli and Palestinian peoples, which, however, reflects Hare's general concern with values and what people believe in so that their lives are meaningful. Not surprisingly, *Via Dolorosa* says that the fighting in the Middle East is not meaningful, but disastrous and contradicts the main values of the two peoples involved, values clearly expressed at the end of the text: Mohammed's statement that all worldly affairs are only little 'strifes' from which one must always "return to the greater. The strife of the soul." And the awareness that the "highest value to a Jew is human life. The idea that stones now matter more than lives is a complete deformation of the Jewish religion. A deformation!" (42–43). The faith, the strong belief that makes people even kill others or themselves, which Hare wanted to find in the Middle East and contrast with the lack of faith in the West, "where nobody believes in anything any more" (4), thus turns out to be destructive and empty, a deluding myth and definitely no alternative to Western disbelief. Hare has become aware of the fact that "for some time [his] subject as a playwright has been faith" (6), and faith as that which makes people behave in a certain way, the source of their actions and lives, is an essential element in political activity and political playwriting. Hare's speech at Westminster Abbey, delivered in May 1996 and published with *Via Dolor-*

osa, "When Shall We Live?", claims that in a world based on human activity, where people are responsible for the state the world is in, everything depends on people knowing what they really believe in and want to achieve in their lives, because "we must work to make it [i.e. life] right now", as it will not be put right by God later.[23]

Faith is important in *Via Dolorosa* and so is history, as the text clearly deals with the historical and political situation in the Middle East; it refers back to people and events in the past and points out the urgent need for creating a better future. Hare's *My Zinc Bed* (2000) is also very much about faith or rather its conspicuous lack in contemporary Western societies, and it portrays three representative characters in London at the end of the 20th century: Victor, a successful business man in his early fifties, Elsa, his wife, about 20 years younger, and Paul, an unsuccessful poet in his early thirties, who takes on odd jobs in order to survive. For Victor, Paul has low self-esteem and belongs to "the confessional class. The class most people belong to nowadays" (21), because it allows people to speak about their weaknesses and keep them. What people believe in is of particularly great importance in this culture: "Nothing is but what is believed. Everything becomes a question of confidence." (103) This basic motif is connected with fundamental questions: What determines people's lives? To what extent are human beings in control of their lives? What are people after? Can one ever love somebody? To what extent do we and does our concept of reality depend on the language we believe in?

The play shows that one indeed needs faith to go on living and to live a life worth living, but faith in itself is not enough: "It's what you have faith in that matters." (105) Only words or only form without content are not enough, language must also be meaningful in the sense that it refers to something and is connected with human activity. Victor expresses the key question that combines all the others and reveals an important problem of contemporary culture: "Now we live longer, we expect to live many lives, not one. Freelance culture persuades us to believe we may start again. But is it true?" (125) The play suggests it usually is not true, but the complete denial of this possibility is also false. Victor has changed from a communist into a capitalist. Elsa, however, who first seems to represent perfect human freedom of choice, in the end says that one is never cured of one's shortcomings and addictions (alcoholism in her case), that one is what one is "for life" (121). Victor also speaks of "the illusion of choice" (52), and he describes himself as a person who "went from believing people could do everything for each other to wondering whether they could do anything" (123).

The importance of addiction in contemporary life is seen as a sign of the sense of worthlessness and the lack of identity that many people have and try to cover up. There is an evident need for people to invent themselves and others constructively, but this does not mean that one has total freedom in doing so. Victor's almost tragic flaw is that he thinks he can liberate himself and others "from the facts" (24). The facts are that human beings cannot depend on people's love (humans are too fickle), and also that when only today matters, when people disregard the past and the future, human beings can never obtain any value and identity, any sense of stability. Life thus has "possibility", but "not perfection" (36). Though life is full of contradictions, the play does not agree with Victor, who thinks "we can't know", "we shall know nothing until we are laid on our zinc beds" (72). One must know sooner, although absolute knowledge is impossible. But one needs to find out the options that life in this specific culture offers and that are least destructive to oneself and others. One needs to be purposeful, even though Paul claims: "It's so wonderful not to be purposeful for a while. Let go and let God!" (81) These, however, have for him always been moments when he has destroyed his own life and that of others, too. One needs to "find life that isn't in a bottle" or in any other form of addiction (96), because all these forms are destructive. Anger at the world and disease in it can never be absolutely avoided or eradicated, they are part of reality, but that is no reason to give up or simply accept them. That is the message the poet and "the philosopher always bring" (108). One needs to affirm life, and one should not run away from problems, even though one does not always get the rewards one may have deserved. One quite evidently cannot control one's life completely, but one should nevertheless try as much as possible. This is Hare's message in this play, and it is not fundamentally different from what his more directly political plays say. *Skylight* (1995) or *Amy's View* (1997) are other plays with characters typical of contemporary society, where Hare makes similar statements and writes political plays without the traditional strong emphasis on a nation, its institutions, history, and overt political comments. As John Peter put it in his review: "*Skylight* is a political play in the sense that Ibsen's and Chekhov's plays, or Shakespeare's *Measure for Measure*, are political plays. They are all rooted in the passionate belief that yes, there is such a thing as society, and that society and its members create and re-create one another in an unending process of mutual needs and pressures. This is the very soil of politics".[24]

David Edgar's political plays have also quite significantly left behind national boundaries, but they are clearly concerned with history and have adopted a conspicuous European perspective. His trilogy on the political situation in Europe after the break-up of the Eastern bloc, *The Shape of the Table* (1990), *Pentecost* (1994), and *The Prisoner's Dilemma* (2001) is not about England or Britain but about the disintegration of communist Eastern Europe and the difficult integration of a new Europe. Even though political plays have always dealt with problems of general human concern, it now is quite evident that the national element has become less important and been replaced by international issues. The main questions dealt with in these plays now are of global and cultural significance, so that the first play, for instance, deals with the transferral of power from one regime to the next with the successor avoiding to become like its predecessor, the question of how language can be used to obscure or reveal power and its abuse, and how negotiating power in committee meetings is always different from the public images and celebrations of power passing from one authority to the next. The shape of the table is variable, it changes in the course of the play, and this is the most important metaphor of what happens to reality. But who decides what reality should be like, and what is the position of the individual in the new world order? These are questions of perennial relevance in political plays, and they are also dealt with by Edgar.[25]

In the last of these plays the political situation connected with these questions is appropriately defined as a dilemma, and the idea of the dilemma works on the individual level as well as on the communal and global levels addressed in the play. On the most comprehensive level, the play reveals that neither a global form of capitalism nor any kind of fundamentalist nationalism provides a solution for the problems of multiethnic communities living together. Not every ethnic group can reasonably become a nation of its own, but how can several ethnicities with very different value systems, different histories and cultures live together in one nation? There are parallels in this situation and in the play with the Middle East and Ireland. The "Selective Chronology" of "War and Peace after the Cold War" at the end of the published text also includes South Africa and Bosnia,[26] but the setting for the play is the Balkan Peninsula. The play thus refers very explicitly to contemporary history and points out significant problems. Its ending leaves the spectators with the dilemma and all problems unsolved. The dilemma is thus the spectators' and the world's dilemma, and everybody is imprisoned by this situation, which cannot be avoided or neglected, but still requires a satisfactory solution in Ireland, the Balkan, the Middle East as well as in various regions of Africa and Asia.

It is quite intriguing to see that what Edgar does in his trilogy is what George Bernard Shaw already did with *Heartbreak House* (1919), the play David Hare points out as the first state-of-the nation play. Shaw dealt not only with England but with Europe before the Great War, and his play very critically depicts the European culture drifting towards destruction. Edgar points out similar dangers, but he leaves more room for hope than Shaw inevitably did after the war. Edgar's hope is connected with an awareness that Shaw also had and that Leo expresses in *Pentecost*: "We are, involuntarily, each other's guests".[27] This implies that in spite of all ethnic differences human beings share essential similarities and depend for their survival on each other and on peaceful coexistence. There might even be a basis for universal human values and human rights here, which is also expressed in the play's title referring to the pentecostal event of communities of difference relating to each other while maintaining their own identities, speaking in various tongues, but expressing the same message. The message in Edgar's plays is clearly political and urges the public to understand the past and the present in order to actively influence the future.

3. *Political Ethnicity and Ethnic Politics in Ayub Khan-Din's* East is East

Ayub Khan-Din's play *East is East* is also concerned with different cultures living together, but the focus here is on two generations of a Pakistani family living in Salford in the 1970s, and the problem presented is again a very realistic one; the play has in fact many autobiographical elements.[28] The title is, of course, a reference to Rudyard Kipling's "The Ballad of East and West", claiming that "East is East, and West is West, and never the twain shall meet", but also that "there is neither East nor West, Border, nor Breed, nor Birth, / When two strong men stand face to face, / though they come from the ends of the earth!"[29] The men facing each other in this play are all nominally from the same culture, but in reality they are not, because there is a great divide between the generations of the father of the family, who came to England and wants to preserve his Pakistani culture there, and the second generation born in England, who cannot accept everything of that culture any more, because they are strongly influenced by the new Western culture. The play's title is, therefore, ironic, because the East is not simply and in an undivided form Eastern, there are different kinds of East. This is what the play shows and presents in connection with the father-son problem: the children of this Pakistani immigrant, who is married to an Englishwoman, lose their freedom of choice in important life decisions, especially in the question of whom they shall marry, when their father selects Pakistani women for them and forces them to act in accordance with his rather than their own will. The play is also about why these men facing each other are not really strong, and it suggests that they lack an awareness of who they actually are and why they do what they do. This is, however, not a point seriously developed in the play, which concentrates on the generation problem and ends with the majority of the children (six sons and one daughter) opting for the freedom of the West, which is – again quite realistically – in this play only the very limited freedom of a consumer society. Education, spiritual values, and getting a job that provides more than just money are not really significant topics. So the play is clearly political in its reflection of contemporary British reality and of the problems that arise when different cultures meet and people are forced to make a decision between divergent cultural values. It also reflects history, but does not make any strong suggestions how the future can be improved; it is rather open-ended in this respect. The characters are basically the victims of the culture they are born into, they do not in any significant way determine their culture themselves, nor are they even ultimately in command of their own lives, they are mainly driven by the unconscious desire to indulge in the material goods the West offers.

4. Direct and Oblique Forms of Politics in Plays by Women: Caryl Churchill, April de Angelis, and Judy Upton

One of the strongest points of feminism has always been its emphasis on the human ability to construct at least parts of one's own life and to change the influence of strong systems, such as (patriarchal) society or language, that want to deter people from using their freedom. Caryl Churchill's political plays have always emphasised this freedom and especially revealed the dangers of not really using it, as most typically and successfully in *Top Girls* (1982). In the 1990s, she has portrayed this danger most strikingly in *The Skriker* (1994), "*a shapeshifter and death portent*" representing in this play most of all the lethal attractions and seductive powers of contemporary media.[30] Churchill has also written about the situation in Eastern Europe after the decline of communism in her play *Mad Forest* (1990) about the revolution in Romania, the damage done to people's lives by years of repression, and the painful difficulties of bringing about lasting change. Churchill's plays of the 1990s continue a strong trend in her own work and in literature generally, namely the mixing of genres and the inclusion of music and dance in plays. This is an important element in *Lives of the Great Poisoners* (1991), where the ability of human beings to change and transform themselves and others is highlighted, as it already had been in *A Mouthful of Birds* (1986).

Churchill's latest plays, *This is a Chair* (1997) and *Far Away* (2000), have been described as haunting impressions of urban alienation and self-obsession, as revealing the increasing surreality of modern life, and they surprisingly indeed seem to emphasise destruction and deconstruction much more than the need to construct a better world. These plays are political when one sees them as depictions of reality so negative that the urge to reconstruct something better is evoked as a necessary response. They do not quite have the political directness of *The Skriker* or *Mad Forest*, even though the headlines provided in *This is a Chair* all refer to events and problems in the political and cultural reality of the end of the 20th century, such as "The War in Bosnia", "The Labour Party's Slide to the Right", "The Northern Ireland Peace Process", or the fundamental medical and ethical problem of "Genetic Engineering".[31] By not really dealing with these topics in the text, the play points out enormous differences between what people say and what they do. These are differences the play already addresses in the title and on the front page, where the statement "*This is a Chair*" is contradicted by the image of a pipe. The statement also needs to be seen in the context of Magritte paintings making similar claims, but always revealing and insisting that what is represented is never reality as such, but only an image, a simulacrum. Churchill, however, does not want to repeat the postmodern claim (often made by Frenchmen, such as Baudrillard [1997]) that there are only simulacra and never a 'reality', but in this as in her other plays she points out (in a rather typically British kind of pragmatism, which is also favoured by most feminists) that there is a reality after all, which needs to be taken account of and must be dealt with constructively. This is the essential clue to her play, which, therefore, makes very critical use of the predominant context of the 1990s, which often emphasised personal and private perceptions of reality much more than that reality itself. In this context, her play is very political indeed and can even be read as a severe criticism of people disregarding the most important problems in their real lives.

The plays by April de Angelis and Judy Upton are also not as directly political as one might perhaps expect when one hears de Angelis say in the introduction to her collected plays that *The Positive Hour* (1997) is about feminism 25 years after its beginnings: "[G]round that had seemed well established in terms of feminism appeared to be being eroded".[32] The play then reveals this erosion very neatly: there is absolutely no solidarity among the women presented, each woman fights on her own for some kind of survival in a society where there are no spiritual values, and where some women do not even have the simple means of subsistence. The play is political in this portrayal of a harsh, loveless reality, but it is also deliberately "ambiguous" in the end, which can be interpreted as either "frightening" or as "hopeful", and where Nicola "stands unsure" now,[33] even though she started with the well-known feminist assumption that it is "a positive thing for women to meet in this way. To share and empower".[34] There is, however, no sharing and no empowering in the society presented in the play, not even among women, and the spectators are dismissed with this feeling of uncertainty and unease. It is, after all, up to them to change society, and de Angelis has shown that change is urgently needed.

De Angelis began writing plays in the 1980s, whereas Judy Upton is one of the important newcomers of the 1990s and, therefore, also belongs into the next group. Born in 1966, she is of the same generation as Kane and

Ravenhill, and has many similarities with them. One is a strong sense of frustration that life is not as splendid as it is usually presented in the jargons of politics or advertising, and her *Ashes and Sand* (1994) portrays this frustration among demoralised working-class kids. The setting of *Bruises* and *The Shorewatchers' House* (1996) is the 1990s, and the plays depict important aspects of contemporary Britain. *Bruises* presents the damage done to battered children and how these children then later beat others, too; it is about failed lives, defective relationships in families, the negative effects of alcohol, unemployment, etc. The play gives a realistic portrait of children in such families and broken up relationships. It is political in this sense, but it nowhere suggests any possibility of change. The play thus ends with one of the characters saying "I don't know what we're going to do" (58), and the three-act form is not connected with any development, apart from an increase of violence. History is of importance with regard to what is passed on from one generation to the next, but the only suggestion of how history may be different in the future is a vague reference by the beaten boy's father to some outside help. The characters in this play cannot help themselves, but whether society offers any help or whether they are simply the result of contemporary society, its victims, is left undecided.

The Shorewatchers' House is about "an ageing nuclear reactor" contaminating the land and the people (65) and about two men loving one woman. At first, one of the men claims, "We all make our own luck", implying that everybody is responsible for his or her own life (98), but that was a belief of the past; now he believes "in fate, in things out of my control" (99). People are shown to be as incapable of fighting as of hating or loving. Freedom is presented as a total illusion and so is every suggestion of change. Even though the characters living in the house next to the reactor have packed everything for leaving the house for good, they remain where and what they are. This decision is clearly not the result of a free choice, and the play is political in showing people without freedom and without a conscious planning of the future of their lives. The nuclear power plant can be interpreted as an image of the powerful influences on human beings that the young people in the play like to protest against, but which nobody can really change. This image, which since the 1950s has been used as a typical example of how human beings can influence their own lives, has in the play of the 1990s significantly become an image of destructive forces that are passively accepted by society. Again the play is particularly political when this internal acceptance is not adopted by its spectators in their own lives and in the external reality, when people refuse to be the victims that the play represents.

5. *Politics in Plays by New Male Playwrights: Nick Grosso, Anthony Neilson, and Nick Stafford*

Nick Grosso, Anthony Neilson, and Nick Stafford have written plays with political implications very similar to what has already been noted with regard to Judy Upton. There is a clear emphasis on personal experiences in their plays, which nevertheless reveal the society the characters come from and invite criticism, which, however, is hardly ever voiced directly in the plays themselves. Nick Grosso's *Peaches* (1994) and *Sweetheart* (1996) are about the Blank Generation or Generation X, a society of slackers who talk but don't act. For Peter Ansorge, the first play "is an engaging round of male chat-up and eventual disappointment".[35] The second play reveals the emptiness of spirit, the gnawing insecurity, and the meaningless banality of this society, and both plays show the disaffection and disorientation of Thatcher's children: people who don't know what they want or how to get it and whose only concern is material, i.e. money and consumption, including peaches, which, of course, means women. Grosso's interest in male groups is again evident in *Real Classy Affair* (1998), which, however, also reveals a great problem of many of these plays, especially when they are without political relevance: there is no real dramatic conflict here. The play simply presents us with a group of males and basically one woman. The woman betrays her husband with one of his 'friends', the men form different alliances amongst themselves, and each one has a particular role in the group. So there is absolutely nothing new or surprising in this play. It is, therefore, not really classy, and this has much to do with Grosso's disregard for plot, for explanations or revelations. He wants to portray banal everyday life with suggestions of things happening on a psychological or subtextual level.[36] There is nowhere a strong point in the play, certainly not a political one, and this unfortunately results only in the resignation and disappointment Ansorge has already expressed with regard to Grosso's earlier plays.

The case is very different with Anthony Neilson, who is also not an overtly political writer, but, as Sierz puts it, "acutely sensitive to questions of social justice".[37] Neilson wants to address the emotions first of all, and this is achieved in *Penetrator* (1993), a play about the destructive force of sexuality bringing about paranoid fantasies of being violated in the protagonist, but leaving the spectators with feelings and hardly any insight. *Normal. The Düsseldorf Ripper* (1991) is more interesting, because of the similarities between the ripper and Nazi Germany and the attraction of violence on the middle class. The play seriously questions common assumptions about what is normal. *The Censor* (1997) is another good example of how political institutions, like censorship, are presented in the 1990s: the play shows that one censors what is somehow defective in oneself. The censor is strongly influenced in his work by personal and emotional factors. This is not really a new claim, but what is conspicuously significant in the play is its emphasis on the importance of looking for meanings. This emphasis is provided by the female film director, who opposes the censor and wants to force him to look beyond the surface of her film (consisting of naked bodies) and to find meanings in it that are not directly evident. So the play emphasises the need to find new signifieds for a given signifier and not to remain on the surface level of signifiers. It is, therefore, not postmodern, but evidently plays with postmodern elements. In the postmodern context of the 1990s, this is a highly political claim, even connected in the play with the need for a pragmatic approach to reality.

Nick Stafford's *Luminosity* (2001) is a late example of a more directly political play, explicitly discussing the enormous influence of the past on the present and claiming that "the versions of the past [...], the stories we choose to tell about our past, decide our present, and our future" (67). History is shown to be partial, and everybody is personally responsible for the past as well as the present and the future. Children need not be like their parents, and the play shows that human beings have choices and can change their lives substantially. Light shines, when the past and the present suddenly meet and reveal surprising similarities in a sort of epiphany (61). The play raises important questions, expressed by Debra, the black woman adopted by a white family: "What should we do, now? […] How should we be?" (59) Thinking about such questions and dealing with them constructively brings light and hope into human life. The play neatly sums up what recent years have made people aware of in both the sciences and the arts, namely that not even the past is unchangeable and that human reality depends strongly on human actions. Three periods of human history are juxtaposed in the play to make this point: 1799, 1899, and the present.

6. *Politics in Private Worlds: Peter Barnes, Peter Whelan, Hugh Whitemore, and Simon Gray*

The group of playwrights revealing that the private is political is enormously comprehensive and includes Patrick Marber and most of the new writers, but also older writers like Harold Pinter, whose *Ashes to Ashes* (1998) focuses on a key political and epistemological question: How do we define reality? Does the play represent a scene in a Nazi camp, or the memories of such a scene, or, as Pinter himself says, are we confronted with the images, ideas, concepts, and feelings the present has connected with the Third Reich? The play thus emphasises the importance of schemata in people's minds: "So in *Ashes to Ashes* I'm not simply talking about the Nazis; I'm talking about us and our conception of our past and our history, and what it does to us in the present".[38] The significance of people's minds for their approach to and grasp on reality and politics is also investigated in different ways in plays by Peter Barnes, Simon Gray, Peter Whelan, and Hugh Whitemore, who provide good examples of the work done by this group.

Peter Barnes' *Jubilee* (2001) is a satire on the long tradition of the Shakespeare industry. It presents this tradition at its starting point with David Garrick's Stratford Jubilee of 1769, but it also points out how this process has been continued and increased in the present, e.g. by confronting Garrick with the ghosts of 20th century directors of the Royal Shakespeare Company, who would have been forced to look for other jobs, if Garrick's project had failed. Nobody in this satire is in any way interested in Shakespeare's works, they all simply use him in order to make themselves famous, create their own glory, and above all make a profit. The play is thus an appropriate attack on the mean- and money-mindedness of the present as well as the past.

Peter Whelan's *Divine Right* (1996) deals with the political question of whether England should stay a monarchy or not and suggests that after the reign of Elizabeth II the new generation in the royal family will understand that they must find new jobs. So the play does not force this decision on to the Windsors, but allows them the freedom to find the answer themselves. Hugh Whitemore uses Harold Macmillan and the Profumo affair of the 1960s in order to make his point in *A Letter of Resignation* (1997). The point in this very subtle, but strong play is that nobody should resign and give up because of personal loss and unhappy relationships, but that one should accept the things one cannot change and act responsibly and constructively in every situation. The political world of the Macmillan era is thus used to emphasise everybody's general and very specific responsibility for their lives, which for Whitemore evidently needed to be emphasised again in the context of the 1990s, when this responsibility and the freedom of choice connected with it was very often rejected or simply neglected.

Simon Gray's plays have always discussed the problem of finding and realising important values in life, and his plays of the 1990s continue this tradition.[39] *Simply Disconnected* (1996) and *Life Support* (1997) again portray the spiritual paralysis that Gray already depicted in *Dog Days* (1976): people are very seriously (and also funnily) simply disconnected from everything that makes life meaningful and valuable. Simon, who was already the protagonist of *Otherwise Engaged* (1975), is again the protagonist in *Simply Disconnected.* He has by now learned, though, that one "always ends up paying for" (35) every neglect of reality and for all endeavours to make life easier than it is. Simon Hench has always been otherwise engaged, never with the significant things, which has made him a henchman of destruction for the people around him and has also destroyed his own life. His egoism and emotional emptiness, his "deadness of spirit" are the reasons why he has never "learnt how to live a life" (42–43). The protagonist of *Life Support* equally neglected the support he was given by his wife, who is now comatose and mechanically kept alive in hospital. But it is actually the husband who has always been on the brink of death, because he has never known how to really live. According to him "nothing can be helped" and life is "entirely random" (26–27), but this attitude is clearly rejected by the play. The alternative is expressed at the end and includes the awareness of history, but no decisive plans for the future: "I'm getting on with my life and staying in touch with my past. What more could a man want?" (45). The plays are very personal, but in their depiction of typical behaviour in contemporary society, their straightforward presentation of this behaviour as negative and destructive to life, and their strong suggestions that human beings should really want and do more than simply to get on in the usual way, they are also political.

7. The Political Modernity of Plays in the 1990s

These remarks on political plays in the 1990s have necessarily referred to only a limited number of authors and plays, but they have addressed essential characteristics of this kind of playwriting and provide insights that are of general significance in this decade. In spite of a common tendency to avoid direct political comments, the plays reveal their inevitable relationship to the culture from which they come and refer to political signifieds, even when these are not always directly addressed. Quite surprisingly, the state of playwriting is rather healthy, even though the society depicted for many reasons is not. This health in an unhealthy world is another of the many paradoxes in modern society, paradoxes that were already presented in the plays of Shaw and Oscar Wilde and that continue to be of great relevance in the (political) playwriting of the 1990s. The world has become even more complex and paradoxical, the need to find meaning and a sense of direction in it is even greater than at the beginning of the 20th century, but the greatest danger in these plays is not absurdity, but rather indulgence, conformity, greed for entertainment and consumption, and the loss of hope for improvements in life. The plays reveal an enormous variety in form and content, they depict reality and ways of seeing, acting, and living in it in multifarious ways, and the presentation of violence, of the physical as well as the psychological worlds is far more direct than it ever was in that century. The most progressive writers, like Churchill, Hare, Edgar, and Pinter, also show how important the mind is for people's approach to, awareness of, and behaviour in reality and politics.

Even though Simon Gray is the only writer who in the plays described has a character explicitly say that one always ends up paying for every neglect of reality and for all endeavours to make life easier than it is, this is actually an awareness contained in all plays. This understanding of reality is another indication that we have not yet left the modern world, in spite of postmodernism, that we are rather in a 'second modernity' (Beck 1998) – a notion which makes much sense, especially when one looks for political plays. Gray's awareness – and that of all the other playwrights mentioned – was already expressed by Friedrich Nietzsche, who thus provides us with a typically modern comment on reality and practical (political) activity. Nietzsche speaks of the inevitable result when people neglect the task of human life and fail to construct reality actively in spite of all difficulties. Then, he says, people become ill, the society is unhealthy. Nietzsche in his own words describes a basic paradox of human life that political plays of the 1990s have also emphasised:

> Krankheit ist jedesmal die Antwort, wenn wir an unsrem Recht auf *unsre* Aufgabe zweifeln wollen, wenn wir anfangen, es uns irgendworin leichter zu machen. Sonderbar und furchtbar zugleich! Unsre *Erleichterungen* sind es, die wir am härtesten büßen müssen! Und wollen wir hinterdrein zur Gesundheit *zurück*, so bleibt uns keine Wahl: wir müssen uns *schwerer* belasten, als wir je vorher belastet waren ...[40]

Notes

1 Edgar (1999: 3).
2 Sierz (2000: 39).
3 Dromgoole quoted in Sierz (2000: 37).
4 *Ibid.*, 53.
5 Edgar (1999: 28).
6 Ravenhill (1999: 50).
7 The years given behind all plays mentioned in this article refer to the first publication, not the first production of the plays.
8 Marber quoted in Sierz (2000: 191).
9 *Ibid.*, 177.
10 The first quotation is from Bond's "A Note on Dramatic Method" (see Bond 1978: xv); the second repeats the last words in the play itself (*ibid.*, 78).
11 Cf. Fukuyama (1992).
12 The tradition referred to here is that of Erwin Piscator, Berthold Brecht, and British political playwriting since the 1950s. Cf. Müller (1993).
13 The institutions were the church, the law, and the political parties, and the three plays Hare wrote about them, *Racing Demon* (1990), *Murmuring Judges* (1991), and *The Absence of War* (1993), are the best examples of traditional po-

litical plays in the 1990s. For an extensive discussion of Hare's trilogy cf. Müller (2000: 232–257).

14 Bond (1978: 80).

15 Cf. de la Tour, Martin & Greig (1999: 66), where Greig says: "[M]ost importantly, political theatre has at its very heart the possibility of change." Greig's play *Victoria* (2000), produced at the RSC and set in a rural community on the Scottish coast, reflects the shifting political and social fabric of Britain in the 20th century.

16 *Ibid.*, 62–63.

17 Herbert quoted in Sierz (2000: 163).

18 Cf. Rabey (1986) and Fischer-Lichte (1997).

19 Cf. my favourable description of Barker's work (Müller 1997) with Tomlin (2000), who has some strong points in her criticism of Barker as strengthening the prevailing individualistic right-wing climate and naively discrediting the ethics of socialism. Barker expressed his provocative, but by now well-known concepts again at the CDE conference in Vienna in 2001 (forthcoming in Contemporary Drama in English 10). Rabey (1989) investigated politics in Barker's plays up to 1987.

20 Cf. Müller (2001).

21 Sierz (2000: 120).

22 Hare (1998: 3). Further references to this edition will be included in the text.

23 *Ibid.*, 71: "I happen to think it a matter of great importance that we do work out exactly what we believe."

24 Peter (1995: 10.20–21).

25 See Painter (1996: 129–166) for very useful discussions of further questions raised by the earlier plays. She also quotes Edgar expressing the central problem his plays deal with: "How communities of difference relate to each other in an increasingly globalised but also fractured world is the big human question we will confront in the new century. Because it is an essentially cultural question (as opposed to the questions posed by traditional Marxism or entrepreneurial liberalism), it will inevitably put the arts in the foreground, particularly the narrative arts, as people seek ever more desperately to construct, deconstruct and reassemble stories that make sense of the world." (149)

26 Edgar (2001: 139–140).

27 Edgar (1994: 104). The idea is an essential element in Shaw's life-force philosophy; it is expressed in *Heartbreak House* by Hector: "We are members one of another." (Shaw 2000: 87) Cf. Hare's preface in the same edition.

28 Cf. Khan-Din's introduction to the film edition of the play (1999: vii–xii).

29 These are the essential lines of the identical first and last stanzas in Kipling's narrative poem. Cf. Eliot (1976: 111–116).

30 Churchill (1994: 1). See Müller (2000: 283–332) for a comprehensive discussion of these and other plays by Churchill.

31 Churchill (1997: 7, 12, 28, 29).

32 De Angelis (1999: xi).

33 *Ibid.*, 323.

34 *Ibid.*, 251.

35 Ansorge (1999: 40).

36 Cf. Sierz (2000: 181–186).

37 *Ibid.*, 66.

38 Pinter (1998b: 66).
39 Cf. Reitz (1991) for a useful interpretation of this tradition in Gray, which Nothof (2000) depicts far too negatively, especially by not detecting any political elements in Gray's work, but by seeing it as the personal and private expression of the author's frustration.
40 Nietzsche (1969: II, 1055).

Bibliography

Ansorge, Peter: "Really a Golden Age?". – In David Edgar (Ed.): *State of Play. Playwrights on Playwriting*, London, 1999, pp. 37–47.
Barnes, Peter: *Jubilee*, London, 2001.
Baudrillard, Jean: *Simulacra and Simulation*, Ann Arbor, 1997 [repr. of the 1994 translation of the French text of 1981].
Beck, Ulrich: *Die Moderne der Moderne. Entwürfe zur Zweiten Moderne*, Aachen, 1998.
Bond, Edward: *The Bundle or New Narrow Road to the Deep North*, London, 1978.
Brenton, Howard (with Tariq Ali): *Moscow Gold*, London, 1990.
–: *Berlin Bertie*, London, 1992.
Butterworth, Jez: *Mojo*, London, 1995.
Churchill, Caryl: *A Mouthful of Birds*, London, 1986.
–: *Mad Forest*, London, 1990.
–: *Lives of the Great Poisoners*, London, 1991.
–: *The Skriker*, London, 1994.
–: *This is a Chair*, London 1997.
–: *Far Away*, London, 2000.
De Angelis, April: *The Positive Hour*. – In A.d.A.: *Collected Plays*, London, 1999.
De la Tour, Andy: *Briefing for Landslide*, London, 1997.
–, Cheryl Martin & David Greig: "Plays on Politics". – In: David Edgar (Ed.): *State of Play. Playwrights on Playwriting*, London, 1999, pp. 62–70.
Edgar, David: *The Shape of the Table*, London, 1990.
–: *Pentecost*, London, 1994.
–: "Provocative Acts. British Playwriting in the Post-War Era and Beyond". – In D.E. (Ed.): *State of Play. Playwrights on Playwriting*, London, 1999, pp. 1–34.
–: *The Prisoner's Dilemma*, London, 2001.
Eliot, T.S. (Ed.): *A Choice of Kipling's Verse with an Essay on Rudyard Kipling*, London, 1975 [repr. of the first edition of 1941].
Fischer-Lichte, Erika: *Die Entdeckung des Zuschauers. Paradigmenwechsel auf dem Theater des 20. Jahrhunderts*, Tübingen, 1997.
Fukuyama, Francis: *The End of History and the Last Man*, London, 1992.
Gray, Simon: *Simply Disconnected*, London, 1996.
–: *Life Support*, London, 1997.
Grieg, David: *Victoria*, London, 2000.
Grosso, Nick: *Peaches*, London, 1994.
–: *Sweetheart*, London, 1996.
–: *Real Classy Affair*, London, 1998.
Hare, David: *Racing Demon*, London, 1990.
–: *Murmuring Judges*, London, 1991.

–: *The Absence of War*, London, 1993.
–: *Skylight*, London, 1995.
–: *Amy's View*, London, 1997.
–: *Via Dolorosa & When Shall We Live*, London, 1998.
–: *My Zinc Bed*, London, 2000.
Khan-Din, Ayub: *East is East*, London, 1997 [film version 1999].
Kureishi, Hanif: *Sleep With Me*, London, 1999.
Lavery, Bryony: *Behind the Scenes at the Museum*, London, 1995 [based on a novel by Kate Atkinson].
Levy, Deborah: *The B File*, London, 2000.
Marber, Patrick: *Closer*, London, 1997.
Müller, Klaus Peter: "Theater als Sinnsuche und Geschichtsschreibung. Signifikante Entwicklungen im englischen Theater der Gegenwart". – In K.P.M. (Ed.): *Englisches Theater der Gegenwart. Geschichte(n) und Strukturen*, Tübingen, 1993, pp. 3–58.
–: "Cultural Transformations of Subversive Jacobean Drama. Contemporary Sub-Versions of Tragedy, Comedy, and Tragicomedy". – In Nicole Boireau (Ed.): *Drama on Drama. Dimensions of Theatricality on the Contemporary British Stage*, London, 1997, pp. 30–58.
–: *Wertstrukturen und Wertewandel im englischen Drama der Gegenwart*, CDE Studies 5, Trier, 2000.
–: "British Theatre in the 1980s and 1990s. Forms of Hope and Despair, Violence and Love". – In Bernhard Reitz & Heiko Stahl (Eds.): *What Revels are in Hand? Assessments of Contemporary Drama in English in Honour of Wolfgang Lippke*, CDE Studies 8, Trier, 2001, pp. 81–107.
Neilson, Anthony: *Normal. The Düsseldorf Ripper*, London, 1991.
–: *Penetrator*, London, 1993.
–: *The Censor*, London, 1997.
Nietzsche, Friedrich: *Werke*. Ed. Karl Schlechta, sixth edition, 3 vols., München, 1969.
Nothof, Anne: "The Pictures of Simon Gray. Dramatizing Degeneration", *Modern Drama* 43, 2000, 56–65.
Painter, Susan: *Edgar. The Playwright*, London, 1996.
Peter, John: "The Price of Love", *The Sunday Times*, 14 May 1995, 10.20–21.
Pinnock, Winsome: *Water*, London, 2001.
Pinter, Harold: *Ashes to Ashes*, London, 1998a.
–: "Writing, Politics and Ashes for Ashes" [1996]. – In H.P.: *Various Voices. Prose, Poetry, Politics 1948–1998*, London, 1998b, pp. 58–70.
Prichard, Rebecca: *Yard Gal*, London, 1997.
Rabey, David Ian: *British and Irish Political Drama in the Twentieth Century. Implicating the Audience*, London 1986.
–: *Howard Barker. Politics and Desire. An Expository Study of his Drama and Poetry, 1969–87*, London, 1989.
Ravenhill, Mark: *Shopping and Fucking*, London, 1996.
–: "Plays about Men". – In David Edgar (Ed.): *State of Play. Playwrights on Playwriting*, London, 1999, pp. 48–51.
Reitz, Bernhard: "'What is the point of caring?' – Lebenslüge und Sinnverlust als strukturierende Motive bei Bennett, Gray and Nichols", *anglistik & englischunterricht* 45, 1991, 95–115.

Shaw, Bernhard: *Heartbreak House. A Fantasia in the Russian Manner on English Themes*, London, 2000.
Sierz, Aleks: *In-Yer-Face Theatre. British Drama Today*, London, 2000.
Stafford, Nick: *Luminosity*, London, 2001.
Tomlin, Liz: "The Politics of Catastrophe. Confrontation or Confirmation in Howard Barker's Theatre", *Modern Drama* 43, 2000, 66–77.
Upton, Judy: *Ashes and Sand*, London, 1994.
–: *Bruises & The Shorewatcher's House*, London, 1996.
Whelan, Peter: *Divine Right*, London, 1996.
Whitmore, Hugh: *A Letter of Resignation*, London, 1997.

Mark Berninger, Mainz

Variations of a Genre. The British History Play in the Nineties

I.

A view on 'the history play in the nineties' only looks at part of the continuing development of a time-honoured genre. The history play is not a new form of theatre that has emerged in the last ten years. Apart from the general habit of considering developments in decades, there is little reason for defining the 'history play of the nineties' as something set off entirely from earlier plays. The development of the history play in the nineties must be seen as the culmination of a long-term movement towards new forms of the genre.

Despite the fact that history plays have enjoyed continuous presence on the British stage, the genre itself (not individual plays or authors) has attracted comparatively little critical attention.[1] This leads to unhelpful definitions such as 'a history play is a play that contains either historical characters or displays historical events'[2] still being widely perpetuated with the result that a large number of contemporary history plays are not considered because they do not fit the definition or are misinterpreted under the auspices of a misleading definition. The great variety of history plays written in the last decade therefore makes it necessary to propose a new definition of the history play which does justice to all the different plays which have emerged.

My suggestion for a useful definition is consequently as encompassing and also as simple as possible: a history play is a play that deals with history. Underlying this, on the surface quite commonplace statement, are a number of important details. First of all, it is necessary to note that the history play is a play defined by its topic. This allows for combination with other genres which are not defined by topic. It also makes clear that there are various different forms of history plays dependent on factors other than topic. Since a play can also contain more than one topic, it is clear that a history play need not be exclusively or even mainly concerned with history.

Secondly, it is important to note that my definition does not state what is to be understood as 'history'. It allows for various concepts of history, as indeed exist. The understanding of what is to be considered as history is not fixed but rather subject to change and discussion. From this follows that a history play needs to be considered in the context of the understanding of history upon which it is based. There is no reason why this principle, which is commonly accepted for older history plays, should not apply to contemporary plays.

'To deal with history' in my definition should not be understood as 'to present past events'. By no means should 'history' be identified solely with 'the past'. This concept, which is implicit in most traditional definitions of the history play, restricts the understanding of history to the positivist view of history of Leopold von Ranke ('to find out what really happened'). This was the dominant concept of history in western culture in the second half of the 19th century and the first half of the 20th century, which demonstrates the limitations of the concept. It is not useful to base a definition of the history play on this concept of history alone, when the definition should also apply to plays written before or after that period or with reference to cultures other than western culture or not belonging to the mainstream of western culture. The second half of the 20th century has seen an increasing criticism of the positivist concept of history[3] and this does indeed manifest itself in the history plays of the nineties. Therefore, the metahistorical discussion about different concepts of history is highly important for this survey.

I suggest that the relationship of a play to 'history as presented in historiography'[4] should not be considered as the central feature for distinguishing between history plays and other plays but as one method of differentiating between different types of history plays. The spectrum of possible relations towards documented history runs from a purely documentary play, which includes nothing but documented facts, to an extremely fictionalised history play which entirely disregards documented history. On a larger scale, this can be seen as a parallel to the relationship between 'reality' and 'fiction' or between 'mimetic' and 'non-mimetic' forms of drama. Thus, a similar spectrum has naturalistic drama as one pole and an extremely anti-mimetic drama as the other. The position of a history play between these poles can be identified by the amount of documentary material which is included (directly or indirectly) in the play and by the use of fictional elements and of non-mimetic techniques, e.g. anachronisms, role-doubling or other such devices.

The level of self-reflexivity of a play is another important feature which is useful for distinguishing different types of history plays. If a history play reflects on its character as a history play, it contains elements dealing either with the theatricality of the play, or with the nature of history, or both. Consequently, the use of metatheatre and of metahistorical discussion can be used to differentiate between various forms of history plays.

Additional levels of self-reflexivity can include an examination of the status of the play as literature (i.e. in relation to other literary texts) and a discussion of the status of history on a more general level (e.g. history in relation to literature and science). Thus, the use of intertextual references (other than documentary sources) and meta-scientific discussions also indicate different forms of history plays.

Finally, one of the main criteria for distinguishing between different types of history plays is the existence of a dominant type of history play which has been considered the genre-model for a long time. I call this 'the traditional history play' because the greater number of history plays in the nineties and the decades before engage with this genre model critically in order to reinvent the genre and develop new forms of history plays. To simplify things and to enhance the contrast to new forms of history plays, I identify the traditional history play with the following features: Interest in the central (mostly male) figures of history, concentration on political and military events (on what has been called 'Haupt- und Staatsaktion' in German), Eurocentrism, use of stage realism (in the paradoxical form of 'historical realism'), chronological presentation of events, adherence to documented history but with the addition of fictional elements (which do not undermine the plays' claim of historical authenticity), and a subscription to the dominant view of history and the prevailing interpretation of the historical events presented. Connected elements include: 'tushery'[5], the use of archaic speech, 'costume drama', hero-worship, and a tragic plot. If history plays engage with this genre model critically, the criticism can be on the level of content (hero-worship, Eurocentrism, the reading of the historical events etc.) or of the dramatic mode of presentation (realism, chronological presentation etc.). A combination of the revision of form and the revision of content is, quite naturally, also possible.

In drawing all this together, it appears suitable to define the following five types of history plays:[6]

1. The **documentary history play** is dominated by the extensive use of documentary material. Fictional elements are avoided as far as possible. Thus, the documentary history play often reaches a high mimetic level and places historical authenticity as its first priority. As concerns the setting, the documentary history play uses either a neutral setting without any distracting and inauthentic details, or a setting similar to the one of the original event.[7] A chronological presentation dominates, ideally the unity of time is also observed. Court procedures lend themselves easily to this form of history play since they are confined to a limited space, a limited time, a limited number of participants and since they are usually well documented.
2. The **realistic history play** can mainly be identified with the traditional history play. Most importantly, it contains a mixture of documented material and fictional elements which do not contradict his-

toriographical knowledge and the dominant interpretation of the events. Formal features of the realistic history play also coincide with the 'traditional history play' (chronological presentation, stage realism, etc.).

3. The **revisionist history play** can be defined *ex negativo*, i.e. by its critical stance against the realistic history play. It challenges and revises elements of the realistic history play. Depending on whether the criticism is directed mainly against the formal characteristics of the realistic history play or against the content represented, the revisionist history play can be subdivided into plays of formal revision and revision of content. The driving force behind most revisionist history plays is the perception of inconsistencies and misrepresentation in the dominant version of history against which an alternative (in terms of form or content) is presented.
4. The **metahistorical play** is dominated by self-reflexivity. Central to this type of history play is the discussion of different views of history or a discussion of how history is made. As a consequence it very often contains two time levels (past and present), between which the process of history-making can be debated. Metadramatic, metascientific and intertextual elements quite naturally combine with the metahistorical.
5. In contrast to the traditional understanding, the **posthistorical play** is probably the most problematic type of history play since it transcends most extensively the limits of what is traditionally seen as a history play. It contains a high degree of fictionalised history. Whether an event is documented or not is irrelevant. Quite to the contrary, the posthistorical play thrives on unrecorded 'gaps of history'. History is understood as similar to fiction, fiction as historically relevant. The distinction between history and myth is challenged. Alternative forms of narrative accounts of the past are employed instead of the use of document-based historiographic discourse. The posthistorical play uses various forms of non-mimetic drama such as symbolism, non-mimetic language (verse, 'absurd' speech, symbolic language, sounds), a non-realistic setting, and undefined or unfixed identities of the characters. Linear chronology is irrelevant, anachronisms are frequent. The logic of time is secondary to and shaped by the dramatic logic. Thus, the posthistorical play breaks radically with the conventions of stage realism.

II.

It is important to note that the first three types of the categories defined above (i.e. the documentary history play, the realistic history play, and the revisionist history play) are all dominated by the view that there is 'one true history', which is to be represented on stage. The differences lie only in the mode of presentation (realism or alternative forms), the importance attributed to the adherence to documentary material, and the content presented. Quite interestingly, history plays revising the content of history have frequently made extensive use of documentary material to strengthen their claim of presenting the true history which is meant to replace a misrepresentation in the usual historical perspective. Only with the introduction of the self-reflective element does the possibility of the parallel existence of different concepts of history gain full force. Yet, as the establishment of an alternative history implicitly contains the idea that various forms of history (or at least readings of history) are possible, the revisionist history play contains an implicit metahistorical statement and thus borders on the metahistorical play, which allows for various degrees of explicitness of the metahistorical element. The posthistorical play can be seen as the extreme form of the revisionist history play, both in terms of form and content. However, it shares the idea of the relativity of history with the metahistorical play. The metahistorical play, in contrast to the formal extremism of the posthistorical play, often adheres (at least partly) to the conventions of stage realism. Both the realistic history play and the posthistorical play use the gaps in documented history to fictionalise history. From this it becomes clear that the five types which have been sketched above are not to be understood as entirely separate categories but rather as a spectrum which allows for overlaps between the different types.

It has to be said that this spectrum contains an implicit element of linearity which runs contrary to these cross-connections. The linear development which could easily be extracted from this typology is a movement from the traditional type of history play, the realistic history play, towards new forms of history plays.[8] The first step in this development would be criticism of form and a revision of content. Thus, alternative versions of history and alternative forms of presentation are presented. From the awareness of alternative versions of history rises an understanding of history as a relative construction. This is reflected in a growing self-reflexivity and in the introduction of metahistorical argument. Radicalised to an extreme extent, this process leads to the posthistorical play. This linear development describes in many ways the development of the history play over the last 40 years, from conventional costume drama and stage realism to postmodern forms of the history play. Yet, like most linear descriptions, this formula is misleading. It suppresses the cross-connections between the different types of history plays and the existence of early examples of new history plays which would upset the chronological sequence, such as Edward Bond's posthistorical play *Early Morning* (1968) or John Arden's formal revision of the history play in *Armstrong's Last Goodnight* (1964), *The Hero Rises Up* (1968), and other plays. Most importantly, the description of such a linear development would tend to suggest that once a new variation of the genre has developed, the older forms might become obsolete. That this is not the case will be demonstrated by a set of examples drawn from recent history plays, which will illustrate my typology and show that all forms of history plays continue to be written and produced.

III.

Nuremberg – The War Crimes Trial (1996), edited by Richard Norton-Taylor, is an example of a highly documentary history play. The script consists entirely of excerpts from the transcripts of the Nürnberg trials. Consequently, the 'author' of the play, Richard Norton-Taylor, appears only as 'editor' of the play. It is quite telling that Norton-Taylor does not fit the usual profile of a playwright. He is a journalist and historian, who has turned to the theatre as an additional medium (beyond non-fiction books) to present his findings. Quite consequently another of his plays, *Half the Picture*, a stage-adaptation of the Scott 'Arms to Iraq' Inquiry in which he collaborated with John McGrath, has won both the 1994 Freedom of Information Campaign Award and the 1994 Time Out Drama Award. In the same way *Nuremberg* can be seen as a mixture of information and drama.

Quite typically for a documentary history play, it focuses on court proceedings. What has been said at Nürnberg is documented word for word. Thus, the Nürnberg trials can count as an unusually well-documented historical event. Yet, uneasiness remains that a court procedure had to be chosen instead of other, less well documented events. The crimes which are presented in the case exist only as reports or figures, yet it is the war crimes and crimes against humanity which are the actual focus of all the proceedings. The play is doubly remote from the 'actual events' (being a play about the trial which followed the events). This is reflected in the difficulties of the prosecutors in proving the personal involvement of the defendants in the criminal actions. Thus, the play can be read as containing an implicit metahistorical statement which is concerned with the necessity and difficulty of establishing historical truth in order to prosecute criminal actions. In his introduction Norton-Taylor makes clear that he is most deeply interested in promoting the idea of international tribunals for war crimes, which until recently found little support. The fact that this play was presented together with other documentary plays on more recent atrocities and the subsequent court procedures (*Ex-Yu* by Goran Stefanovski, *Haiti* by Keith Reddin, *Reel Rwanda* by Femi Osofisan, and *Srebrenica* by Nicholas Kent) underlines this perspective.

Albert Speer (2000) by David Edgar is another documentary history play on a related topic, but in comparison with *Nuremberg* it displays a greater amount of authorial freedom with the material. Edgar states in the subtitle of the play that it is "[b]ased on *Albert Speer: His Battle with Truth* by Gitta Sereny", yet has to admit that in order to adapt this 720-page book for the stage he "had to conflate scenes and concentrate the incidents on which they are based".[9] Quite logically he identifies himself as the author of the play but maintains: "As ever, the aim of this is better to reveal the truth" (ix). This shows how strongly he is oriented towards the ability of historiography – here in the shape of Gitta Sereny's book, which is "written with the utmost historical rigour" (*ibid.*) and "whose moral credentials and dignity of purpose were questioned by no one" (149) – to identify historical truth. Edgar admits differences between historiography and drama though:

> However passionate its author, a work of history [i.e. historiography] has an essentially magisterial relationship with its readership. Like the French legal system, the medium invites sober consideration of the evidence, the balancing of arguments and the disinterested search for truth. Like the British courtroom, a play tends to the adversarial, demanding that the jury identify with one side. (149–150)

In identifying drama with the British legal system, he invests drama with a similar authority as historiography (if this is not to be understood as a criticism of British legal procedures). Edgar's play thus shares both the theme and the documentary approach with *Nuremberg* (*Albert Speer* also contains a court scene which is, naturally, very similar to Norton-Taylor's play), with the one important difference that, to present Speer's story fully, Edgar feels the need to expand beyond the fully documented procedures of the courtroom. Consequently, scenes of Speer's career in Nazi Germany, of his imprisonment in Spandau and of his life after his release in 1966 are included. Here, fictional elements quite necessarily have to be included. The dialogue with the chaplain at Spandau, Casalis, for example, which serves as a narrative frame for the first part of the play, in which Speer's past in Nazi Germany is revealed, must count as 'fiction based on documents'. A chaplain named Casalis is documented to have spoken with Speer frequently in Spandau but the actual words of the text are not documented and rather follow Edgar's dramatic need for a frame.

This also shows how Edgar has to manipulate the documentary material into a (dramatic) narrative.

As in *Nuremberg*, a metahistorical element about the problem of establishing historical truth is included in *Albert Speer*. Edgar mentions this in relation to his efforts to transfer Gitta Sereny's book to the stage: "This is a vulnerable procedure in a play based on a biography in which truth is pursued but also questioned" (ix). At numerous places in the text, Edgar presents various forms of establishing the truth (court procedure, confession, memoirs, archival work, a lecture with questions asked etc.) but they all prove inefficient in establishing the real truth about Speer. Edgar tries to explain this with a quote by W. A. Visser 't Hooft, which precedes Act Two: "People cannot find a place in their imagination (or allow themselves to remember) [*sic*] unimaginable horror. It is possible to live in a twilight between knowing and not knowing." (89)

IV.

Alan Bennett's *The Madness of George III* (1991) contains all the features which have been identified with the realistic history play. Bennett tries to include only information which is either documentary or compatible with documented history. He accounts for this in his 16-page introduction, which describes his historical research and findings. He states that "[t]he characters are largely historical"[10] and includes additional information about the political background of the play. Bennett "struggled to mince these chunks of information into credible morsels of dialogue" (*ibid.*) but "often felt it would have been simpler to call the audience in a quarter of an hour earlier and give them a short curtain lecture on the nature of eighteenth-century politics before getting on with the play proper" (xiii).[11] At the same time Bennett also feels free to invent details in accordance with documentary history as the inclusion of one of George's servants, Fitzroy, shows:

> I thought I had invented Fitzroy but discover that in 1801 George III had an aide-de-camp of this name, who was later the heart-throb of the king's youngest daughter, Amelia. He was 'generally admitted to be good-looking in a rather wooden sort of way, he had neither dash nor charm and seems to have been on the frigid side into the bargain', which describes our Fitzroy exactly. That he was playing a double game and was an intimate of the Prince of Wales is my invention. (xiii-xiv)

The play follows a linear chronology and adheres to the conventions of stage realism with only one exception at the very end of the play, when a modern doctor, Dr Ida MacAlpine, enters the scene and converses with George's servants about the nature of the king's illness. This very short scene, which serves to pass on to the audience medical information about George's madness (not available to 18th-century physicians and thus impossible to include in a strictly realistic play), is the only anachronistic break of an otherwise intact stage illusion of the 18th century. Bennett constructs this illusion by the usual means of employing period music (Händel's music is played frequently), period costume,[12] and period language:

> NICHOLSON: I have a property due to me from the crown of England.
> KING: The poor creature's mad. Do not hurt her, she's not hurt me.
> NICHOLSON: Give me my property or the country will be drenched in blood. (1)

As concerns the setting, Bennett wrote his play with a number of period settings in mind and had to admit "[h]ow to stage the succession of scenes [...] that were more like a script for a film than a play, I had no idea" (xxi). It is not surprising that the play has successfully been turned into a film, a medium which usually has fewer restrictions concerning costumes and setting.

The plot is centred on the important historical figures of George III and the Prince of Wales. Grouped around them are – no less important and historically documented – Prime Minister William Pitt and his opponents Fox and Sheridan. The focus of the play is mainly on the political significance of the events, and Bennett repeatedly stresses in his introduction and in the play that the personal condition of the king in the 18th century was a matter of utmost political importance. Thus the play consists entirely of 'Haupt- und Staatsaktionen' and because of this it fits the traditional model of the history play exactly. The only revisionary elements of the play are to be found in Bennett's wish to clarify the audience's idea of George's 'madness' and to counter the Whig interpretation of history in which "George had been written up as a villain and a clumsy tyrant" (v). Yet since both these aspects were subjected to revision in historiography decades ago, Bennett does not exceed the limits of the 'agreed facts of the past' or the dominant interpretation of the past.

V.

As Stephanie Kramer and Gilbert/Tompkins have shown in their respective studies,[13] the revisionist approach towards the history play is typical of numerous feminist history plays and postcolonial plays. Revision here concentrates quite naturally on the content but also extends to the inclusion of alternative forms of drama, which are either identified as typically female or postcolonial, in any case as opposed to male-dominated, eurocentric stage-realism. In *The Gut Girls* (1988), Sarah Daniels presents an unexpected picture of Deptford at the turn of the century. Her revision of the "accepted historical picture" contains a number of aspects. Firstly, she concentrates on women, which is, seen against the dominance of male figures in history plays, an act of fundamental revision. Secondly, the play is not about a single character but about a group of women, the 'Gut Girls', and can thus be seen as an alternative to the presentation of a single hero. Thirdly, the women represent the working class, not the powerful and commonly historically visible members of society. Instead they are members of the 'silent (or silenced) masses'. As the misrepresentation of the working class has inspired a great number of political history plays, this aspect of *The Gut Girls*, the appalling working conditions, the exploitation, etc. is probably the least unexpected feature of historical revision. Of course, it combines easily with the focus on gender, as working class women were doubly exploited, which Daniels does not forget to point out in her play. The most important act of revision lies in the fact that the women working in the gutting factory are not depicted as subdued but as economically and also intellectually independent. They are 'strong women' to an extent which makes them appear more like a contemporary feminist ideal than like a representation of historical reality. This can be seen as an act of counter-revision of history by Daniels, who sketches her gut girls as a counter-image to the common expectation of the (either silent and invisible or subdued and victimised) working-class woman. Quite paradoxically, Lady Helen's attempt to improve the Gut Girls' lives turns out to be the end of their independence. Forced into respectability and serfdom as chambermaids, they lose their freedom and also their group identity. This can be seen as a parallel to postcolonial history plays which depict the fall from an ideal, independent pre-contact phase into the subjugation of colonialism.[14]

Another clearly revisionist history play is Sue Glover's *Bondagers* (1991), which deals with the lives of female farm workers in Scotland in the mid 19th century. In concentrating on the bondagers (female subworkers who had to be hired by each male farmworker to work alongside him), Glover also places the topic of female work centre-stage.[15] Her focus on Scotland and the inclusion of Scots dialect constitutes another aspect of the revision of history and the traditional history play, which is usually not only Eurocentric but also highlights English (or even only London) events at the expense of the regional margin. This places *Bondagers* in a long line of Scottish and Scots history plays, which runs from e.g. Robert McLellan's *Jamie the Saxt* (1937) via John MacGrath's *The*

Cheviot the Stag and the Black, Black Oil (1973) and John Arden's *Armstrong's Last Goodnight* (1964) to Liz Lochhead's *Mary Queen of Scots Got Her Head Chopped Off* (1987).[16] Glover's play is, in many ways, an invocation and reclamation of the lost lives of the bondagers, who are now nothing but 'ghosts in the fields'. At the end of the play one of the bondagers, Sara, tells about the vision her young friend Tottie had:

> She would tell me these stories, she said they were true.
> She 'saw' them, she said, on the moor, in the mist.
> In a hundred years – more –
> We'll be ghosts in the fields,
> But we'll cry out in vain,
> For there'll be no one there.
> Fields without folk.
> Machines without horses.
> A whole week's harvest
> All done in one night,
> By the light of great lamps …
> Not the light of the moon,
> They won't wait for the moon … no need for the moon …[17]

A revisionist history play which combines revision of both form and content is *A Dead Woman on Holiday* (1991) by Julia Pascal. This becomes obvious in comparison with *Nuremberg* and *Albert Speer*, with which it shares the topic of the Nürnberg trials. Building it around identical material,[18] Pascal constructs a different story and a very different play. Instead of focusing on the (male) war criminals, her play follows the character of Sophia Goldberg, an Alsacian Jew married to a British soldier who works as an interpreter at the trials. This fictional character is based on the journalist Martha Gellhorn, who – as Pascal describes in her introduction[19] (7) – reported on the trials. Again, a marginalised figure becomes the centre of the action. Pascal describes that she "was fascinated to read how individual lives were totally shattered by the act of interpreting the Holocaust".[20] Instead of presenting the trials objectively or realistically, Pascal stages them (and with this the Holocaust) through the deliberately subjective perspective of the interpreter, e.g. when Sophia and her colleagues have to memorise the French equivalents of special vocabulary necessary for the trials (like 'to shoot', 'annulment', 'assassination', 'atrocities', 'annihilation', 'forced labour', 'wholesale deportation', 'mass killings', etc.). This becomes an almost musical scene (entitled 'Boogie'), which consists solely of the staccato rhythms of the English words and their French translations. That the play is not going to follow the usual conventions of stage realism is established right from the beginning when two stand-up comedians introduce the scene (Nürnberg in 1946) in cabaret style.[21] In the course of the play the linear narrative of Sophia's life during the trials is punctuated by fragmentary scenes which show the ravings of a dyed-in-the-wool Nazi woman, court scenes in which the various languages (Russian, German, French and English) overlap, a stylised baseball game, etc. Finally, the play closes with a scene in which its various threads (the trial, Sophia's private life, and the ravings of the Nazi woman) interweave. Factual mixes with fictional and symbolical, the private with the public. In comparison with the documentary style of *Nuremberg* and the more realistic, yet document-based style of *Albert Speer*, Julia Pascal's play presents a formally alternative version of the history of the Nürnberg trials.

VI.

The tendency inherent in the revisionist history play towards the metahistorical is well exemplified in Sheila Yeger's *Self Portrait* (1990). The play is clearly dominated by the wish to write a hitherto neglected (female) artist into history. The painter Gwen John, who is overshadowed both by being the sister of Augustus John and the mistress of Auguste Rodin, is the central character of the play. Her paintings have suffered from a lack of public recognition due to a male-oriented interpretation of art history, which saw in Gwen John no more than a second-rate painter related to the important figures of Rodin and Augustus John. Thus, the official record has rendered her and her paintings invisible. Sheila Yeger presents an alternative interpretation of Gwen John by setting the play at a memorial exhibition which tries to do justice to Gwen John's paintings and the story of her life. The scenes at the exhibition change without interruption into scenes set during John's lifetime and thus Yeger can juxtapose different views of John's paintings and life with the past. It is helpful that Gwen John's paintings have autobiographical subjects, i.e. they show objects which can be related to John's biography, most obviously in the self-portrait which gives the play its title. Thus, they can function as relicts of the past which contain the forgotten (or suppressed) story of John's life and which serve as 'starting points' for scenes dealing with the time and situation of the production of the paintings.

Yeger includes a great amount of documentary evidence about Gwen John in her play to strengthen her revision of John's work and life. This ranges from the presence of the paintings to biographical information presented as a slide-show with commentary from a tape recorder at the exhibition. In her introduction Yeger informs the reader that she has conducted extensive research on Gwen John, e.g. reading through the 3000 love letters John wrote to Rodin. This, in combination with a bibliography Yeger provides on the subject of Gwen John, strengthens her claim to present a historically accurate alternative account of Gwen John's life.

So far, key features of the revisionist history play can be detected but by giving the factual scenes of John's life the fictional frame of the exhibition, Yeger opens the play towards a more general discussion. The central theme, beyond the individual case of Gwen John, is the question of the marginalisation of the female artist. With this, Yeger enters the metalevel of the discussion on how the historical image of Gwen John and her marginalised status have been constructed and how they should be reconstructed differently. The role doubling as well as the double plot situated both in the past and present also enables a juxtaposition of numerous versions and interpretations of the past. At the same time, the process of marginalisation and of rehabilitation can be presented. Yeger shows how strongly an interpretation of Gwen John's work and life depends on the view the interpreter takes, which she demonstrates as being utterly dependent on the character of the interpreter. The chauvinist male critics Frank and Robert find John's work unimportant and reduce their interest to the erotic details of John's life and her relation to her famous brother. Female viewers generally judge the pictures and the story of her life differently. The art student detects her technical skill and sees her as a role model. The same is true for the writer Barbara, who can identify not only with the artist John but also with the problems of her life since she shares several of her experiences. The nun Sister Mary Ursula interprets John as a spiritual model, and for the organiser of the exhibition, Karen, she is a prime example of a marginalised female artist. It must be noted that, although Yeger clearly has sympathies for the female interpretations – or rather antipathies against the male-dominated interpretation – the play does not decide on a 'true version' of Gwen John's life and work. It becomes clear that the traditional image of her is wrong but several alternatives are presented. The question of how John should be seen is answered 'from multiple perspectives'. Therefore, the play illustrates the movement from the revisionist type of history play towards the metahistorical play.

Another indicator of the play's tendency towards a(n implicitly) self-reflective metahistorical approach is the extensive use of role-doubling. This device is highly significant as characters in one plot of the play are, beyond the need to economise on the number of actors required, doubled systematically with characters on the second level of the play. The only exceptions are the central characters Gwen John and Barbara. The role-change happens directly on the stage as the scenes change without interruption from one time-level to the other. This underlines the connections between the present and the past, as the doubled characters share traits, but it also stresses implicitly the theatricality of the action.

VII.

David Edgar's *Pentecost* (1995) is a very good example of a dramatic text which does not fit into the traditional definitions of the history play but must nevertheless be considered as part of the genre. Although no scene plays in the past and no historical characters appear on the stage, *Pentecost* is highly concerned with history. I will illustrate this in the following by focusing only on the central element of this complicated play, the church fresco which literally forms its background. This painting is a piece of history which is brought back into the present. In this process the various purposes which are served by this discovery (financial, nationalistic, artistic, religious) are thematised and thus addressed on a metahistorical level.

The setting of the play is a derelict church in some unspecified Eastern European country. The scene does not shift from there but the setting and most notably the state of the painting changes slightly with every scene. At the opening of the play no part of the fresco is visible as it is hidden behind a brick wall with a revolutionary mural. During the first scene part of the wall is removed and a small section of the fresco is revealed.

> [I]n Scene Two it is in the process of being cleaned, in Scene Three it is being covered with a gauze and canvas facing [to remove the fresco from the wall], a procedure completed by Scene Four. In the second act, the facing is removed but the painting remains largely in darkness until the beginning of Scene Seven. We do however see reproductions and outlines of sections of the painting, and the whole in a blown up photograph.[22]

At the end of Act Two the painting is destroyed as anti-terrorist commandos break through the wall with the fresco – "It is, apparently, the weakest wall" (104) – and the last scene shows mainly rubble, debris and a gaping hole in the wall. From this, it becomes clear how symbolically charged the realistic setting is. It represents the various stages of a process of historical (re)construction: discovery, removal of distracting details,[23] making the painting readily available by trying to remove it from its original surroundings, reproduction, comparison with similar paintings (Giotto), reduction to an outline, abuse (as a hostage in an act of 'art terrorism') and finally destruction due to practical necessities.

All these uses or abuses of the painting are just a continuation of the "chequered history" (xx) of the church, which has, over the centuries, already served various purposes depending on those in power. It became an Orthodox church when the Slavic influence dominated and Catholic when the Hungarians ruled. Under Turkish rule it became a mosque, in the Napoleonic wars it was used as a stable, then as a prison or 'Transit Centre' during the time of German occupation in WW II. After that, under communist rule, it was converted into a "Museum of Atheism and Progressive People's Culture" (5) and finally into a foodstore. In the course of the play the church is discovered to be the birthplace of perspective painting, then it also becomes a refuge for a group of persecuted immigrants from various countries and finally the site of a 'counter-terrorist' strike with numerous dead. The local art historian Gabriella sums up the fate of the church:

> Church. Mosque. Stable. Torture centre. Foodstore. Fortress. Cemetery.
> *Slight pause.*
> *Middle Europe theme park? Sure. (104)*

The church is a striking example of a 'semantisation of space' or palimpsest as various historical levels are present in the same space at the same time. As the play opens, Gabriella uncovers the church's history layer by layer for the British art expert Oliver. She shows him the prisoners' signatures under the socialist painting. Underneath that, the holes where catholic paintings of the stations of the cross had been hung are visible. Then, under a layer of whitewash, orthodox paintings appear and at the very end, underneath these orthodox paintings, the fresco of the 'Lamentation of Christ' she has discovered. It is telling, how each ruling power has taken pains to paint over the previous history, to whitewash the walls and reuse the church, or in other words 'the commodified past', for its own purposes. Now, the church with its paintings is instrumentalised again, by priests, politicians, art historians, nationalists, refugees and soldiers. They all insist that different layers of the church history must be seen as the most important one. With the charged, multi-layered space of the church, Edgar thus illustrates the use and abuse of history as well as the influence history has on the present.

Quite typically for a metahistorical play, *Pentecost* adheres to conventions of stage realism but is mainly fictional. The plot of the play is highly fictional but stays (just) within the limits of the realistically imaginable. References to documented history and reality exist (e.g. the connection of the church fresco to Giotto paintings) but often they remain unfocused and inaccurate (e.g. the fact that the play takes place in an unspecified country which bears strong resemblance with Bulgaria but is not identified as Bulgaria). Also quite typically metahistorical, the printed text is embellished with supplementary quotations from various sources (from Leonardo da Vinci to Samantha Fox and newspaper commentaries), which add new metalevels to the different themes discussed in the play.

VIII.

The definition of the posthistorical play as given above was written with an eye to the plays and theoretical writings of Howard Barker. In his collection of essays, *Arguments for a Theatre*, Barker is quite explicit about the relation of his theatre towards history: "I discovered that the only things worth describing now are things that do not happen, just as the only history plays worth writing concern themselves with what did not occur."[24] He makes clear that he has little regard for authenticity in the usual sense and is not interested in basing his plays on documentary material: "The drama which I practice creates its own world, it does not require validation from external sources, either of ideology or of spurious realism, which is itself an ideology. It is compellingly imaginative and without responsibility to historical or political convention." (29)

Thus, his plays are decidedly anti-mimetic and attacks against the idea that theatre reproduces reality: "Drama [...] is not life described but life imagined, it is possibility and not reproduction" (30). In this he proposes a radical drama which concentrates on the poetic (or poesis) instead. He does not understand this as a restriction against dealing with the historical, quite on the contrary. A great number of his plays are concerned with history but in a sense that differs from the positivist understanding of history. Being deeply suspicious of 'truth' as a tool of ideology, Barker stated for his own works: "The theatre is not a disseminator of truth but a provider of versions. Its statements are provisional. In a time when nothing is clear, the inflicting of clarity is a stale arrogance" (45). Thus, his plays are full of ambiguities and this also characterises his historical method. He sees the process of constructing history as "the anodyne reconciliations which pass for public history" and cause "the annihilation of individual pain in collective orthodoxy" (59). Consequently, he defines the purpose of the history play as counteracting these movements, often by employing methods of the theatre of cruelty. Yet, he states that he is not interested in 'correcting' a false historical perspective (as a revisionist history play would) and replacing it with (an equally biased) different version.

He does not believe in either confirming the audience's expectations about history ("Do you want to pay £ 10 to be told what you knew already? That is theft." [47]) or 'winning the audience over' ("Do you want to agree all the time? That is flattery" [*ibid.*]). As he thinks that "[t]he audience itself must be encouraged to discover meaning" (49), he lays his texts and the history they contain open to a multiplicity of readings. He does not want to teach the audience anything about history, not even how history is constructed (as metahistorical plays do) since he upholds "that the play is not a lecture" (55).

Thus freed of "naturalistic bondage" (56) and of "the statement of loyalties, to gender, to ideology, to concepts of the progressive, even to melancholy" (123), his claim is that he is free to explore "dramatic beauty" (56), "to establish the primacy of [...] experience over the public interest" (59) and thus to write for a theatre which "replaces loyalty with an aesthetic of will to experience" (123).

Thus, his history play is radically anti-naturalist, ambiguous, metaphoric, elitist, anti-documentary, poetic, and audience-related. As a consequence, he has turned to imaginary histories, which combine the historical, mythological and fictional on a symbolic level.

The Bite of the Night (1988) is "4 ½ hours of an imaginative unearthing of the layers of Troy"[25] with Barker's typical imaginative creation of both historical and mythical characters. Barker himself has said about this play: "*The Bite of the Night* is not contemporary, nor satirical, neither is it short. It is mythical, tragic and very long" (1993: 38–39). Thus, it defies the audience's expectations to be entertained or taught something. Concerning the historical character of the play, Barker has remarked: "The ahistoricity of this journey is obvious, the collapsing of time and narrative signalling to the audience that it must forsake its conventional expectations of meaning" (*ibid.*, 83).

Hated Nightfall (1994) is an exemplary play of Barker's technique of imaginary history. He uses the 'unrecorded gap' in history which is still left after all the information about the final days of the last Russian Tsar and his family has been collected. In this historical void (which has given rise to all sorts of speculations about what really happened), he sets his deliberately imaginary history play. Little to nothing in the play is rooted in documented history. The references to reality are just sufficient to relate it to the historical events at Ekaterinburg in 1918. Whenever the identification with recorded history becomes too close, Barker introduces additional references which stress the ambiguity of the play. There is, for example, no distinct reference to the Russian character of the scenery or any attempt to include 'historical flair'. Instead of 'comrades', revolutionaries are addressed as 'citizens', which is more reminiscent of the French Revolution than of the events of 1918. The identities of the historical figures become blurred. Instead of Alexandra, the wife of the Tsar is called Caroline, which connects her more with English Queens of the 18th century than with the Russian Tsarina of 1918. Theatrical and symbolic images like the sleeping posture Caroline assumes on a chair, are more central to the play than historical references. The language of the play is far removed from any historical sources or from 'period speech', but it is also distinct from normal contemporary discourse. Instead, it is dense, fragmented, poetical, and symbolic. Just as the sentences of the characters are disrupted by pauses and sudden leaps in unexpected directions, the plot disregards conventional realist patterns. The execution of the royal family is imminent but not carried out in the course of the play. Instead, the anticipation and the repetitious killing of other characters structures the play. Barker thus demonstrates that his 'theatre of catastrophe' is much closer to the radical anti-mimetic dramaturgy of the Theatre of the Absurd than to any form of (even revised) stage realism.

The technique of approaching history non-realistically and metaphorically is radicalised in *Found in the Ground*, one of Barker's most recent plays.[26] Instead of imagining history in unrecorded gaps of historiography, he constructs a play on symbolic images alone. There is no attempt to connect the play directly with any recorded past event, yet the dramatic metaphors Barker invents are charged with historical allusions. The symbolic images of the play contain, among many others, a naked, headless woman who walks again and again across the stage, a number of nurses who carry trays with heaps of earth or peat on them, and a pyramid of smouldering books which is fuelled occasionally by a workman who tips new piles of books into the fire.

The naked, headless woman turns out to carry the name 'Macedonia'. As she is identified as an allegorical figure, contemporary allusions to the wars in Yugoslavia might spring to mind, yet she also assumes a more generally metaphorical function:

> (*A blurred, enlarged portrait photograph descends and stops over the shoulders of the headless woman*) [...]
> MACEDONIA: I am all the Ann Franks (*Pause*)
> All the Ann Franks me (*Pause*)
> The ditches full of (*Pause*)
> The pits of (*Pause*)
> Composers
> Violinists
> Physicists (*Pause*)
> I am all the Ann Franks (*Pause*)
> All the Ann Franks me (310)

The name 'Ann Frank' here is less a concrete historical reference to a distinct Jewish girl, but a historical symbol. It makes clear what the title of the play hints at, that Barker attempts a theatrical engagement with the buried history of human suffering and especially with the holocaust. A comparison with the documentary history plays *Nuremberg* and *Albert Speer*, and with the revisionist history play *Dead Woman on Holiday*, underlines the posthistorical character of Barker's play. *Found in the Ground* makes no attempt to reproduce reality in any form. Everything in the play is symbolic, not factual. Images substitute references to reality. Instead of presenting the proceedings of the Nürnberg trials in any form, the central character of the play, Toonelhuis[27], is identified as a (fictional) dying judge of the Nürnberg trials. The books burnt in the background are Toonelhuis's library and files which he wishes to be burnt before his death. The allusion to the book burnings of the Nazis and Heinrich Heine's famous prophecy[28] is made explicit when Denmark, his librarian, tries to save the books:

Denmark: The books should not be burned
Vastly better
If burning must take place
Humans burn (327)

The earth or peat on the trays of the nurses are the remnants of various Nazis who were sentenced to death by Toonelhuis. He revels in rummaging in and eating the remains of his convicts, which is his method of reviving memory. Images of the past, as well as the ghost of one of his convicts and of Hitler (who appears as a 'casual visitor') haunt him.

To reduce these images to unambiguous messages would mean reading against Barker's explicit intention. As the author doesn't claim higher insight into his plays ("As the artist chiefly responsible for what occurs on the stage I claim no superior insight or even the status of a visionary, let alone a just man with a conscience" [Barker 1993, 89]), it seems that "[t]he critic must suffer like / everyone else. / The play is important. / The audience is divided / and goes home / disturbed / or / amazed" (*ibid.*, 71). Just as he claims,[29] Barker makes a fetish of contradiction:

Clarity
Meaning
Logic
And Consistency

None of it
None[30]

Most importantly, Barker's play is not concerned with moral judgements, which seem unavoidable in a play that alludes to the Holocaust.[31] The experience of suffering gains prominence over easy moral judgement and the connected narrative strategies:

BURGTEATA: In the great plagues in the great wars this was mundane this was commonplace the apotheosis of normality every cottage every manor-house the duckpond thick with rotten sheep the corps all seed the thatch squashed by the thumb of incomprehensible malevolence I say thatch I say duckpond I am picturesque I have to be sentimental how it suffocates me why else did I run to filthy hospitals only to keep the sentimental off only to blind the sentimental with a pan of scalding squalor (*Pause*). (347)

IX.

A number of general topics and tendencies of the history play in the nineties have already become apparent in the exemplary plays discussed above. The development towards higher self-reflectivity and fictionalisation, which gave rise to the metahistorical play and posthistorical play, appears as central. This is reflected in the growing number of metahistorical and posthistorical plays and in the tendency to include metahistorical elements even in documentary plays (e.g. in Edgar's *Albert Speer*). This development can be easily connected with general postmodern tendencies towards increased self-reflexivity, but the most distinctly dramatic feature shared by history plays in the nineties is the continued interest in the exploration of the relationship between history and the specific possibilities and characteristics of drama beyond the limits of the traditional form of the genre. This interest in combination with postmodern self-reflexivity is most directly discernible in the use of metadrama, for example in Timberlake Wertenbaker's *After Darwin* (1998), which presents, in alternating scenes, a history play about Darwin and the efforts of a present-day theatre group to develop and stage that very play. Discussions about the possibility of presenting history on the stage and the chances and problems arising from this are interwoven in Wertenbaker's play with corresponding 'historical' scenes.

Objects as traces of the past which can bridge the gap between past and present achieve a central role in several plays. The paintings in *Self Portrait* or the various objects (letters, the apple, various books, the tortoise, etc.) which circulate freely between the two time levels in *Arcadia* are good examples, but the use of charged objects becomes most obvious in the most potent trace of past life, the dead body. Several new history plays are centred around the discovery of a dead body, e.g. Shelagh Stephenson's *An Experiment with an Air Pump* (1998) or the Theatre de Complicite's *Mnemonic* (1999). In Howard Barker's plays, the dead body is a recurring symbol of the unearthed or unburied suffering of the past. It is not only the most telling trace of past life but also demands an explanation, it demands to be brought back to life, to have its story told. This becomes the starting point for history's process of construction, as alternative stories of the past can be constructed around the 'evidence' of the dead body.

Since space is a very concrete category for drama, more than for example for the historical novel, the semantisation of space, the coexistence of past and present in the same space becomes a central feature of many new history plays. Often the theatrical space becomes a palimpsest. In Edgar's *Pentecost* the simultaneous existence of several historical layers (of paintings) forms the background of the play. Tom Stoppard's *Arcadia* (1993) is an example of a carefully arranged gradual entanglement of past and present, which alternate in a setting which remains constant until they coexist and overlap in the final scene.[32] In *Poetry or Bust* (1993) and *The Kaisers of Carnuntum* (1995) Tony Harrison makes use of the semantisation of space in a rather different way. In transporting the theatre to the exact location of the historical event,[33] he brings the audience and the stage action in direct contact with a highly charged space. In doing so, Harrison has no interest in documentary authenticity but rather in a poetical invocation of a tell-tale ghost image of the past. This is achieved through a mixture of authentic, poetic, and anachronistic elements, for example in the setting of *The Kaisers of Carnuntum*, which consists of the Roman arena, live animals (lions and tigers) under the tribunes, in the centrepiece of the arena a stylised map of the Roman Empire with the model of the Colosseum in the middle, and modern border watchtowers behind each tribune. This mixture of authenticity, poetry and anachronism also extends to the level of language and sound. The play starts with passages from Marcus Aurelius' "Meditations" recited from one of the watchtowers in ancient Greek. This is followed by the verses of a 'Chorus of Women', by cello music, modern sounds ("*sirens, machine-gun fire* [...] *and the sound of a searching helicopter as if someone unauthorised is crossing a border*"),[34] and then finally by the entrance of Commodus with his very own anachronistic couplets:

> [...] Is this Carnuntum? Thumbs up or thumbs down!
> And is this the arena of that ruined Roman town?
> [...]
> I have something to tell you. But first
> in Marcomannisch: *Ich habe Durst.*[35]

Language itself as a trace of and a symbol for the past is a recurring theme. The most basic form is the use of period speech in realistic history plays to enhance the illusion of historical realism. In revisionist history plays language can become a tool of revision as the alternative version of the past is, literally, 'voiced', e.g. in the working class argot of the female workers in *The Gut Girls* or in the Scots of *Bondagers*. In metahistorical plays, language contains traces of the past and is also the medium of the narrative (re)construction of history.[36] In *Pentecost* all the various languages of the refugees contain stories which reveal their identity and individual history. The effort to translate the past from one language into another in the Nürnberg trials is the central event in *A Dead Woman on*

Holiday. *An Experiment with an Air Pump* is, among other things, a play about the 18th-century scientist Peter Mark Roget and his efforts to categorise the whole vocabulary of the English language, in the play a symbol of the scientific optimism of the past, which is juxtaposed with postmodern scepticism.

Some plays also depict non-verbal communication as a means of constructing the past, e.g. Nigel William's *Country Dancing* (1986), in which disappearing folk dances and fiddle tunes are collected by Cecil Sharp, a folklorist. The dances and tunes form the central historical and narrative metaphors of the play as Sharp notes down the memories of the old fiddler Ted, who remembers the past through dances and music. In *Bondagers* dance is shown as part of the lost life of the bondagers, as part of their rural culture. The 'kirn', the great dance and harvest festival, is the central event both in the working year of the bondagers and in the plot of the play as the events reach their climax there. Dance also appears in the very contrary works of Howard Barker and Peter Barnes. In Barker's *Hated Nightfall* the central figure bears the telling name 'Dancer' and his dance with an enormous wedding cake becomes an ambiguous symbol for his sexual desire for Caroline and has historical undertones:

> DANCER (*hacking another slice*): **Let them eat cake!** (*He tosses it wildly over his shoulder.*) She was not cruel ... she was struggling with incomprehension, Marie Antoinette ...[37]

In Barnes' *Dreaming* (1999) the characters dance their way through the war-torn landscape of England after the Battle of Tewkesbury in 1471:

> Bess: [L]ife is a dance.
> *She takes out a handful of sand, throws it across the ground and dances a soft-shoe / sand-dance on it.*
> (*Singing*.) Shh / Listen, listen / It's the sound of time running out / Don't you hear life pour away / Every second of the day? / Shh. It's all written in the sand / All the things we've every done / They're all written down in sand ...[38]

Another main theme of the history plays of the nineties lies in the attempt to connect the past directly with the present. Interest in historical dimensions has increased under the influence of recent events, such as the changes in Eastern Europe, which were the starting point of the historical panorama in *Pentecost,* or the discovery of the bronze-age man 'Ötzi' in a glacier in 1991, which forms the central metaphor in *Mnemonic*.

A number of significant anniversaries also gave rise to history plays. The French Revolution forms the background for Howard Barker's *Golgo* (1989) and for Peter Barnes' *Revolutionary Witness*, a series of four short scenes written for BBC Television and broadcast in July 1989. Barnes also wrote *Bye Bye Columbus* for BBC Television in 1992. The same event is remembered in *Columbus and the Discovery of Japan* (1992) by Richard Nelson. Barnes' most recent play, *Jubilee*, was "[c]ommissioned by the RSC to commemorate David Garrick's Shakespearean festival of 1769 – the first celebration of the great man's life and works", which Barnes uses as a chance to write a "mischievous satire on the foundation of the Shakespeare industry".[39] As the plays discussed above show, the 50th anniversary of the end of WW II and the Nürnberg trials also gave rise to a number of plays. The explosion of Hiroshima echoes in Robert Lepage's and Ex Machina's *The Seven Streams of the River Ota* (1994–96) and in Tony Harrison's film/poem *The Shadow of Hiroshima*, which was broadcast by Channel 4 exactly fifty years after the bomb was dropped. Michael Frayn's *Copenhagen* revolves around the discussion about the infamous meeting of Niels Bohr and Werner Heisenberg in 1943, which might well have determined the fate of the atomic bomb. The firestorm of Hamburg is unmistakably the historical resonance in David Harrower's *Presence* (2001), which deals with the German experience of the early Beatles.

From these commemorative works, which have often been commissioned specially for the anniversaries, it becomes obvious that the traditional dividing line between playwrights and screenwriters has dissolved to a large extent. Authors change freely from one medium to the other and the history play has proved extremely fertile ground for connections between film, TV, radio, and theatre. The most ostentatious example was given by Tom Stoppard, who co-authored the screenplay for the most successful historical romance (about theatre!) of recent years, *Shakespeare in Love* (1998).

This shows that this survey could easily be extended in several directions, e.g. by the inclusion of works by playwrights for TV or the cinema. But not only media boundaries are crossed regularly. With *Translations*, an Irish play has already been mentioned and more plays by Brian Friel, or by Frank McGuinness, Sebastian Barry, Daragh Carville and others could have been added and have only been excluded because this volume – for good reasons – does not subsume Irish drama under the heading of British drama. In their quality as history plays Irish plays are at the forefront of the revision and reinterpretation of the genre. The same is true for American and Canadian authors, who have also been added to my list of examples (Richard Nelson and Robert Lepage). But not only national and media boundaries become blurred by authors and plays – with the reinterpretation of the history play as a genre it has opened towards other forms of drama – a process which has taken place over the last fifty years and reached its climax in the last decade. Comic and farcical history plays are now just as possible as historical romance and tragedy have always been. The thematic and formal repertoire of the history has been expanded vastly. Historical topics merge with mythic narratives as the boundaries of traditional history as based on historiographic research are torn down. Alternative histories are staged and connect the history play with socialist, feminist and postcolonial drama. As the process of 'making history' is understood as similar to the workings of individual memory, the history play blends with the memory play. All forms of drama are employed to stage history. Tony Harrison writes history plays in verse and also film/poems with historical themes. Howard Barker's plays are much indebted to the Theatre of the Absurd and also close to the renaissance of the Theatre of Cruelty in recent years ('In-Yer-Face Theatre'). Surrealist dream sequences mix with the historical and realistic in Robert Lepage's highly visual drama. Tom Stoppard's plays easily combine a historical focus with a great number of other, equally important themes. This trend towards hybridisation and variation of the genre can be seen as most prominent. To remain productive, a genre has to reinvent itself. For the history play this process is in full swing.

Notes

1 A number of good surveys on special topics have appeared, e.g. Brown (1996) on Scottish history plays, Schneider (1991) and Imhof (1999) on Irish history plays, Sakellaridou (1993) on history plays by female playwrights and myth, Kramer (2000) on female biographies in contemporary drama. Yet, a survey of the new forms of the history play is still missing. German monographs mainly date back to the seventies and early eighties, e.g. Schnabl (1982), Hammerschmidt (1972), Tetzeli von Rosador (1976), and Hinck (1981). A good, but all too short, survey is included in Krieger (1998: 145–154).

2 The greater number of surveys of the history play base their definition on the authenticity of the characters or plot depicted in the play, e.g. Hammerschmidt (1972: 11–12). Other problematic definitions are based on equating history with the past: "Die naheliegende Begrenzung auf Stoffe aus der Vergangeheit wird problematisch, wenn gefragt wird, welcher Zeitraum zur Vergangenheit, welcher noch zur Gegenwart gehört, wo die Grenze zwischen Geschichtsdrama und Zeitstück verläuft." Düsing (1998) Or they are rooted in the difference between the 'past depicted' and the 'present time of the author': "Handlung [, die] erkennbar in spezifischen Epochen, die nicht identisch mit der Zeit des Autors sind, lokalisiert ist" Broich (1987: 154). The helpful approach of Kurt Tetzeli von Rosador (1976), who suggested basing the definition of the history play on the concept of history prevalent in the play and thus distinguishing between different types of history plays has, unfortunately, found little resonance.

3 The ongoing discussion about positivist and other concepts of history (e.g. Hayden White's understanding of history as a narrative construct) is well documented in Jenkins (1997).

4 In the following I will distinguish between 'history' and 'historiography'. 'Historiography' is meant to describe the academic process of producing accounts of the past. Historiography is defined as strictly non-fictional, document-based

and quasi-scientific discourse. I use the term 'history', on the other hand, to denote all forms of narrative accounts of the past which are considered historical.

5 In the sense of R. L. Stevenson's use of the word as a romantic and escapist way of presenting history. Cf. Krieger (1998: 145).

6 The typology I suggest here is indebted to the typology of the historical novel as developed by Linda Hutcheon (1988) and Ansgar Nünning (1995) and as applied to the field of drama by Stephanie Kramer (2000).

7 Ideally, the play takes place in the exact place of the original event. This enhances authenticity to a level which is unattainable for most other forms of historical and documentary literature. The same is conceivable for the characters involved. In extreme cases the difference between actor and role could be minimised by the presence of the very persons who actually participated in the historical event. Yet, it must be said that such an overlap of reality and drama is not only impossible in most cases but also directed against the very constituents of drama (i.e. its fictional, theatrical character), so that such performances must be seen as lying outside of drama. Instead they come close to other forms of performance such as e.g. historical re-enactments of battles.

8 A special position has to be attributed to the documentary history play, which does not fit into the picture. Documentary elements have been used both as a method to strengthen alternative versions of history and to support metahistorical discussions. On the other hand, the documentary history play is, influenced by other documentary genres such as documentary films or writing, something like the positivist answer to the growing relativism of postmodernism.

9 Edgar (2000: ix). Further references to this edition will be included in the text.

10 Bennett (1991: xiii). Further references to this edition will be included in the text.

11 Exactly such a lecture is part of Tom Stoppard's metahistorical play *Travesties* (1974). Stoppard does not "call in the audience a quarter of an hour earlier" but starts the second act with 'Cecily's Lecture'. In *Travesties* this piece of historiographic discourse is one version of the past which stands in stark contrast to the rest of the play, which is dominated by the erratic and highly subjective version supplied by the main character, Henry Carr.

12 Bennett prescribes full state robes for the King and Queen in the very last scene of the play, for example. Unfortunately he discovered that realism in the theatre also has its practical limits and had to admit that this was "*a fond stage direction, as it turned out there was no money left out of the National Theatre budget to run up some state robes so it was just their everyday royal togs*" (1992: 93).

13 Cf. Kramer (2000) and Gilbert & Tompkins (1996: Chapter 3: "Post-colonial Histories").

14 Gilbert & Tompkins (1996: 110) point out the problematical character of such an account of the past as it means "perpetuing misconception about the past by positing a harmonious pre-contact period in contrast to the fraught post-contact past and present". The wish to establish or re-establish an indigenous tradition leads to the construction of a competing history which might then itself be subjected to revision because it is revealed as being fuelled by ideology.

15 The all-female cast underlines this. Men exist only as absent characters and in the stories of the bondagers. Sometimes the male voice of a dialogue is simply cut out, as in Act II, Scene 9, where Maggie, one of the bondagers, is sum-

moned before the master for interrogation. The audience sees only Maggie and hears only her answers. This is an inversion of the usual historical narrative which gives a voice only to the powerful and male.

16 Cf. Brown (1996: 85): "One of the great achievements of the Scottish stage in the last twenty-five years, following the post-war experiments, has been the variety and complexity of the ways it has dealt with history and the particular significance of its use of the past for the present stage of Scottish culture and history".

17 Glover (1991: 72).

18 For example the report of the engineer Graebe on the mass executions of Jews at Dubno in 1942 appears both in Pascal's play (2000: 61–63) and in *Nuremberg* (Norton-Taylor 1997: 50–52).

19 Pascal (1991: 7).

20 *Ibid.*

21 This formal device was used in a similar way by Caryl Churchill in the last scene of her revisionist history play *Vinegar Tom* of 1976, where two witch-hunters, Kramer and Sprenger, appear as comedians (Churchill 1997).

22 Edgar (1995: xx). Further references to this edition will be included in the text.

23 Edgar connects this cleaning of the fresco with ethnic cleansing. Thus, the process of cleaning and removing one layer of the church's history becomes problematical as it suppresses and destroys unwanted and less valued layers.

24 Barker (1993: 23). Further references to this edition will be included in the text.

25 Reitz (1997: 253).

26 As yet unproduced. Published in Barker (2001a). Further references to this edition will be included in the text.

27 'Toonelhuis' seems to be a variation of 'toneelhuis', which means 'theatre' in Dutch ('toneel' = stage, 'huis' = house). His daughter is called Burgteata, a name which needs little explanation in Germany and especially Austria. By hinting at the function of theatre, the names of these characters open up a level of metatheatrical interpretation in the play.

28 "Das war ein Vorspiel nur, dort wo man Bücher / Verbrennt, verbrennt man auch am Ende Menschen" *Almansor* (1821).

29 "We can make a fetish now of contradiction" (Barker 1993: 22).

30 Second Prologue to *The Bite of the Night* (Barker 1988: 3–4), see also Barker (1993: 43).

31 "A further offence Tragedy commits against ethical dramaturgy is that nothing it proposes is susceptible to argument, it evades debate to the extent that every action, every ordeal, is both just and unjust, indeed it makes justice [...] a redundant concept, it produces silence in the audience, a moral hiatus." (Barker 2001b)

32 Cf. also Christopher Innes' article in this volume.

33 *Poetry or Bust* – a play about the Romantic poet John Nicholson, the Airedale Bard – was performed at Salts Mill, Saltaire "two minutes away from the river Aire, where John Nicholson died" (Harrison 1996a: 3). The setting of *The Kaisers of Carnuntum* was even more directly connected to the historical events as it was performed in the Roman arena of Carnuntum (Petronell, Austria), a place of high significance for the central character of the play, the Roman emperor Commodus (son of Marcus Aurelius): "Staging the story of Commodus in the actual space where as a child he must have seen buckets of blood gives

The Kaisers of Carnuntum great resonance, amplified still more by the political implications of the site." (Harrison 1996b: xviii) Carnuntum/Petronell is situated near the Austro-Hungarian-Czech border.

34 Harrison (1995: 68).

35 *Ibid.*

36 One of the most unmistakably metahistorical and metalinguistic history plays is the Irish play *Translations* (1980) by Brian Friel, which depicts the attempts of British soldiers to cartograph a Gaelic-speaking region of Ireland. In this process the Gaelic place names are replaced by English transcripts. As the English version only conserves the sound (if at all) the story behind the names is lost. This serves as a metaphor for the overall process of colonialisation and loss of history and identity (see Friel 1981).

37 Barker (1994: 43, his emphasis).

38 Barnes (1999: 26).

39 Barnes (2001: back cover text).

Bibliography

Barker, Howard: *The Bite of the Night. An Education*, London, 1988.

–: *Arguments for a Theatre*, second edition, London, 1993.

–: *Hated Nightfall*. – In H.B.: *Hated Nightfall / Wounds to the Face*, London, 1994.

–: *Found in the Ground*. – In H.B.: *Collected Plays 5*, London & New York, 2001a.

–: "The Ethics of Relevance and the Triumph of the Literal". Paper given at the CDE conference in Vienna on 26 May 2001b, forthcoming in Contemporary Drama in English 10.

Barnes, Peter: *Revolutionary Witness*. – In P.B.: *Plays 3*, London, 1996a.

–: *Bye Bye Columbus*. – In P.B.: *Plays 2*, second edition, London, 1996b.

–: *Dreaming*, London, 1999.

–: *Jubilee*, London, 2001.

Bennett, Alan: *The Madness of George III*, London, 1992.

Broich, Ulrich: "Einleitung zum Symposium: Das Europäische Geschichtsdrama nach 1945", *Literaturwissenschaftliches Jahrbuch* 28, 1987, 153–165.

Brown, Ian: "Plugged into History. The Sense of the Past in Scottish Theatre". – In Randall Stevenson & Garvin Wallace (Eds.): *Scottish Theatre since the Seventies*, Edinburgh, 1996, pp. 84–99.

Churchill, Caryl: *Vinegar Tom*. – In C.C.: *Plays 1*, second edition, London, 1987.

Daniels, Sarah: *The Gut Girls*. – In S.D.: *Plays Two*, London, 1994.

Düsing, Wolfgang: "Einleitung. Zur Gattung Geschichtsdrama". – In W.D. (Ed.): *Aspekte des Geschichtsdramas. Von Aischylos bis Volker Braun*, Mainzer Forschungen zu Drama und Theater 19, Tübingen & Basle, 1998, pp. 1–10.

Edgar, David: *Pentecost*, London, 1995.

–: *Albert Speer. Based on* Albert Speer: His Battle with Truth *by Gitta Sereny*, London, 2000.

Frayn, Michael: *Copenhagen*, London, 1998.

Friel, Brian: *Translations*, London, 1981.

Gilbert, Helen & Joanne Tompkins: *Post-Colonial Drama. Theory, Practice, Politics*, London & New York, 1996.

Glover, Sue: *Bondagers*. – In S.G.: *Bondagers & The Straw Chair*, London, 1997.

Hammerschmidt, Hildegard: *Das historische Drama in England (1956–1971): Erscheinungsformen und Entwicklungstendenzen*, Wiesbaden, 1972.
Harrison, Tony: *The Shadow of Hiroshima and other Film/Poems*, London, 1995.
–: *Poetry or Bust*. – In T.H.: *Plays 3*, London, 1996a.
–: *The Kaisers of Carnuntum*. – In T.H.: *Plays 3*, London, 1996b.
Harrower, David: *Presence*, London, 2001.
Hinck, Walter: *Geschichte als Schauspiel. Deutsche Geschichtsdramen. Interpretationen*, Frankfurt a.M., 1981.
Hutcheon, Linda: *A Poetics of Postmodernism. History, Theory, Fiction*, New York & London, 1988.
Imhof, Rüdiger: "The Past in Contemporary Irish Drama". – In Jürgen Kamm (Ed.): *Twentieth-Century Theatre and Drama in English. Festschrift for Heinz Kosok on the Occasion of his 65th Birthday*. Trier, 1999, pp. 589–610.
Jenkins, Keith: *The Postmodern History Reader*, London & New York, 1997.
Kramer, Stephanie: *Fiktionale Biographien. (Re-)Visionen und (Re-)Konstruktionen weiblicher Lebensentwürfe in Dramen britischer Autorinnen seit 1970. Ein Beitrag zur Typologie und Entwicklung des historischen Dramas*, CDE Studies 6, Trier, 2000.
Krieger, Gottfried: *Das englische Drama des 20. Jahrhunderts*, Stuttgart, 1998.
Lepage, Robert & Ex Machina: *The Seven Streams of the River Ota*, London, 1996.
Nelson, Richard: *Columbus and the Discovery of Japan*, London, 1992.
Norton-Taylor, Richard (Ed.): *Nuremberg. The War Crimes Trial*, London, 1997.
Nünning, Ansgar: *Von historischer Fiktion zu historiographischer Metafiktion*, Trier, 1995.
Pascal, Julia: *A Dead Woman on Holiday*. – In J.P.: *The Holocaust Trilogy*, London, 2000.
Reitz, Bernhard: "*Granite Crucibles* – The Theatre of Howard Barker". – In Uwe Börker & Hans Sauer (Eds.): *Anglistentag 1996 (Dresden)*, Trier, 1997, pp. 251–258.
Sakellaridou, Elizabeth: "Feminist Heterologies. Contemporary British Women Playwrights and the Rewrite of Myth and History". – In Robert Clark & Piero Boitani (Eds.): *English Studies in Transition*, London & New York, 1993, pp. 306–319.
Schabl, Gerlinde: *Historische Stoffe im neueren politischen Drama Großbritanniens*, Heidelberg, 1982.
Schneider, Ulrich: "Staging History in Contemporary Anglo-Irish Drama: Brian Friel and Frank MacGuinness". – In Geert Lernout (Ed.): *The Crows Behind the Plough. History and Violence in Anglo-Irish Poetry and Drama*, Amsterdam, Atlanta, 1991, pp. 79–98.
Stephenson, Shelagh: *An Experiment with an Air Pump*, London, 1998.
Stoppard, Tom: *Travesties*, London, 1976.
–: *Arcadia*, London, 1993.
Tetzeli von Rosador, Kurt: *Das englische Geschichtsdrama seit Shaw*, Heidelberg, 1976.
Theatre de Complicite: *Mnemonic*, London, 1999.
Wertenbaker, Timberlake: *After Darwin*, London, 1998.
Williams, Nigel: *Country Dancing*, London, 1987.
Yeger, Sheila: *Self Portrait*, London, 1990.

Mary Luckhurst, York

An Embarrassment of Riches. Women Dramatists in 1990s Britain

To write about 'women dramatists' is to enter dangerous territory. Women who write plays are understandably cagey about the ghettoising implications of the term when designations such as 'men dramatists' and 'male playwrights' are not in currency. Clare McIntyre and Winsome Pinnock focused on the troublesome politics of labelling at David Edgar's 'About Now' Birmingham Theatre Conference in 1997, McIntyre fuming at the literary and theatrical territories which tend to be automatically marked out and ascribed to women writers,[1] and Pinnock arguing that labelling can "construct an identity for the writer which excludes a kind of complexity of interpretation".[2] The fact that such public debates were part of the nineties was significant, first because the agenda moved on from a preoccupation in the eighties – the relative scarcity of professional productions of plays by women – and second because the visibility of established and new women playwrights improved throughout the decade. In other words, enough work by female playwrights was produced both to make more sophisticated debate possible and to allow various theatre-makers to develop more inclusive policies. Indeed, women playwrights in 1990s Britain enjoyed a level of visibility that they had never enjoyed in the past as theatre repertoires and publishers' lists testify. It was no accident, therefore, that Cambridge University Press commissioned a *Companion to Modern British Women Playwrights* during the nineties – the last decade has given its editors, feminist theatre historians Elaine Aston and Janelle Reinelt, much food for thought.

In the early nineties women writers in particular suffered from the post-Thatcherite malaise afflicting the theatre industry and from the consequences of a reluctance to stage new plays. Thatcher's curious philistinism coupled with her economic policies in the eighties (notably the abolition of the Greater London council) saw the demise of funding for many alternative theatre companies and in the nineties just two high-profile women's theatre groups kept afloat: Sphinx (formerly the Women's Theatre Group) and Clean Break. The country waited for John Major's Conservative Party to complete its dance of death and from 1990–1994 pronouncements of doom and gloom on the crisis affecting the production of new plays were frequent and shrill. Between 1970–85 new plays were calculated as forming twelve per cent of the repertoire of mainstream theatres; from 1985–90 this dropped to seven per cent; and from 1990–95 it dropped to five and then rose back to seven per cent.[3] The proportion of new plays by women was struggling to reach one per cent from 1970–85 but climbed to two per cent from 1985–95. Women writers, who have never known anything other than a climate of crisis, began to make progress.

In the mid to late nineties the situation vis-à-vis new play production took a turn for the better. The reasons for this are complex and relate to a shift in attitudes from producers and directors, to changes in economic structures brought about by lottery moneys awarded to certain mainstream theatres and companies, to changes in the political climate that encouraged new work and new voices in the arts as well as private sponsorship deals, and not least to the upsurge in artistic confidence and productivity in Wales, Scotland and Northern Ireland as the notion of a uniform Britain diminishes and the expression of alternative identities becomes a matter of political expediency.

The shift in attitudes in the theatre industry itself gained concentrated expression through the temporary re-housing of the Royal Court theatre in St. Martin's Lane, the heart of London's West End, while its actual premises in Sloane Square underwent major re-building work. The temporary location brought the Royal Court under a more than usually intense period of scrutiny which in turn provided Stephen Daldry, then artistic Director, with a surge of new creative ideas. Despite her limited experience and lack of exposure, Daldry decided to back Sarah Kane's *Blasted* (1995) and in so doing brought about the theatrical scandal of the decade. He also ensured a subsequently lively quest by theatres to stage plays by women and in particular to find a sub-Kane bratpack of new writers. This quest amongst others was in part enabled by lottery funding, the full effects of which have yet to be analysed, but the most obvious example of direct gain by women playwrights was the new writing initiative at the Birmingham Repertory Theatre, which received three million pounds of development funding. Blair's inauguration in 1997 certainly hailed a new era of artistic 'Cool Britannia' spin,[4] but it also injected a renewed interest in young, new voices and women playwrights have benefited accordingly (though the political implications of association can be problematic for those involved.)

Some of the names from the eighties maintained their high profile during the nineties. Caryl Churchill was as unpredictably inventive as ever and began the decade with a political play about Romania, *Mad Forest* (1990), performed by students at the Central School of Speech and Drama. She experimented with physical and dance theatre in *Lives of the Great Poisoners* (1991) and *The Skriker* (1994) and moved on to linguistic and formal explorations inspired by the absurdists with *Heart's Desire* (1997), *Blue Kettle* (1997) and *This is A Chair* (1997). April de Angelis reworked a successful West End revival of *Playhouse Creatures* (1997) for

Peter Hall's theatre company and wrote *The Positive Hour* (1997) and *A Warwickshire Testimony* (1999). Pam Gems honed her skills on the biographical play, enjoying a West End run with *Marlene* (1996) and a hit with *Stanley* (1996) about artist Stanley Spencer. Anne Devlin penned a fine second play, *After Easter* (1994), to follow *Ourselves Alone* (1985), and once more represented different women's perspectives on the Irish question – an undertaking that is also the province of Christina Reid. Winsome Pinnock, who has Jamaican origins, continued to explore issues of immigration and identity in her plays *A Hero's Welcome* (1990) and *Talking in Tongues* (1991), and wrote *Mules* (1996) – a devastatingly powerful script for the prison company Clean Break about women caught in the poverty trap of drug-running. Timberlake Wertenbaker's decade was uneven: *Three Birds Alighting on a Field* (1991) was greeted favourably at the Royal Court, but the non-Court productions *The Break of Day* (1995) and *After Darw*in (1998) lacked dramatic impetus and were structurally ragged. There was much talk behind the scenes that Wertenbaker needed the nurture of an institution like the Court in order to write at her best – something one never hears said of male playwrights, though she certainly believed that the Royal Court propagated a 'backlash' against women playwrights in the nineties.[5] At any rate, her latest play *Credible Witness* (2001) has been hailed by some as a return to form. Clare McIntyre followed *Low Level Panic* (1988) with *My Heart's a Suitcase* (1990) and *The Thickness of Skin* (1996), all at the Royal Court, but has not had a play produced since 1996 and feels increasingly marginalised by an industry run overwhelmingly by men.[6] Sharman Macdonald's *When I was a Girl, I used to Scream and Shout…* (1984) answered perfectly to conservative notions of what a 'feminist play' might be in the eighties, but *The Winter Guest* (1995), *Borders of Paradise* (1995), and *Sea Urchins* (1998), despite being more sophisticated and mature plays, did not strike the same critical chorus. Though formally conservative, Macdonald can write hauntingly well and is an interesting writer to track. Bryony Lavery was as prolific and as exasperatingly erratic as ever, but she wrote four plays that stood out: *Her Aching Heart* (1990), *Nothing Compares to You* (1995), *Goliath* (1997), and *A Wedding Story* (2000). *Goliath*, which depicts the multiple personalities of a woman abused in childhood, is a minor masterpiece and deserved a great deal more attention than it attracted. Louise Page and Sarah Daniels, on the other hand, were names that were conspicuously absent from the stage. Daniels was active as a writer for television serials and soaps, and *Morning Glory*, a play she composed many years ago but re-worked for production in 2000, showed a clumsy hand and a strangely dated quality of dialogue. Daniels, it seems, has been unable to modernise her stage writing to suit contemporary speech patterns and *Morning Glory* smacked too much of the old-style issue play.

The Royal Shakespeare Company (RSC) and the Royal National Theatre (RNT) have notoriously poor records for producing the work of female playwrights and grudgingly showed themselves willing with Churchill, de Angelis, Devlin and Gems. Churchill's *The Skriker* seemed to baffle the institutional mechanisms and orthodoxies of the RNT and was too peculiar a beast for the Cottesloe; unused to dance theatre, the director, Les Waters, did not find a consistent visual language for the play and the movement, choreographed by Ian Spink, remained a thing apart from the spoken word. Gems's *Stanley* was a play much more in the tradition of the RNT and fared well commercially. De Angelis was commissioned by the RSC to write *A Warwickshire Testimony* using particular manuscripts and materials provided for her, a process she found strange,[7] and it was perhaps particularly unadventurous and constraining of the Literary Manager to use the writer to address what was one of the management's preoccupations – the criticism that they were no longer appealing to local audiences. Devlin, by contrast, was granted a free hand to write the play she wanted for the RSC.

Churchill's recent plays, to be sure, do not sit easily on large stages and require intimacy. Her anti-realist experiments go against the grain of the repertoires of the RNT and the RSC but so too does her chameleonic facility to reinvent herself with every play. Churchill has no public face, very rarely gives interviews, and does not pronounce on theatre in the manner of Hare or Barker. Unlike Pinter she does not act or direct, and whilst Beckett's silences only layered intrigue upon intrigue, Churchill's render her yet more invisible. She exists through her plays, is with Pinter England's greatest playwright. But she has always had a far from straightforward relationship with mainstream theatre. *Top Girls* (1982) is a canonical text at schools and universities, but it is a single example in a range of plays that are astonishingly different from one another. Given her achievements, it is a shameful testament of the sexism at the RSC and the RNT that more has not been done to facilitate and promote her work. Though both institutions are including more plays by women in their repertoires, they have not led on the issue, and their equally lamentable record of appointing female directors does little to instil any confidence that they are acting much beyond tokenism. Neither establishment has yet been run by a woman Artistic Director and possible high-profile candidates have made known their disinclination to manage what they regard as a gentleman's club. Many top women directors choose to free-lance or to construct their own working spaces by setting up companies in response to the resistances they encounter.[8]

On a happier note a decided feature of the nineties was the commercial emergence of a collection of strong women writers who found theatres and companies interested in their work and enjoyed considerable success.

Marie Jones, a founder of Charabanc Theatre Company in Belfast, made significant inroads on the regional touring circuit with her comedy *Women on the Verge of HRT* (1996). *A Night in November* (1994) and *Stones in His Pockets* (1999) both explored Irish-American axes; the former representing a journey of self-discovery for a man who comes to understand the meaning of his Irish roots on a trip to New York, and the latter mapping the effect of a Hollywood film crew and their offensive, idealised constructions of rural Ireland on the local townsfolk. *Stones in his Pockets*, a two-hander, demanded virtuoso performances from actors required to play multiple roles, and the tautness of Jones's writing, her comic skill in depicting a dizzying array of maverick characters, and the fact that Irish plays were very much in vogue in London, made it first a West End and later a Broadway hit. Charlotte Jones, a namesake but no relation, rose to prominence during the nineties and at the time of writing has a critically acclaimed play on at the RNT called *Humble Boy* (2001). *Martha, Josie and the Chinese Elvis* (1999) and *In Flame* (1999) brought her the Critics' Circle Award for the Most Promising Playwright and were the plays that established her name so rapidly. Certainly popular with audiences, Jones's two plays in 1999 relied on worn comic tropes and stereotypes and betrayed a superficiality that was sadly all too prevalent on mainstream London and regional stages. *In Flame*, in particular, leant heavily on age-old representations of Yorkshire folk as comic yokels and, disturbingly, London audiences regarded it as prime entertainment. I left feeling chilled to the bone.

Born and raised in County Offaly, Ireland, Marina Carr cannot be classified a British writer but her impact on the London stage in the 1990s was profound. *Portia Coughlan* (1996), the story of a working-class woman who drowns herself in the river like her twin brother before her, was extraordinarily haunting, consummately well-constructed, and the richest poetic play of the decade. *On Raftery's Hill* (2000) was received with less critical rapture but was as bleakly atmospheric as *Portia Coughlan*, portraying a farming community in the Irish midlands rife with incest, sexual abuse and brutality. Carr's ear for the rhythms of language is precise, her debt to Beckett clear,[9] and there is no one who can currently match her moving portrayals of the inarticulate. For the moment she seems to be one of the few playwrights who can blend poetics with realism in ways that are startlingly evocative.

Shelagh Stephenson, like Churchill, honed her writing skills for radio before she began composing stage plays. *The Memory of Water* (1996), which was a West End hit and won the Laurence Olivier Award for Best Comedy, dissects the individual crises in the lives of three sisters on the eve of their mother's funeral. *Five Kinds of Silence* (2000) anatomises the domestic dictatorship, sexual abuse and brutality endured by a mother and her two daughters at the hands of the husband/father. The women commit a shocking collective murder that also symbolises an act of traumatic liberation; by the end of the play, after the stresses of a trial, they are tentatively planning new lives for themselves and trying to accustom themselves to the idea of a hopeful future. In 1998 Stephenson caught the mood for the dawning millennium with *An Experiment with an Air Pump* by creating dual narratives set on new year's eve in 1799 and 1999, and by exploring scientific advancements and ethics, romance, and death at the end of both centuries. In a memorable final tableau the figures from 1799 gather round a coffin containing the body of a young woman as the bells chime midnight on new year's eve and riots sound from the distance. Awe-struck the characters stare into the dark, as one whispers: "Here's to whatever lies ahead ... here's to uncharted lands ... here's to a future we dream but cannot know ... here's to the new century."[10] Stephenson is perhaps at her best writing tense psychological drama from a woman's point of view and her mastery of craft exploits suspense and atmosphere in ways that make for a compelling night at the theatre.

Three notable nineties plays were inspired by issues related to the Sho'ah: Julia Pascal's 'The Holocaust Trilogy' incorporating *Theresa* (1990), *A Dead Woman on Holiday* (1991), and *The Dybbuk* (1992); Diane Samuels' *Kindertransport* (1995); and Moira Buffini's *Gabriel* (1997). Pascal's *Theresa* was revived throughout the decade and toured on the continent. Based on the true story of a Jewish woman deported from Guernsey during the Second World War and murdered in Auschwitz, the play unpicked the tale of collaboration and anti-Semitism on the Channel islands, which British historians have been slow to cover and which rather belies the perception that many British citizens have of the nation's heroic past. Pascal's play is still censored in Guernsey, and the screen version was dropped by the BBC because of worries about political sensitivity.[11] *Theresa* contains the real names of the collaborators and Pascal mixes a documentary style of reportage (quoting from archival documents) with a Brechtian structure that also borrows from expressionist and cabaret styles of performance. Its contents are explosive and it is no surprise that Buffini's *Gabriel*, a much less politically thrusting play which skirts a lot of tricky issues, casts itself more as detective drama and refuses to end unhappily, was embraced wholeheartedly by the mainstream and won the awards. *Gabriel* is altogether more palatable in that it does not point the finger and it concentrates on those few who tried to save lives and ignores the many who did not. Samuels' *Kindertransport* focused on the plight of German-Jewish children who were sent to Britain as refugees in 1938–39 and the way in which their world was turned upside-down by the separation from their parents and their settlement in a foreign country. Samuels concentrates on a daughter's struggle to comprehend her mother, who has concealed her past out of shame, anger, and horror, and on the mother's refusal to reconcile herself with her own mother's 'banishment' of her from Germany. Stimulated by the desire to investigate "the cost of survival"[12] and to tell a narrative that she felt had been passed over, Samuels anatomises cycles of deprivation, pain, and punishment with exquisite emotional precision. If it turns out to be the only stage play of Samuels to find success, she has certainly made a mark with it.

Three Scots who had established their playwriting credentials before the nineties, Liz Lochhead, Sue Glover and Rona Munro, continued to produce interesting work. Glover and Munro became significantly more high-profile and the 'grande dame' of women poet/playwrights in Scotland, Lochhead, waited until 2000 before penning a brilliant adaptation of *Medea* for Theatre Babel which showed the same edge and wit as *Mary Queen of Scots Got Her Head Chopped Off* (1987). *Medea* was a blessed relief after *Perfect Days* (1998) which disappointed and bemused many with its conventional realism and tired, banal feminism for the (apparently hysterical) pre-menopausal woman; it never overcame the idea of the 'Late-30s Woman Desperate For A Child', a construction which has besieged the sitcom in the absence of more original concepts. Lochhead's Medea blazed onto the stage, spitting words with spin-doctorish venom, she was ironic, witty, tender, spiteful and a mass of other passions but never the victimised weakling. Audiences walked a tightrope between laughter and fear, and teenagers queued up in theatre foyers after the show to buy Lochhead's modernised, wise-cracking text. The language was Scots and it vaulted between high-flown diction and the spicily colloquial: men and lives were dispatched at a thrilling pace. To give the barest taste of the play, witness Medea's deliciously controlled, implacable scorn in the face of Kreon's attempt to banish her:

> I've heard this before
> I'm oppressed by my reputation
> the evil one the witch the clever woman
> don't educate your daughters Kreon!
> clever men are envied
> and despised the world has no use for them
> fools think them foolish
> the clever fear them
> put them down can't take the competition
> but a clever woman
> fie it is to fly in the face of nature
> an abomination
> fear me? I can't be very clever can I
> or I'd not be in this pretty situation?[13]

Lochhead wrote the part for her friend, Maureen Beattie, and given the astonishing power of the piece it might be interesting to encourage her to write again with a specific actor in mind – a practice that was the norm in former times and which in this case yielded a remarkable result.

In *Bondagers* (1991) Sue Glover depicts the lives of six women working on the Border farms in the 1860s, exploring the social, economic and sexual oppressions they were forced to endure. In a matter of two to three years *Bondagers* became a modern classic and re-affirmed Glover as a playwright who is especially concerned with garnering female narratives in Scots history which have been marginalized or silenced. Her most recent play *Shetland Saga* (2000) examines the collision between a local Shetland community and a crew of stranded Bulgarian sailors. Rona Munro experimented with different forms during the nineties and was more prominent in the first two thirds of the decade than the last third when the marked looseness of structure in a play like *Snake* (1999) was not sufficiently compensated for by character, content, or language. A feisty, grimly humorous play, *Bold Girls* (1990), won her the Susan Smith Blackburn Prize. It represents the lives of three Catholic women in Belfast whose men have died or been killed by the British army. *Your Turn to Clean the Stair* (1992) was a psychological whodunit centred on Lisa, a vulnerable young woman, and had moderate success, but her most ambitious play was *The Maiden Stone* (1995), a modern epic reminiscent of *Peer Gynt* which is "about the landscape in North East Scotland"[14] and was inspired by the writings of a 19th-century touring actress who had seventeen children and outlived two husbands. The two central female characters are strongly linked to the harsh natural landscape and are as destructive as they are positive and nurturing. Like *Bold Girls* the play depicts women of extreme courage and resistance, but its folk-tale elements, story-telling components, use of dialect, and its evocation of a particular part of Scotland all implicate it in an interrogation of traditional forms of Scots theatre-making.

One phenomenon of nineties theatre was, of course, Sarah Kane and many retrospectives privilege her. Sierz for example argues that she "pioneered a new aesthetic – more blatant, aggressive, confrontational – that opened up new possibilities in British drama".[15] In a sensitive introduction to the *Complete Plays* David Greig describes both her writing and her suicide as "defining moments in British theatre".[16] Sierz's is the received view of Kane as a progenitor of the New Brutalism, as wild genius of the theatrically shocking. I am not of the view that Kane was a great writer nor that her plays represented a defining moment. In *Blasted* (1995) and *Cleansed* (1998) the dialogue is undistinguished, and the extreme representations of violence created technical staging problems which, particularly with *Cleansed*, threatened to turn the production into a fiasco. At

Cleansed I was sitting next to audience-members in combat gear who had come to laugh at the multiple mutilations inflicted on one of the characters. Kane seemed to be reinforcing the very agenda she was trying to challenge. Until then the Court had always been associated with leftist politics but their publicity material did its best to appeal to violently inclined factions of the public traditionally associated with the far right.

There are two aspects of Kane's work that are interesting: her theatrical vision and her pursuit of an agenda which rigorously interrogates the limits of representation. I still find the impossible stage directions in *Blasted* extraordinary, especially in the final scene: they are reminiscent of Artaud's theatre scenarios, themselves notoriously difficult to translate into stage performance and evidence of an almost ludicrously ambitious project. Violence and scandal are not new in theatre; on the contrary, they are the stuff of received history, but Kane began where others left off and though I find her plays politically conservative and her writing stilted, I admire her wilful refusal to be confined by the mundane practicalities of staging. Every play was a call into battle for the actors and a summons to the frontline for the director.

The media frenzy around Kane raised up all the prejudicial constructions of women playwrights that normally bubble just beneath the surface of critical opinion. The fact is that, had Kane been a man, *Blasted* would not have received the attention it did. The tabloids professed astonishment and outrage that a young woman should be responsible for such atrocities and positioned themselves in the well-worn role of Suburban Disgust. At the time of *Blasted* there was one critic who thought that Sarah Kane could write; before *Cleansed* even opened the broadsheet critics had about-turned and were hailing a 'Wunderkind'. The constructions of Kane by the artistic establishment followed the example of sensation artists like Damian Hirst and Tracey Emin: theatre needed a decent Rebel, one that was exportable and fitted in with 'Cool Britannia' – Kane was perfect material. Time may lend moderation to constructions of Kane and her plays, but her suicide added to the mythology, and in the manner of Plath, critics seem to find it impossible to see her work through anything other than the lenses of gender and mental instability.

The year before Kane hit the headlines, Rebecca Prichard gained considerable praise for *Essex Girls* (1994) and clearly displayed a talent for capturing the concerns and cadences of ordinary teenagers. In 1998 Prichard's *Yard Gal* was co-produced by the Royal Court and Clean Break. A two-hander, *Yard Gal* showed masterful formal control and a brilliant ear for dialogue and rhythm. It looked very much as though Prichard was moving towards the top-rank playwrights, but as yet we are still waiting for the next play and hoping that her best work is not confined to the past. 1994 brought visibility for Judy Upton with *Ashes and Sand*, the blurb on the backcover describing it as 'a vicious little hand-grenade of a play'. Set in a sea-side resort it depicts the nasty exploits of a girl-gang and was a sort of seedy English spin on a Tarantino film. *Bruises* (1995) and *The Shorewatchers' House* (1995) confirmed Upton's strength as a writer, but more recent plays such as *Confidence* (1998) and *Sliding with Suzanne* (2001) seem to have slipped into formulaics and Upton urgently needs to move beyond violent plays set in English coastal towns. Tamsin Oglesby and Catherine Johnson are also a new generation and are in the early stages of development. Oglesby's *Two Lips Indifferent Red* (1995) showed promise but *My Best Friend* (2000) was of a different order and displayed a maturity and knack for creating the unexpected climax. Stephanie McKnight's *The Cub* (1997) anatomised the relationship between a mother and her son with gruesome precision and she continues to be worth watching. The Soho Theatre initially helped to develop Tanika Gupta's writing talents and produced *Skeleton* in 1997. *Skeleton* was inspired by a short story by Rabindranath Tagore and is a beguiling story of love and possession set in Bengal. Gupta's *The Waiting Room* (2000) premiered at the RNT and focused on a dead woman, Priya Banerjee, who has just three days on earth before she can enter the Waiting Room of spirits. It received moderately welcoming reviews, but for the present Gupta's ideas for plays are more compelling than her ability to write them. The late nineties were marked by the rise of Zinnie Harris, whose play, *By Many Wounds* (1998), was born out of the author's experience of her parents' suffering when it was confirmed that their friend, Lucy Partington, had been a victim of serial killer Fred West. Her most high-profile play *Further Than the Furthest Thing* (2000), which plundered the recent history of the remote Atlantic island of Tristan da Cunha, transferred to the RNT to great acclaim.

It would be remiss not to include the French writer Yasmina Reza in any retrospective of theatre in nineties Britain. Her witty play *Art* (1995), translated by Christopher Hampton, has been one of the new play hits of the West End and is still running. *The Unexpected Man* (1998), *Conversations After a Burial* (1999) and *Life x 3* (2001) have also been significant commercial successes. An American trio Phyllis Nagy, Naomi Wallace, and Rebecca Gilman also had a distinct impact on mainstream stages. Nagy, who has not found success in the States, blazed in like a comet with a trail of smart, inventive, and audacious plays including *Weldon Rising* (1992), *Butterfly Kiss* (1994), *Disappeared* (1995), and *The Strip* (1995). Her blend of fantasy and reality was a whacky concoction and characters were simultaneously crazy and street-wise, but by the late nineties she was struggling to get productions and recent work has not matched past form. Wallace and Gilman consistently produce outstanding work and must rank amongst the best playwrights produced in Britain, with Wallace leading Gilman by an edge. Both are driven political writers whose understanding of the complexities of structure is thorough and whose approach is intellectual. Wallace's *Slaughter City* (1996), about the ruthless exploitation of textile workers, may have overloaded audiences with its message, but it was visually a stunningly conceived piece and audiences at the RSC were silenced by its power. In *The Trestle at Pope Lick Creek* (2001) Wallace has corrected the tendency to verbal overload and produced a work steeped in haunting images and poetry. Gilman's *The Glory of Living* (1998) shocked with its representation of an uneducated and abused young woman's complicity in serial killings, and *Spinning into Butter* (2001), about political correctness, demonstrated that too many British playwrights are timid about addressing big political issues.

Though a glimpse at West End and mainstream theatre listings immediately reveals that women playwrights are still vastly under-represented, the nineties was a decade which gave female playwrights a greater visibility than ever before. My survey is far from exhaustive and is much influenced by the levels of critical attention playwrights received. There are large gaps – Welsh women writers, who have been notably more marginalised than many other constituencies (another story), and site-specific and post-modern writers like Rose English and Jyll Bradley, whose work currently defies critical vocabularies. The drive by the major publishing houses Faber & Faber, Nick Hern, Methuen, Oberon and Samuel French to get more women's plays into print in the nineties was remarkably concerted and has paid great dividends. In comparison with the past women's plays poured from the presses. There are more productions of women's plays than ever before. But there can be no rest. The situation could so easily become perilous once more, and post-feminists be hanged! – we *must* ensure that this is only the beginning of what must be far greater changes in the future.

Notes

1 Edgar (1999: 56).
2 *Ibid.*, 58.
3 *Ibid.*, 19.
4 Smith (1998: 4–5).
5 Edgar (1999: 75).
6 *Ibid.*, 56–57.
7 Cf. Luckhurst & Rebellato (forthcoming).
8 Giannachi & Luckhurst (1999: 120).
9 Stephenson & Langridge (1997: 147).
10 Stephenson (1998: 96).
11 Luckhurst (2000: 138–148).

12 Samuels (1995: vii).
13 Lochhead (2000: 12).
14 Munro (1995b: v).
15 Sierz (2001: xii).
16 Kane (2000: ix).

Bibliography

Aston, Elaine & Janelle Reinelt (Eds.): *Modern British Women Playwrights*, Cambridge, 2000.
Buffini, Moira: *Gabriel*, London, 1997.
Carr, Marina: *Plays 1*, London, 1999.
–: *On Raftery's Hill*, London, 2000.
Churchill, Caryl: *Plays 1*, London, 1985.
–: *Plays 2*, London, 1990.
–: *Plays 3*, London, 1998.
–: *Blue Heart*, London, 1997.
–: *This is a Chair*, London, 1999.
De Angelis, April: *The Positive Hour*, London, 1997.
–: *Plays 1*, London, 1999a.
–: *A Warwickshire Testimony*, London, 1999b.
Devlin, Anne: *Ourselves Alone*, London, 1986.
–: *After Easter*, London, 1994.
Dromgoole, Dominic: *The Full Room*, London, 2000.
Edgar, David: *State of Play. Playwrights on Playwriting*, London, 1999.
Gems, Pam: *Stanley*, London, 1996.
–: *Marlene*, London, 1998.
Giannachi, Gabriella & Mary Luckhurst: *On Directing*, London, 1999.
Gilman, Rebecca: *The Glory of Living*, London, 1999.
–: *Spinning into Butter*, London, 2001a.
–: *Boy Gets Girl*, London, 2001b.
Glover, Sue: *Bondagers* & *The Straw Chair*, London, 1997.
Gottlieb, Vera & Colin Chambers: *Theatre in a Cool Climate*, Oxford, 1999.
Gupta, Tanika: *The Skeleton*, London, 1997.
–: *The Waiting Room*, London, 2000.
Harris, Zinnie: *By Many Wounds*, London, 1998.
–: *Further Than the Furthest Thing*, London, 2000.
Johnson, Catherine: *Shang-a-Lang*, London, 1998.
Jones, Charlotte: *Martha, Josie and the Chinese Elvis*, London, 1999.
–: *In Flame*, London, 2000.
Jones, Marie: *A Night in November*, London, 1995.
–: *Stones in his Pockets*, London, 2000.
Kane, Sarah: *Complete Plays*, London, 2000.
Lavery, Bryony: *Plays 1*, London, 1998.
–: *A Wedding Story*, London, 2000.
Lochhead, Liz: *Perfect Days*, London, 1998.
–: *Medea*, London, 2000.

Luckhurst, Mary: "The Case of Theresa: Guernsey, the Holocaust and Theatre. Censorship in the 1990s" – In Irena Swiderska, Jerzy Jarniewicz & Adam Sumera (Eds.): *Jewish Themes in English and Polish Culture*, Lodz, 2000, pp. 138–148.
—& Dan Rebellato (Eds.): *On Playwriting. Interviews with Playwrights*, London, due out in autumn 2002.
Macdonald, Sharman: *Plays 1*, London, 1995.
McIntyre, Clare: *My Heart's a Suitcase* & *Low Level Panic*, London, 1994.
–: *The Thickness of Skin*, London, 1996.
McKnight, Stephanie: *The Cub*, London, 1997.
Munro, Rona: *Bold Girls*, London, 1991.
–: *Your Turn to Clean the Stair* & *Fugue*, London, 1995a.
–: *The Maiden Stone*, London, 1995b.
Nagy, Phyllis: *Plays 1*, London, 1998.
Oglesby, Tamsin: *Two Lips Indifferent Red.* – In *Bush Theatre Plays*, London, 1996.
–: *My Best Friend*, London, 2000.
Pascal, Julia: *The Holocaust Trilogy*, London, 2000.
Pinnock, Winsome: *Mules*, London, 1996.
Prichard, Rebecca: *Essex Girls.* – In *Coming on Strong. New Writing from the Royal Court*. London, 1998a.
–: *Yard Gal*, London, 1998b.
Samuels, Diane: *Kindertransport*, London, 1995.
Sierz, Aleks: *In-Yer-Face Theatre. British Drama Today*, London, 2001.
Smith, Chris: *Creative Britain*, London, 1998.
Stephenson, Heidi & Natasha Langridge (Eds.): *Rage and Reason. Women Playwrights on Playwriting*, London, 1997.
Stephenson, Shelagh: *An Experiment with an Air Pump*, London, 1998.
–: *The Memory of Water* & *Five Kinds of Silence*, London, 2001.
Upton, Judy: *Ashes and Sand.* – In Pamela Edwardes (Ed.): *Frontline Intelligence 3*, London, 1995.
–: *Bruises* & *The Shorewatchers' House*, London, 1996.
–: *Confidence*, London, 1998.
Wallace, Naomi: *Slaughter City*, London, 1996.
–: *Birdy*, London, 1997.
–: *The Trestle at Pope Lick Creek*, London, 2001.
Wertenbaker, Timberlake: *The Break of Day*, London, 1995.
–: *Plays 1*, London, 1996.
–: *After Darwin*, London, 1999.

Heiko Stahl, Mainz

'There ain't no black in the Union Jack' vs. 'England is de place for me'. Black Women Playwrights in Britain in the 1990s

1. Introduction

'There ain't no black in the Union Jack' ran a racist rhyme that certain groups of English football fans would sing during the seventies and eighties.[1] It highlights questions of identity and identification for immigrants from former British colonies and their second and third generation descendants. But these questions about what it takes to be British are even more complex and can be extended to 'Englishness' as well. In her study on British drama and film, May Joseph asks: "What, for instance, are the implications of 'Englishness' [...] for peoples of African, Caribbean and Asian descent as they inscribe themselves into the narratives of nation and culture in Britain? How do these groups interrupt the narrative of 'Englishness' through their marginality?"[2] In other words, immigrants are influenced by their 'host'-culture, but they, in turn, also have an effect on this culture as they become part of it – however marginal. Cultural influence, therefore, is a reciprocal process. An attempt at solving certain problems of terminology can be seen in the distinction between 'Englishness' and 'Britishness' – not an easy task as the recent discussion of these terms shows, a debate which culminated in the controversy over Jeremy Paxman's book *The English* (1998) and Lord Parekh's report of the Commission on the Future of Multi-Ethnic Britain (2000).[3]

Due to its history of colonialism, British culture is a place in which many ethnicities are represented – from Africa, Asia, the Caribbean, Europe, and the Middle-East – and the British stage has become a strategic arena for the representation of these cultural collisions.[4] In Britain, these various ethnicities, with the exception of the Europeans, are referred to as 'black'; hence this term can and at times does include people from all 'non-white' backgrounds. 'Black Theatre' therefore, encompasses a wide range of different ethnic groups with diverse cultural and theatrical backgrounds. Due to limitations of space, I will concentrate on playwrights of African and Caribbean descent, and I will limit the meaning of the term 'black' to this group. My aim is to try to find answers for questions such as: what is the state of black, i.e. African and Caribbean drama in Britain in the final decade of the 20th century? Is there a crisis? Can it be pigeonholed as postcolonial, immigrant, or British drama?[5]

There are quite a number of black playwrights living and working in Britain, and the following list is certainly not complete: Biyi Bandele Thomas, Paul Boakye, Trish Cooke, Fred D'Aguiar, Killian Gideon, Michael Ellis, Alfred Fagon, Bonnie Greer, Tunde Ikoli, Jackie Kay, Maria Oshodi, Winsome Pinnock, Caryl Phillips, Jacqueline Rudet, Naomi Wallace, Edgar White, Roy Williams, Benjamin Zephaniah and Zindika. Not all of these playwrights see their plays performed or even in print, and women playwrights still have to face additional problems to those they share with their male colleagues. Within the scope of this paper, I will take a closer look at three texts by black women playwrights – *England is De Place for Me* by Killian M. Gideon (1987), *Running Dream* by Trish Cooke (1993) and *Talking in Tongues* by Winsome Pinnock (1991). In their focus on first and second generation immigrants from the Caribbean in recent and contemporary Britain, these three dramatists represent black British playwriting in the 1990s, but despite this common denominator there are substantial differences in topical and theatrical orientation. The plays cover a wide spectrum of perspectives and angles. You can find the look backward, the look inward and the look at the present, even into the future; there are observations of the past with its ancestral heritage, of psychological questions and of the reality in our contemporary society. In these plays, European theatre tradition moves alongside and overlaps with Caribbean and African forms of staging and storytelling.

2. *Black British Drama Since the 1950s*

After the arrival of the Empire Windrush, a first ship with migrants from the British West Indies, on 22 June 1948, London changed for good, because "the image of the Caribbeans filing off its gangplank has come to symbolise many of the changes which have taken place here".[6] Both British residents and newcomers experienced vast cultural shocks at this clash of the periphery and centre of the former global Empire.[7] The Caribbean émigrés however, having experienced British colonialism for generations, "knew more about England and the British, than the British knew of them",[8] as actress Pearl Connor-Mogotsi puts it. In an opening address to an international bookfair in 1995, she gave a comprehensive overview of blacks in the field of arts in Britain since the 1950s, with a special focus on the performing arts and theatre practitioners, a field in which she herself had taken an active role. In 1956, together with her husband Edric Connor, she established the Edric Connor Agency to represent black artists in the performing arts.[9]

1956 marks the beginning of a new era in British theatre not only because of John Osborne's *Look Back in Anger*, but also because of the Trinidadian playwright Errol John, who won an *Observer* drama award for *Moon on a Rainbow Shawl*, a play about working-class blacks living in Britain.[10] The play was produced at the Royal Court Theatre's mainstage, since the Royal Court,[11] together with the Theatre Royal, Stratford East,[12] was one of the first theatres to stage plays by African and Caribbean playwrights such as the Nigerian Wole Soyinka, then a student at Leeds University, and Athol Fugard from South Africa. The Notting Hill Carnival with its street theatres helped to promote Caribbean artists as of 1965. For the following decade Connor-Mogotsi states that "Black representation in quality drama was clearly absent in the 1970s",[13] though she sees the increasing influence black directors and producers gained towards the end of and beyond that decade: Anton Phillips (Carib Theatre), Yvonne Brewster (Talawa), Joan Ann Maynard (Black Theatre Co-operative), Alby James (National, Temba and Royal Court), and Malcolm Frederick (independent).

Generally, the "most serious setback facing black theatre practitioners is the need for permanent premises as part of the British theatre establishment".[14] Connor-Mogotsi observes and mentions the successful example of Yvonne Brewster and her Talawa at the Cochrane.[15] Bernadine Evaristo seconds her remarks by saying that "Black theatre has diminished since the days of the now defunct Greater London Council [abolished in 1986] which had an active funding commitment to support the Black Arts".[16] At the same time, Kadija George highlights a different emphasis by finding "fewer Black theatre companies, yet improved quality",[17] for instance at the Black Theatre Co-Operative, the Black Mime Theatre, the Theatre Centre, and again, the Talawa.[18]

George finds one reason for the enormous problems Black theatre groups have to face in present day Britain in the "assumption that Black people are only capable of singing, dancing and playing the fool, with serious drama being put onto the back-burner".[19] Evaristo looks at this phenomenon from a slightly different angle; she describes the fact that Black audiences of late seem to be interested in Caribbean comedy. "The emphasis shifted from the exploration of serious drama to treating black theatre as a commercial commodity. [...] [T]his means producing theatre which has the lowest common denominator – music, humour with a little dance thrown in".[20] Yvonne Brewster is also aware of this trend: "Sometimes we are our own worst enemies because we put forward the idea that this is what we really want to do. 'We want to go to the theatre? We want to laugh. I am not going into the theatre unless I can laugh'. So sometimes Black people themselves are responsible for the prejudices".[21] George, Evaristo and Brewster agree that there is a need for serious Black drama in contemporary Britain. Brewster stresses that "[s]ome of the best writing in English nowadays is produced by people who are not English, that is, not Anglo-Saxon English",[22] and continues by mentioning Ben Okri, Salman Rushdie, and the Nobel prize winners Wole Soyinka and Derek Walcott – a list to which one might want to add the latest laureate, V.S. Naipaul.

With her anthology, George provides a space for "nationally achieved writers [...] who have at last been taken out of the realms of specialisation and rid of the term 'ethnic minority' and into the national framework where they rightfully belong".[23] Brewster sees an ongoing osmosis of Black theatre traditions into the British mainstream.[24] One of the 'mission statements' of Brewster's Talawa Theatre reads as follows: "to use black culture and experience to further enrich British theatre".[25] Moreover, in her series of anthologies, *Black Plays*, Brewster features up and coming but also well-established Black playwrights. Since 1982 the Albany Empire in Deptford, South London, has also offered a framework, the Second Wave, for woman writers to find a 'Room of Their Own' – in the spirit of Virginia Woolf. Since 1986 its festival for young women playwrights has provided an opportunity to see their work on stage.[26] The first two plays to be discussed here are from that background. Like the third text, they focus on issues such as displacement, uprootedness and pain – issues that are, however, translated very differently into action on stage, with topics including controversies about gender, sibling and sexual questions.

3. Killian M. Gideon, England Is De Place for Me *(1987)*

Killian M. Gideon's two-act play, *England Is De Place for Me* (1987),[27] shows two immigrant couples from Jamaica in London from the 1960s to the late 1980s. The play could be categorised as kitchen sink realism mixed with storytelling elements. Set in various apartments, the action is at times halted when characters address the audience to provide background information; the characters speak Jamaican *patois*. The plot evolves around five characters – Wilma and Dickie, Rose and Winston, and their landlord Parkie – who struggle to make a living in the UK. They arrived from Jamaica in the late 1950s with the plan of returning home always at the back of their minds. Eventually only Wilma and Dickie return, Parkie emigrates to the US, while Rose and Winston, after their separation, both stay in Britain.

Act One is set in 1966. The sixties are characterised by racist violence and conflicting gender roles. Winston's believable but nevertheless untrue story of having been beaten up by 'Teddy Bwoys'[28] refers to the ever present threat of racially motivated violence:

WINSTON	[…] Two Teddy Bwoy come up to me and ask me de time. You know something, dere was four more standing behind de two …
DICKIE	*(surprised)* Teddy bwoys?
WINSTON	Eh heh. Well I tell dem de time not suspecting what dem was up to. … All suddenly de ruction start. As I turn my back to go one of dem shout … Oui nigger piss off back to your own country. Suh I ask him who him ah call nigger. Next ting I know him ah try fling punch inna my face
ROSE	*(suspicious)* You mean big 1966 and Teddy bwoy still about? You sure dem was Teddy? (25)

Even though in this case, Winston has invented the attack, discrimination was commonplace in the sixties. Parkie later relates his version of race riots in Notting Hill in 1958/1959: "Nothing but pure fighting inna de streets, between black and white wid bottle, razor and ting" (30).

Another issue first-generation immigrants to the UK had to face were diverging perceptions of gender roles. When Wilma announces her plan to invest her first wage into fashionable "short, short mini skirts" (23) her husband is not amused:

DICKIE	*(putting down paper violently)* Mini-skirt? […] You not gong to wear no short, short mini skirt and walk anywhere behind me you hear …
ROSE	Behind? *(sucks her teeth)*
WILMA	And wha wrong wid me wearing ah mini skirt?
DICKIE	Suh dat odder man can look pon your batty?! You mussee tink you is one teenagerto guh showing off your whole foot like dat
WILMA	Dickie why you carrying on suh … is only a skirt
DICKIE	Maybe de English man naw mind him whoman dress suh, but dat is not fe me. Hear me good. You naw guh buy no minki or mini skirt and bring it come in here! (23)

Of course she does and he tears it to shreds. Different culturally-defined gender roles are illustrated by this passage. The women enjoy their increased freedom – Wilma wants to dress like other British women and rejects West-Indian notions of how husband and wife walk together in public. Despite the English environment, Dickie is not ready to let go of his convictions about how the wife of a Caribbean man should behave. A similar situation takes place between Rose and Winston when she proposes to take on a part-time job:

WINSTON	You willing to teck ... Wait ah minute is who are de man here? Is who gwine look after de pickney and Nigel while you wuking suh damn hard?
ROSE	Well we just wuk someting out and teck turn baby-sit
WINSTON	(*shocked*) Who ah guh baby-sit?! Me? Whoman you crazy (35)

Very much like his white fellow citizens, Winston has a hard time accepting the changing gender roles in the sixties.

In Act Two, ten years later in 1976, both couples experience the problems of the generational gap; they no longer understand their children who, quite literally, speak a different language. As Wilma points out to Rose, "[s]ometime Leo ah talk some breed ah Cockney me naw understand. I haffe tell him to slow down ... ah no Cockney in dis house" (55). Moreover, both cannot understand why Rose's son Nigel has joined the Rastafarian movement, which represents a form of protest new to them. The parent generation has adapted to the reality of the 'mother country'. Wilma and Dickie own a house and their children are in college. Although they have got used to the country and the life style, the couple consider a return to Jamaica "after sixteen years in dis place" (48) – a plan they successfully realise during the following ten years by working overtime. Rose and Winston, though, represent the less successful immigrant couple who didn't 'make it' economically, who got divorced, and who never really felt at home in England. At the end of Act Two, before the epilogue, Winston is disillusioned: "You know someting Dickie ... dis country it eidder make you or bruck you" (64).

The epistolary epilogue, set in the eighties, tells the audience that in the end, only Rose seems to have adjusted to England. The title of the play could have been one of Rose's lines, for in England she found her emancipation. The final statement of the play is Rose's, in which she informs Wilma that she has managed to run down another bulwark of male dominance: "you know seh I pass me driving test. All de best Rose" (66). Wilma and Dickie return to their roots, and although Rose's roots are clearly within the Jamaican culture, she only promises to come for a holiday visit, thus making it clear that now England is the place for her.

4. Trish Cooke, Running Dream *(1993)*

The imagery of roots and trees plays an important role in Trish Cooke's play *Running Dream* (1993),[29] another Second Wave production. Questions of displacement and identity complete a colourful picture of pain and loss; gender issues and racism, major topics in Gideon's piece, play a minor role in this text. *Running Dream* is a two-part play; the setting is divided between the Caribbean island of Dominica and England. Cooke tells the story of three generations of women, grandmother Ma Effeline, her daughter Florentine and her three granddaughters Clementine, Grace and Bianca. Florentine follows the father of her first two daughters to England, leaving Clementine and Grace behind with their grandmother, who raises them. Later – Clementine is a grown woman and herself a mother – Florentine sends money for the passage of her younger daughter Grace. Meanwhile Bianca is born in England. Florentine never finds her luck in the 'mother country', and she lies on her sick-bed throughout most of the play. Grace has difficulties adjusting to the new, colder climate and to her new sister. Clementine is left behind and invests all her feelings of neglect in a doll her mother sent her as a first present from 'Inglan', thus causing pains in her mother's body – a procedure reminiscent of voodoo or obeah[30] practices, but employed rather as a symbol in this play. After having taken care of her sick mother for a long time, Grace returns to Dominica when she learns that Ma Effeline is on her deathbed; Florentine has dreams of Ma Effeline's death. When Bianca travels to her sisters' and her mother's home in the Caribbean, she meets her eldest sister Clementine for the first time.The three sisters and their mother led very different lives, but all of them were running towards a dream they never realised. Clementine would have liked to run too, but was left behind. All she could do was dream of running.

Having read this outline of the plot, one might think that *Running Dream* is a very conventional play. This, however, is not the case. Part One is by no means chronological, and there is a chorus that does much more than merely comment on the action onstage.[31] This first part is a "series of impressionistic, often musical snapshots"[32] of the characters' lives, as Ian Shuttleworth remarks. Part Two follows a chronological line, and the role of the chorus decreases as the characters gain awareness – a "gear-change"[33] in comparison with Part One, in which the audience in a 1993 performance joined the onstage exchanges. The languages of the play are English, French and English *patois*, often supported by drums and music. The two settings are placed simultaneously on one stage and they overlap, especially when they are defined as symbolic places. All the characters, including the chorus, remain present on stage throughout the play, as the following scene helps to illustrate:

(GRACE and CLEMENTINE sing, the distance between them is big)
GRACE/CLEM: *(Sing)* You and I / You and I / You and I / You and I Sharing the Sky…
(The singing is interrupted by a baby crying.)

BIANCA: Aaaaaaaaaaagh. *(GRACE looks at BIANCA.)*
GRACE: She was like one of them tiny tears dolls that cried real tears... only she never really cried. She just made the noise.
BIANCA: Aaaaaaaaaagh.
GRACE: ... and I would take the 'kerchief and wipe her nose until the snot reach her temple. And it would stay there and dry up on her face until night time when I had to bathe her. And then she'd cry.
BIANCA: Aaaaaaaaaagh.
GRACE: ... and tell Mammy I do her mischievous.
CHORUS: Méchansté! (Mischievous!)
BIANCA: Mummy Grace pinched me!
GRACE: Chèt up before I bite you! (207, emphasis in the text)

When Grace and Clementine sing their song of separation, they are interrupted by a baby crying (Bianca is being born in England), Clementine is still in Dominica and Grace is already on her way to and, at the same time, arriving in England, while Bianca is born, has grown and is talking already. Time and space melt and mingle in this small scene, as they do in other scenes, in the first part in particular. This element adds a certain magical quality to the unfolding plot, as does the chorus.

The chorus can be defined as being situated somewhere between a classical Greek chorus, African storytelling musicians and an African unison chorus.[34] Its members take on the roles of additional characters in certain scenes and then step back into line. They accompany the scenes with comments, interjections, drums, songs, and even physical interference. In their songs, the members of the chorus employ the Dominican French *patois*, translations into English *patois* and standard British English. The same goes for the other characters. Nation language[35] is used to establish scenes (i.e. in the Caribbean), connections between people (i.e. between mother and daughter), and to emphasise common heritage (i.e. between the English-born sister and her Caribbean siblings). The use of *patois* thus renders authenticity to the emotional level, and the chorus underscores this notion by frequent repetitions, interjections and songs in *patois*. In the following scene, the chorus helps Bianca express her feelings of not belonging, and her interpretation of the sisters' unrest:

(Cadence music is playing in the background. The drummer leads Spotlight on BIANCA.)
CHORUS: Hear de call / Bianca-oi Bianca-oi vini!
Come girl come / Come girl come
BIANCA: I didn't know what I was looking for. I didn't know what I would find.

FLORENTINE: Peace …

CHORUS: … of mind. Peace of mind …

(Cadence music gets loud. CHORUS make fête. They dance, blow whistles. Celebration. As the revelling comes to a close, lights fade. The moon appears. The sound of waves lapping. BIANCA follows the call.)

CHORUS: First the sky appeared / dispelling from it rays of hope,
tormenting my mutancy, / ridiculing my peculiarity,
and I felt that I did not belong.
I searched for the root / but she had drowned in the ocean,
the stem of our tree had wilted in the breeze,
We, the branches, had lost our way / So I searched for a new seed
to give me reason, / and above the rotting earth
I found her still growing in the shade

(BIANCA looks at CLEMENTINE)

Her eyes were bright and she could see beyond my return … (219–220)

The last line expresses Bianca's hope that Clementine might be able to accept her as her sister, because, after all, they have the same roots and are branches of the same tree.

Each sister is jealous of the others and of what each presumes the others had. While Clementine dreams of England, Bianca dreams of a home she never had while Grace is torn between the two. What they really miss is the connection as sisters and the connection as daughters with their mother and their grandmother. Trish Cooke shows the importance of this maternal line and of a sense of belonging. The women in this play are uprooted – each in her own specific and painful way.

5. *Winsome Pinnock,* Talking in Tongues *(1991)*

Winsome Pinnock's *Talking in Tongues* (1991)[36] is a two-act play set in London at a party and in Jamaica at a holiday resort. The protagonists belong to the next generation of black British – they could be the children of Gideon's or Cooke's characters: they were born in the UK, they grew up there, they speak the language without any foreign accent, they see themselves as British, and, what's more, other non-British blacks refer to them as English. They are young, urban, upwardly mobile people. The plot revolves around four women and their partners. In Act One, at a New Year's Eve party, Leela's boyfriend Bentley betrays her with Fran, the white hostess, in the cloak-room. Leela and her girlfriends, hidden under the coats, witness the sexual intercourse. Later that night, Jeff, Fran's boyfriend, has sex with Curly, one of Leela's girlfriends. As David Nathan puts it, the topics of "cross-racial sexuality, jealousy and their noxious effects of racial prejudice suggest some interesting parallels".[37]

Claudette	It's always the same when a white woman comes in the room.
Curly	Don't start, Claudette.
Claudette	Our men are straining at the leash like hunting dogs on the scent of the fox. Ow. Careful. […] What do they feel when they're holding her [during the dance]? Have you watched their faces when they're holding a white woman? They look as though they're in seventh heaven. Makes you feel like the invisible woman. […] It's not as if they [white women] want to be your friend. The only time one of them wants your friendship is when she's trying to get her hands on one of our men. (175–76)

Race is as much an issue here as are gender and sex. Within British society, these black women feel disadvantaged, powerless and at times even invisible.

Later in this act, the issue of race is taken to a different level. Jeff, a white man, talks about Othello and how he needed to fit into his society more than any other man because he was black. Claudette strongly disagrees with him and denies the racial component: "Why? Why would he need to fit in? He was the boss. The one who hired and fired, told them what to do, wrote references for them. They had to fit in with him, more like" (199). Her words foreshadow her behaviour in the second act, which takes Leela and Claudette to Jamaica, where Claudette enjoys herself without thinking of any consequences.

Claudette represents the stereotype of a 'sex tourist' in a foreign country to which she has no connection. In turn, to her Jamaican environment she is just another wealthy British tourist who happens to be black. Conversely, Kate, a white woman and a drop-out of British society, tries to make Jamaica her home and raise herself above the standard of the typical tourist. When she has sex with Claudette's lover however, it becomes clear that she and Claudette are on the same step of the international exploitation ladder, although Claudette has the feeling that once again a white woman acts as a "sexual usurper"[38] and takes 'her' man – a man she herself took from another black woman: Sugar. Claudette's revenge is to cut Kate's hair during her sleep, ironically a punishment for adulteresses some centuries ago, but also very recently for women who had fraternised, i.e. had sexual relationships, with the enemy in times of war. Oppression no longer seems to be linked to skin colour. It has to do with power, and power is where the money is. Consequently, it is Sugar who is fired when Kate's brother wants somebody to pay for the mutilation his sister suffered. Sugar is the weakest member in this group of people. Incidentally, her name mirrors Jamaica's former major export product, before tourism became the most important source of income for the island: sugar, made out of sugar cane with the use of slave labour for hundreds of years. Today, Sugar is a modern slave of the tourist industry, as is her husband Mikie.

In this play, language functions as a marker of geographic belonging: Jamaicans speak English with a Jamaican *patois*-tinge to it, all the others, in or coming from Britain, no matter if they are black or white, speak English and they are defined as Englishmen and Englishwomen who constantly talk about the weather. They are foreigners to the island that might have been the home of their parents or grandparents – but this is never an overt issue in this play. But *Talking in Tongues* is also a play about having no words, no language to express oneself. Leela has a deep unnameable feeling of not belonging, of being in the wrong place, of displacement:

> Leela — I've always felt really self-conscious about the way I speak. [...] It's because this isn't my first language, you see. Not that I do have any real first language, but sometimes I imagine that there must have been, at some time. You can feel that sometimes, can't you? If you don't feel you belong to a language then you're only half alive aren't you, because you haven't the words to bring yourself into existence. You might as well be invisible. (195)

She feels invisible at times; furthermore, she feels that English is not her proper language – she is not at home in the culture she lives in, that she is a part of, because she feels she is *not* a part of it. She is the victim of oppression – whether based on racist, gender or class reasons or a mixture of the three is secondary.

Means of storytelling are used to emphasise that this is by no means a new development. In a prologue leading into the play, the Jamaican waitress Sugar tells Leela the story of three women who, once a week, would go to a secret place by a waterfall and engage in some strange obeah practice that would lead one of the women to talk in tongues (cf. 173–174).

Later in the play, although earlier in terms of chronology, Irma provides Leela with an explanation for Leela's mother's complete immersion into similar religious practice:

Irma	Why were you crying? Distance. That's what I'd do. I'd go away. Of course our mothers had religion.
Leela	For all the good it's done them.
Irma	I wouldn't knock it. […] The point is that our mothers found a way of releasing the pain, they never let themselves become victims of it. (194)

By the end of the play, Leela works herself into such a rage that she starts to talk in tongues (cf. 223). She seems to have found a connection with her maternal line and her past. Afterwards, she goes for long walks in Jamaica as if she were looking for the secret waterfall in Sugar's story. She wants to stay in touch with her body in order to be able to vent some of the unspeakable energy that weighs her down, in the same way as her mother was able to release pressure and pain. She wants to become and remain visible.

Most of all, Leela wants to stop running. Black women are seen and see themselves as running from or towards something:

Jeff	Do you remember that perfume ad where the woman's running through the street at night?
Curly	Which perfume ad?
Jeff	It's very striking. There aren't any words. Just this image of a woman running. She just keeps running but doesn't arrive anywhere. […] You're left wondering what she's running to.
Curly	Or, more to the point, what she's running away from. (191)

Curly identifies with this image and sees in it her own displacement and uprootedness. Claudette and Leela run away from invisibility. Interestingly enough, Fran, the white woman, cannot see herself in this ad (cf. 196). She does not have to ask herself the question whether 'England is de place for her'.

6. Black Drama and the Union Jack

The one image connecting these three plays is the image of women running. In *Talking in Tongues* Claudette and Leela, even Kate, keep running. By the end of *England Is De Place For Me*, Wilma, together with Dickie, finally finds her place in Jamaica. She arrives where she started to run from. Rose 'runs away' from her husband and keeps on running, or driving, rather, in England. In *Running Dream* Florentine and her daughters Grace and Bianca run towards a dream or they in turn dream, like Clementine, of running. It is the dream of a better life, together, away from the nightmares of reality.

Killian Gideon, Trish Cooke and Winsome Pinnock belong to a generation of playwrights who "reflect clearly the realities of black life in the British dimension and do not imagine from anecdote, through rose-coloured spectacles, the life and times of recent ancestors".[39] Nevertheless, Gideon's and Cooke's plays are clearly locked in a postcolonial framework of displacement, uprootedness and pain that is located *between* cultures including the British, whereas Pinnock's text discusses the same phenomena *within* this one culture, the British. In an afterword to her play, Winsome Pinnock says, "Racism is a fact of life, but it doesn't mean that we can't (or don't) reach out to each other from across the cultural divide".[40] By implementing the gist of statement in her plays, she depicts a part of contemporary British reality. Moreover, she has, like other black playwrights, become part of the mainstream. I agree with Aleks Sierz when he states that this general development is "a good thing",[41] and Kadija George and Yvonne Brewster would probably also agree (cf. above). Postcolonial and immigrant issues have entered British culture at large – certainly disputed, but they have become part of the mainstream and, therefore, also part of British mainstream drama. In terms of the British stage there is black in the Union Jack. Only it is a somewhat bluish reddish whitish kind of black – in other words, it has become a part of the Union Jack and lost its exclusively black quality – it is British Black, if you will. It is a part of contemporary British reality and it contributes to making it richer and more diverse.

Notes

1 Paul Gilroy, lecturer in sociology at Goldsmith's College, University of London, uses it for the title of his study on racism in the UK. In this study, Gilroy shows the complexity of racial politics in England and discusses concepts such as 'nation,' 'race' and 'class'. Cf. Gilroy (1991).

2 Joseph (1993).

3 Cf. anon., "Commission".

4 Cf. Joseph (1993: 4).

5 For a comprehensive discussion of the terms 'postcolonial' and 'immigrant' within the context of British drama see Dahl (1995:38–55).

6 Anon., "What is Windrush?".

7 Joseph remarks in this context: "The presence of colonised peoples from Africa, the Caribbean, and Asia in the country of their former colonisers leads to

collisions of cultures, histories, and languages. This, in turn, transforms and ruptures the existing cultural codes of the host country" (1993: 3).

8 Connor-Mogotsi (1995).

9 The Edric Connor Agency was later renamed the Afro Asian Caribbean Agency, and was run by Pearl Connor from 1958 until 1974. Cf. Ponnuswami (2000: 217–18).

10 Cf. Dahl (1995: 39).

11 It was also at the RC that Hanif Kureishi ran the Royal Court Young Writers' Group and encouraged Winsome Pinnock to write her first play. Cf. Pinnock (1995b: 21).

12 For portrayals of the Royal Court and the Theatre Royal cf. Raab (1999: especially 22–37).

13 Connor-Mogotsi (1995).

14 *Ibid.*

15 Yvonne Brewster is one of Britain's best established and most respected black theatre directors. Originally from Kingston, Jamaica, she is currently artistic director of the Talawa, a black theatre company she co-founded in 1985. Her productions include the first ever black production of Oscar Wilde's *The Importance of Being Earnest* at the Opera House, Newcastle, an *Othello* based on African-American personalities such as Colin Powell and O.J. Simpson, and numerous plays by African and Caribbean playwrights. Cf. anon. "*Talawa*".

16 Evaristo (1993: 14). The Greater London Council, or GLC, had been established in 1963, but was abolished by the Conservative Government in 1986, after a highly controversial debate during the 1980s. Cf. Oakland (1998: 116–117).

17 George (1993: 6). Cf. also King (2000: 131–136).

18 For a more comprehensive analysis of the effects or the absence of public funding see Ponnuswami (2000: 211–23).

19 George (1993: 6).

20 Evaristo (1993: 14–15).

21 Oni (1993: 18).

22 *Ibid.*

23 George (1993: 7).

24 Cf. Oni (1993: 19).

25 Anon., "*Talawa*".

26 Cf. Gray (1990: 9–11).

27 *England Is De Place For Me* was first performed at the Albany Empire, Deptford, South London, in October 1988. The play was directed by Paulette Randall. Page numbers in the text refer to the following edition: Gideon (1990).

28 In the early 1950s, the press in England referred to a new development in teenage gangs that had appeared in the East End of London as 'Teddy Boys' or 'Teds', because they wore clothes that had been fashionable in the reign of Edward VII (1901–1910). These gangs expressed opposition to authority and terrified English society with their razor attacks and vicious gang fights. The *OED* defines a Teddy Boy as a "youthful street rowdy." Cf. anon. "The Story of the Teddy Boy Movement". Paul Gilroy says about riots in Notting Hill and Nottingham in 1958: "The main emphasis in newspaper reports fell on the issue of law and order which was identified as the appropriate response to the hooli-

ganism of the Teddy boys who were discovered at the core of the events." (Gilroy 1991: 81).

29 Olusola Oyeleye directed the first production of *Running Dream* at the Theatre Royal, Stratford East, London, in March 1993. Subsequent page numbers in the text refer to the following edition: Cooke (1993).

30 "In certain cultures of the Caribbean, the term [obeah, also spelled obia] denotes forms of sorcery and witchcraft, usually overpowering and evil." (*Encyclopdia Britannica. Micropdia*, 15th edition 1985).

31 In Trish Cooke's play *Back Street Mammy* (1989) there was only one character, Dynette. Here, three chorus actors took the additional roles of six further characters. (cf- Cooke 1990).

32 Shuttleworth (n.d. [1993]).

33 *Ibid.*

34 Cf. Small (1993: 9).

35 'Nation Language' is a term created by Edward Kamau Brathwaite to denote forms of Caribbean English that are influenced by the African cultural and linguistic heritage. Cf. Brathwaite (1984). In this context, I took the liberty to expand the meaning of this term to include French Caribbean *patois*, as it is based on an oral tradition as well.

36 Pinnock (1995c). Subsequent page numbers in the text refer to this edition.

37 Nathan (1991: 1044).

38 Church (1991: 1045).

39 Brewster (1995: vii).

40 Pinnock (1995a: 226).

41 Email to the author, 23 October 2001. Sierz is the author of *In-Yer-Face-Theatre. British Drama Today* (2000).

Bibliography

Anonymous: "Commission on the Future of Multi-Ethnic Britain", *The Runnymede Trust*, http://www.runnymedetrust.org/meb/TheReport.htm, date of access: 25 October 2001.

–: "The Story of the Teddy Boy Movement", *Teds News. Authentic Rock'n'Roll Web Site*, http://www.geocities.com/Nashville/7957/historique.htm, date of access: 25 October 2001.

–: "*Talawa*", http://www.talawa.com/, date of access: 19 October 2001.

–: "What is Windrush?", *BBC Online. Education*, http://www.bbc.co.uk/education/archive/windrush/whatis.shtml, date of access: 21 October 2001.

Brathwaite, Edward Kamau: *History of the Voice. The Development of Nation Language in Anglophone Caribbean Poetry,* London, 1984.

Brewster, Yvonne: "Introduction". – In Y.B. (Ed.): *Black Plays 3*, London, 1995, pp. vii–viii.

Church, Michael: "Review of *Talking in Tongues*", *Guardian*, 31 August 1991, reprinted in *Theatre Record*, 27 August – 9 September 1991, 1045.

Connor-Mogotsi, Pearl: "Our Olympian Struggle", *The Chronicle.* http://www.thechronicle.demon.co.uk/archive/mogotsi1htm and mogotsi2.htm, date of access: 19 October 2001. [Address held on 23 March 1995 at the Camden Centre, London, at the 12th International Bookfair of Radical Black and Third World Books].

Cooke, Trish: “Back Street Mammy”. – In Kate Harwood (Ed.): *First Run 2. New Plays by New Writers*, London, 1990, pp. 39–95.
–: “Running Dream”. – In Kadija George (Ed.): *Six Plays by Black and Asian Women Writers*, London, 1993, pp. 187–227.
Dahl, Mary Karen: “Postcolonial British Theatre. Black Voices at the Center”. – In J. Ellen Gainor (Ed.): *Imperialism and Theatre*, London, 1995, pp. 38–55.
Evaristo, Bernadine: “Black Women in Theatre”. – In Kadija George (Ed.): *Six Plays by Black and Asian Women Writers*, London, 1993, pp. 14–15.
George, Kadija: “Introduction”. – In K.G. (Ed.): *Six Plays by Black and Asian Women Writers*, London, 1993, pp. 5–7.
Gideon, Killian M.: “England Is De Place For Me”. – In Frances Gray (Ed.): *Second Wave Plays. Women at the Albany Empire*, Sheffield, 1990, pp. 13–66.
Gilroy, Paul: *'There Ain't No Black in the Union Jack'. The Cultural Politics of Race and Nation*, Chicago, 1991.
Gray, Frances: “Introduction”. – In F.G. (Ed.): *Second Wave Plays. Women at the Albany Empire*, Sheffield, 1990, pp. 9–11.
Joseph, May R.: “Black British Theatre and Film as Postcolonial Discourse”, *DAI* 54, no. 4, 1993, 515A [Ph.D. University of California, Santa Barbara, 1992].
King, Barnaby: “The African-Caribbean Identity and the English Stage”, *New Theatre Quarterly 16*, no. 62, 2000, 131–36.
Morris, Jessica: “Belle @ The Gate Theatre”, *My Village Notting Hill*, Online, http://www.mynottinghill.co.uk/nottinhilltv/arts-belle.htm, date of access: 18 October 2001.
Nathan, David: “Review of *Talking in Tongues*”, *Jewish Chronicle*, 13 September 1991, reprinted in *Theatre Record*, 27 August – 9 September 1991, 1044.
Oakland, John: *British Civilization. An Introduction*, London, 1998.
Oni, Stella: “An Interview with Yvonne Brewster, O.B.E.”. – In Kadija George (Ed.): *Six Plays by Black and Asian Women Writers*, London, 1993, pp. 18–19.
Paxman, Jeremy: *The English. A Portrait of a People*, London, 1998.
Pinnock, Winsome: “Afterword”. – In Yvonne Brewster (Ed.): *Black Plays 3*, London, 1995a, p. 226.
–: “Influences. Winsome Pinnock”, *New Statesman & Society* 8, no. 337, 1995b, 21.
–: “Talking in Tongues”. – In Yvonne Brewster (Ed.): *Black Plays 3*, London, 1995c, pp. 171–225.
Ponnuswami, Meenakshi: “Small Island People. Black British Women Playwrights”. – In Elaine Aston & Janelle Reinelt (Eds.): *The Cambridge Companion to Modern British Women Playwrights*, Cambridge, 2000, pp. 217–234.
Raab, Michael: *Erfahrungsräume. Das englische Drama der neunziger Jahre*, CDE Studies 4, Trier, 1999.
Shuttleworth, Ian: “Review of *Running Dream*”, *London Evening Standard*, http://www.cix.co.uk/~shutters/reviews/93002.htm, date of access: 19 October 2001 [1993].
Sierz, Aleks: *In-Yer-Face-Theatre. British Drama Today*, London, 2000.
Small, Valerie: “The Importance of Oral Tradition to Black Theatre”. – In Kadija George (Ed.): *Six Plays by Black and Asian Women Writers*, London, 1993, pp. 8–11.

Christopher Innes, Toronto

Science on the Stage

I.

In the 1950s one of the leading British physicists of the time, C.P. Snow, famously declared that scientific advances had now divided society into 'two cultures', and that these were incompatible, indeed incomprehensible to each other. In contrast to classical Newtonian physics, which could be illustrated by everyday images like an apple falling on a man's head, quantum mechanics, atomic physics or even theories of light were too abstract and (in dealing with sub-molecular levels) too mathematically intricate to be understood by anyone working in the humanities. And reciprocally therefore, nothing artists or philosophers might say would be of any relevance to scientists.

His position as the government's scientific advisor lent Snow's assertion official status, and it quickly became accepted as received truth – and although in response a decade later scientists like Carl Sagan were mounting television programs to explain science to the masses, up until very recently it was a challenge that dramatists avoided. By and large the theatre, which traditionally held a mirror to the world, restricted its depiction of contemporary life to the standard humanistic subjects of politics, gender relations, observable social behaviour, or very occasionally (as with Caryl Churchill's *Serious Money*) economics. And when something scientific did appear on stage, it was Sci-fi fantasy, or a variation on the mad-scientist stereotype, as with Alan Ayckbourn's plays from the 1980s or early nineties. So Ayckbourn's *Comic Potential* and *Henceforward*, which on the surface address issues of artificial intelligence and cybernetics, are set in a future dystopia and the robots presented as characters are merely the standard mechanistic figures of farce, while in *Body Language*, where the ostensible topic is medical science and transplant surgery, the heads of two women, simultaneously decapitated by the whirling blades of a helicopter, are sewn back onto the wrong bodies by a highly eccentric doctor obsessed by his new experimental technique.

By treating science as dangerous magic, this sort of dramatic treatment effectively confirmed Snow's dictum. Essentially a rejection, it implied that in a time when scientific advances increasingly impinge on every aspect of life, the theatre was unable to deal with a major area of experience – not that fiction or Hollywood movies were doing so either. And this was equally true of European plays that British dramatists might have used as a model. Brecht for example, who was a major influence on British theatre from the 1950s, had indeed dealt with atomic physics and the moral responsibility of scientists – but he did so through a distant analogy to astronomy set far back in the history of *Galileo*. Even Dürrenmatt, who had attempted to discuss the problem head-on in *The Physicists*, resorted to a fantasy of an insane asylum in which the characters are little more than puppets, with the protagonist being named after the Möbius strip: the mathematical model on which the front becomes the back and forward movement reverses itself. Although set in the present, the physical context of the play is (literally) cut off from everyday life, and the grotesque that Dürrenmatt saw as the only possible expression for 'the atomic age' proved too idiosyncratic for other dramatists to emulate.

However, over the last fifteen years two British dramatists have found an approach that makes it possible to put even the most abstract of complex contemporary scientific theory on the stage. These are Michael Frayn and Tom Stoppard, better known for highly theatrical farces like *Noises Off* or *Rosencrantz and Guildenstern Are Dead*. Normally one might expect such an initiative to come from more 'serious' political writers like Howard Brenton or David Hare. But it is no accident that the breakthrough should have come from playwrights known for comedy, who are the inheritors of Bernard Shaw's 'drama of ideas'. Stoppard, the first to focus on modern physics, showed an interest in science from his earliest plays. But although the laws of thermodynamics and relativism had already made an appearance in *Rosencrantz and Guildenstern*, and the moon landing in *Jumpers*, they were incidental in comparison to questions of existentialism and tragic order, fate versus free will, religious faith versus logical positivism. Only two of his plays to date (*Hapgood* and *Arcadia*) have science at their core; and Frayn addresses the subject in just one (*Copenhagen*). Yet because these three plays share certain general stylistic qualities they have an importance beyond their small number, offering a potentially viable model for other dramatists.

II.

In a sense the first of these plays, *Hapgood*, was ahead of its time; indeed, first performed in 1988, strictly it falls just outside the time-frame of this volume. But it deserves inclusion as an initial prototype, showing how Stoppard developed his technique for dealing with scientific themes that emerged so successfully in *Arcadia*. It also illustrates some of the problems in finding a suitable stage-form, *Hapgood* proving less popular than it might have been because the subject appeared abstruse.

Working on his usual principle of blending "entertainment and education as completely as a row of chorus girls explaining Einstein's theory of light",[1] Stoppard has the theory of light explained by glamorous spies in *Hapgood.* But there is nothing simpler than a chorus line, while here the problem was that both levels are complicated, with the spy story genre depending (as it does) on disguise, doubles and deception, which Stoppard multiplies and combines with arcade/computer games. In addition, the plot is full of clichés: a Star Wars secret ('anti-matter') may have been passed to the Russians, if the Russian physicist who has developed it is a Soviet plant (as the authorities have come to suspect) instead of the defector he claims to be, or if there is a mole among the British agents. Hapgood, the title character, who is the Russian's British 'control', is also his lover; and their young son is used as a pawn to untangle the truth. She also takes the role of her bohemian, antiestablishment twin sister – and then has to take on a double role: of her sister disguised as herself – to entrap her subordinate, whom she suspects of being a double agent. He turns out to be not only the opposite of what he appears, but operates by using an identical 'twin' to evade detection, and has 'blown' her 'network ... inside out'. And in the denouement this undercover war between opposing intelligence services is revealed to be a form of cooperation (as in the more cynical novels of Len Deighton or Le Carré). Its sole purpose is "keeping each other in business",[2] since the Star Wars secret to be guarded, or betrayed, has no possible practical value. And although these clichés may have been intended to provide a transparent familiarity – as the physicist, who reads "only [...] spy stories" (12), points out, "they all surprise in the same way [...]. I don't mind. I love the language [...]. Safe house, sleeper, cover, joe" (47) – they also distracted from the level of philosophical and scientific enquiry, which is Stoppard's true focus.

While the spy story genre provides the overall metaphor for the play, the structure follows the intellectual discussion of Newtonian versus Einsteinian theories of light, and mimics the photoelectric effect, which is explicitly related to the characters' search for truth (and by extension, to the way spectators view the play). This is explicitly encapsulated in the spy/scientist's analogy between the action and a laboratory experiment: "Every time we don't look we get wave pattern. Every time we look to see how we get wave pattern, we get particle pattern [...] Somehow light is particle and wave. The experimenter makes the choice. You get what you interrogate for" (49). Indeed the whole play is set up as a test of perception for both characters and audience, in which there is no single correct solution. The sequence of the scenes is designed as an equivalent of the square root of sixteen – to which, as the physicist points out, there are 'two correct answers. Positive and negative' – while the action embodies this in the permutation of 'doubles' and twins, where one person can be two characters, or vice versa. And following this, the proposition that "the act of observing determines the reality" (12) is the key to interpretation, as Peter Wood's 1988 production emphasised. The settings continually required the spectators to reevaluate their perception through *trompe l'œil*, distortions of scale or deceptive perspectives. For instance, the photographer's studio (in which Hapgood plays the part of her own sister) contained an eightfootlong toothpaste tube, monstrously out of scale, while at the zoo (a typical 'meet' for spies) the characters, facing front, gazed idly through the bars of a cage while talking – but the blank reverse of the notice identifying what is inside indicated that it was the audience who were the animals on show.

Yet if all this forces us to question reality, it also refers back to the artifice of the stage, where actors are not the characters they represent, and where all scenery is fake. In the theatrical context only what is unreal is true, gameplaying is the most significant activity; and this too is reflected in the activities of the characters, which might be described as find the odd-man-out, detect the twin, identify the father – all variations of Hunt the Thimble – while the opening sequence is a double level Shell Game, switching both a row of swimmingbath cubicles (marked by towels) and the identical briefcases deposited inside them (marked by a radioactive spray), with the missing radiobleeper in place of the traditional coin under the row of upturned cups. As Hapgood warns her suspect colleague: "[Y]ou're street smart and this is a board game. In Paris you bounced around like Tigger [from the children's classic, *Winnie the Pooh*], you thought it was Cowboys and Indians" (43). However, even more than in Stoppard's previous work, these are intellectual sports. The game of betrayal and state secrets is specifically compared to playing chess without a board against an absent opponent. Indeed the games the characters play are all of this sort: imaginary cards, where one player does not even know what game it is until the other calls out '*Snap!!*', or offstage (and therefore in theatrical terms equally imaginary) football.

Like the spy story, Stoppard also presents modern physics as intellectual games. Thus Euler's advanced mathematics is used to solve the puzzle of the Königsberg bridges, which is explicitly duplicated ("*if not replicate[d]*" [3]) in the opening scene of the play. 'Anti-matter' is (supposedly) the opposite of ordinary physical reality; and *Hapgood* is designed to break new theatrical ground in finding tangible images for scientific abstractions, and by combining physics with metaphysics in a way that reintroduces humanistic values to science. So Stoppard's focus is on "the only real mystery in physics", which his physicist defines as "the missing rung. Below it, particle physics; above it, classical physics; but in between, metaphysics. All the mystery in life turns out to be this same mystery, the join between things which are distinct and yet continuous, body and mind, free will and fate, living cells and life itself" (50). Quantum mechanics, particle versus wave theories of light, Heisenberg's indeterminacy principle, are all used to explore metaphysics. The point is much the same as in Stoppard's earlier play *Jumpers*, where the subject had explicitly been religious philosophy, but here applied to science: "[M]athematics deny certainty, they reveal only probability and chance, and Einstein couldn't believe in a God who threw dice" (49).

III.

Stoppard's next major play, *Arcadia* performed five years later, focuses just as much on contemporary science as *Hapgood*. But in place of particle versus wave theories of light, or Heisenberg's indeterminacy principle – both of which are also explored by Michael Frayn's 1998 play *Copenhagen* - Stoppard directs our attention to chaos theory, fractal geometry, and the laws of thermodynamics. These are combined with English landscape gardening, the history of aesthetics in the switch from rationalist Neo-classical ideals to Gothic Romanticism, Lord Byron and academic biography, making this one of Stoppard's most multi-layered plays. At the same time, in contrast with his earlier attempt to present science on the stage, form and content are inseparable here, making *Arcadia* perhaps the best of all his plays.

The two time-frames of the action – 1809 in the days leading up to a fire that kills the young protagonist of this half of the play, Thomasina, on the eve of her 17th birthday; and at the same country house in the present day – replicate each other, in much the same way as the fractals she is said to have discovered, where repeating (or in mathematical terms, iterating) an equation with the solution to one being fed back into the next produces a constant geometrical pattern. In its simplest terms, as explained by Valentine, a computer expert in the contemporary scenes, the numbers translate into graphs, each graph being identical but formed from "a small section of the previous one, blown up. Like you'd blow up a detail of a photograph, and then a detail of a detail, and so on, forever".[3] He is using the method to find an explanation for historical changes in the grouse population, as recorded in the family game-book. But the point of using it as a structure for the play is that fractals correspond to the workings of nature, since (according to the Royal Society Research Professor cited in the programme for the original production) "complicated, irregular or fluctuating behaviour – weather patterns, marginal rates of Treasury Bonds, colour patterns of animals or shapes of leaves – can be generated by the simplest of rules […;] the mathematics of chaos offers new and deep insights into the structure of the world around us".[4]

In the same way the relationships between the characters in each time frame mirror each other, with variations that expand during the play. In both there is a teacher (Septimus, the family tutor / Bernard, a university professor) who publishes slashing reviews that outrage a writer (the incompetent poet, Chater / the non-academic historian Hannah) and is loved by the daughter of the house (Thomasina/Chloe). In each, one of the family (Thomasina/Valentine) is fascinated by "the behaviour of numbers"[5] and using the same type of mathematics, although in the past the mathematician is also "the genius of the place" (28), while in the present the equivalent spirit of the house is his young brother (Gus), who gave up speaking at the age of five. In each too, Byron is absent, but very much on the minds of everyone else, and – as well as the tortoise which is assumed to be still alive after 184 years – one character is identical in both time frames: the young boy Augustus/Gus (played by the same actor). In addition, the same patterning recurs from scene to scene in the historical frame, with the stage directions to one explicitly stating that it is "[*a*] *reprise*" (67), while the description of the previous scene reminds us that "[*w*]*e have seen this composition before*" (35). At the same time, mimicking the expanding graph of fractals, whenever characters from either era put anything on the table, it remains there, in a multiplying collection of objects.

One of these is an apple – offered by the shy Gus to Hannah; picked up first by Thomasina, who uses a leaf from it to plot an equation that will demonstrate "nature is written in numbers" (37), then by Valentine to explain how a "picture of this leaf" (47) could be made by iterating the right algorithm. The apple, of course, is simultaneously emblematic of Newtonian physics (in popular iconography one falling on Newton's head in an orchard led to his discovering the law of gravity) and of Eve's seduction of Adam in Eden: as Valentine puts it, "The attraction that Newton left out. All the way back to the apple in the garden" (74). And indeed the Biblical Garden of Eden, or its classical equivalent Arcadia, is one of the controlling images in the play. The title is picked up in the landscape of Sidley Park, with Hannah describing the formal Italianate 1730s garden as having been "Paradise in the age of reason" (27); and the Lady Croom of 1809 seeing herself surrounded by the picturesque naturalism of Capability Brown's garden that has replaced it as being "[h]ere [...] in Arcadia" – which leads Thomasina to recall the title of Poussin's famous painting (reproduced in the NT programme) where the "I" of "Et in Arcadia ego!" refers to death (12–13). Indeed this reminder of mortality – also inherent in the Biblical story where Eve's apple is a symbol of both sex and death – is reflected in all the game-shooting (and duelling) that goes on in these idyllic surroundings. And even more centrally in the immolation of Thomasina on the verge of sexual awakening, as well as in the implication of her mathematical discovery.

For Hannah, the 1809 remodelling of the park into a Romantic wilderness, complete with fake ruins and a hermitage, marks "[t]he decline from thinking to feeling" (27), which makes the landscaper with his steam-engine (in Septimus' phrase) "the serpent" in "the scheme of the garden" (4). And it is the steam engine, as well as stirring jam into a bowl of rice-pudding, that brings Thomasina to deduce the principle of entropy by revealing that "the heat equation [...] only goes one way" (87), which as Septimus realises means that "we are all doomed" (93). (Newtonian physics assumed that energy is conserved and therefore the universe is stable because it is limited to the laws of motion, but once the laws of thermodynamics are taken into account then, as Thomasina points out, "the Improved Newtonian Universe must cease and grow cold". [*ibid.*])

This seems a bleak vision of existence; and indeed the play is frequently seen as a statement of existential despair. Thomasina dies, unfulfilled; and we are told that Septimus spends the rest of his life alone in the hermitage, covering mountains of paper in an (apparently) insane attempt to disprove her equations. Yet the final waltz, which unites couples from both time frames, is highly ambiguous. The pairings are patently incongruous – the dumb Gus with Hannah twice his age, and Thomasina with Septimus who has already refused her advances – but it is still a traditional image of harmony. Indeed while entropy (like all human life) may be a one-way passage to extinction, the Newtonian physics it displaced is totally deterministic and rules out free will. And Thomasina's "New Geometry of Irregular Forms" (43) offers a positive alternative, since mathematically it is the opposite of entropy: "In an ocean of ashes, islands of order. Patterns making themselves out of nothing". (76) There is also another form of creation that the play stresses. "The action of bodies in heat" (84) – the definition of thermodynamics – is also a description of sexual activity, which preoccupies all the characters in both time frames. Their behaviour may be disastrous because, whether Septimus being seduced by the promiscuous Mrs. Chater in the gazebo or the modern day Bernard copulating with Chloe in the hermitage, they pursue sex without loving while love, either in Thomasina's feelings for Septimus or the pretended engagement between Valentine and Hannah, remains unconsummated. Even so, sexual attraction is asserted as a force that escapes from all deterministic laws of physics, and the flame that consumes Thomasina is an emblem of passion. In the play it is only the candle she takes to her bed, which burns her up physically – but the clear implication is that this would not have happened if Septimus had accepted her invitation to go to bed with her, changing her historical fate by exchanging the candle for burning emotion.

Other things also get burnt during the play: all Septimus' endless pages of mathematical proofs, letters that would prove the truth about Byron.

And a comparison is made to the burning of the library at Alexandria, in which so much of the literature and scientific writings of the classical age was destroyed. However Stoppard takes much the same view of the latter event as Shaw in *Caesar and Cleopatra.* The present-day scenes demonstrate that ideas never die, and that "[m]athematical discoveries glimpsed and lost to view will have their time again" (38). Even if direct historical evidence vanishes, the truth (as with Byron's supposed duel over Mrs. Chater) can still be intuited. More: facts are 'trivial' since "[i]t's wanting to know that makes us matter" (75). And Stoppard deliberately transforms history, most significantly in the figure of Thomasina. She – and the Byron connection – is clearly inspired by a real mathematical genius of the period, Ada, Byron's daughter who was born in 1815 and first introduced the binary system (on which computer mathematics are based) in place of Charles Babbage's decimal system, which had been the standard method of counting up to then. But although Ada, too, died relatively young, she lived to marry at twenty, becoming Countess Lovelace – a name with significant overtones in terms of *Arcadia* – and bearing two children. As the figure of Wilde remarks in Stoppard's next major play, *The Invention of Love,* "Truth […] is the work of the imagination".[6] So the play itself, with its fractal-like structure that finally breaks through the entropic logic of time in the merging of past and present, becomes the ultimate affirmation of the positive value in human existence. Science, in the form of chaos theory and mathematical algorithms, becomes presented as the guarantor of personal freedom and emotional fulfilment.

IV.

Copenhagen, which followed *Arcadia* just five years later – while it has a happy ending of a sort, and focuses on exactly the same scientific theories as Stoppard's *Hapgood* ten years earlier – is straight intellectual drama. And in contrast to *Arcadia*, even though the characters are all presented as dead, in an afterlife of memory, Frayn takes pains to justify the historical accuracy of the action. At the same time, Frayn also uses a double time-frame, if vestigially, since the consciousness of these characters is located in the present of the performance, while the scenes they replay are events from the 1940s. And still more importantly, however different the tone of *Copenhagen*, it shares the same merging of form and content, like Stoppard using the scientific principles at the core of the discussion as a structure for the scenes.

Revolving around Heisenberg's uncertainty principle and Bohr's theory of complementarity, which together with the Copenhagen Interpretation of quantum mechanics provided the basis for nuclear physics, every aspect of the play is designed to embody the concept of the universe defined by modern science. The characters responsible for ushering in the atomic age are seen in terms of their own theories. They "live inside the atom",[7] and as Heisenberg remarks:

> Copenhagen is an atom. Margrethe [Bohr's wife, who transcribed all his theories] is its nucleus [...,] Bohr's an electron. He's wandering about the city [...]. I'm a photon. A quantum of light. I'm dispatched into the darkness to find Bohr. And I succeed, because I manage to collide with him. (70–71)

Even their status as ghosts parallels Schrödinger's imaginary cat, alive and dead at the same time.

Complementarity is constantly used to define a theme in which "physics [...] is also politics", and where the two opposing scientists are mirror images of each other, while the Uncertainty Principle (or in the more precise term Frayn suggests in his Postscript to the play, indeterminability [cf. 101]) correlates to memory: Heisenberg and Bohr cannot even agree whether they spoke together in German, Danish or English; and when both conclude they did their best work together, Margrethe asserts that each made their fundamental discoveries while alone. Uncertainty also defines the central action, a visit made by Heisenberg to his old mentor Bohr in September 1941 during the German occupation of Denmark: potentially a crucial turning-point in World War II, and much discussed by historians, but about which tantalisingly little is known for sure.

This meeting is revisited in a series of inconclusive variations by the remembering ghosts of the long-dead protagonists, whose afterlife is like the half-life of the atomic radiation that would be the effect of the weapon the conversation circles around. The key question is Heisenberg's motive as the leader of the Nazi nuclear program. Was he looking for Bohr's sanction to developing an atomic bomb? Or trying to get an agreement through Bohr's contacts in the American scientific community, that if he avoided working on it for Germany then the Allies would refrain too? Or more subtly, subconsciously hoping that Bohr would make the moral choice for him either by showing him the solution (which he may have known but suppressed) to a mathematical problem that would make fission practicable, or by not doing so and thus justifying his (possibly willed) blind spot and denying Hitler such a weapon? Nothing can be determined with certainty – except that these particular scientists had the power of God to decide the fate of all the two thousand million people in the world – since, following the principles of quantum physics, the act of observing any event (as the audience are, and as the characters themselves do in re-enacting their conversations) changes its nature. And as Bohr points out, anyone's motives, particularly Heisenberg's given the contradictory pressures he was under during the war, are equated with the theory of light, which is either a wave or a particle (or both) depending which you test for. Still, just as an electron can only be tracked by its effects, so the survival of London, Paris, Amsterdam – which would have been targeted as the Allies advanced, and utterly destroyed if Hitler had had the atomic bomb to hand – can be seen as the effects of Heisenberg's meeting with Bohr. As Frayn puts it in the final words of the play: 'Our children, and our children's children. Preserved, just possibly, by one short moment in Copenhagen. By some event that will never quite be located or defined. By that final core of uncertainty at the heart of things.' And the fact that Heisenberg apparently never considered tackling the crucial mathematical equation is represented as a reversed image of an atomic explosion, in which his "tiny failure" had saving consequences that doubled and redoubled exactly like the chain reaction of nuclear fission, but with the opposite effect. This is also contrasted with the fact that the Allies did develop the atomic bomb and use it to destroy Japanese cities.

The play was given added coincidental relevance by opening within hours of the announcement that Pakistan had just tested its first atomic bomb. But what makes *Copenhagen* so striking is the way Frayn transmutes physics into the human dimension. As Bohr says, it is the philosophical implications of science that matter – the same is true of Frayn himself, one of his earliest books being titled *Against Entropy* (1967) – and the play demonstrates that quantum physics have "put men back at the centre of the universe" (73). Reversing the traditional subordination of people to an omnipotent God or the determinism of classical mechanics, the fact that on a subatomic level observation itself changes reality means the universe is not objective. It exists only "within the limits determined by our relationship with it. Only through the understanding lodged inside the human head" (74). Frayn also suggests this should lead to a "new quantum ethics" (94), recognising that applied (as here in the play) to people, the Uncertainty Principle makes standard moral judgements unjustifiable. There is no attempt to deny the "darkness inside the human soul" identified with Hamlet's Elsinore (60). Yet paradoxically in the face of its discussion of Fascist tyranny, the Holocaust, and the nightmare of the Atomic Bomb, the play affirms the potential of individuals.

V.

In *Copenhagen*, Frayn also challenges the whole traditional basis of drama. If, following the principles of particle physics, we can only be aware of our own existence through observing the reactions of others to our presence, while uncertainty means that motivation cannot be determined even by ourselves, then all conventional characterisation is false. On all levels *Copenhagen* is very much a play for the contemporary age. Much like Stoppard's *Arcadia*, it not only addresses modern science but is structured to express a new vision of life that corresponds to the latest scientific principles. With these plays the potentially disastrous divide between Snow's 'two cultures' has been bridged. Humanistic values are applied to science, while at the same time scientific principles are incorporated into artistic structure. And beyond that contemporary science, whether quantum mechanics, complementarity and the uncertainty principle, or fractal geometry, thermodynamics and chaos theory are asserted as positive forces. For both Stoppard and Frayn these new areas of intellectual exploration offer ethical frames for the world of today that – in the face of death and even the destruction of the world – can serve as a basis for personal happiness in everyday life.

Notes

1 Stoppard's principle derived from his review of a Richard Attenborough film, *The Angry Silence*, *Bristol Evening News*, 8 March 1960.
2 Tom Stoppard: *Hapgood*, London, 1998, p. 87. Further references will be included in the text.
3 Tom Stoppard: *Arcadia*, London, 1993, p. 43.
4 Robert M. May, University of Oxford and Imperial College, London, in the National Theatre programme, 1993.
5 Stoppard, *Arcadia*, p. 45. Further references will be included in the text.
6 Tom Stoppard, *The Invention of Love*, London, 1997, p. 93.
7 Michael Frayn, *Copenhagen*, London, 1998, p. 61. Further references will be included in the text.

Aleks Sierz, London

In-Yer-Face Theatre.
Mark Ravenhill and 1990s Drama

1. Introduction

During the 1990s, there was a revolution in New Writing for British theatre. Although, at the end of the previous decade, it had been fashionable to proclaim the 'death of new plays', by the mid-1990s theatre had become a central part of the much-hyped revival of cultural confidence known as 'Cool Britannia' – indeed, theatre was "listed along with pop, fashion, fine art and food as the fifth leg of the new Swinging London".[1] What I propose to do is to tentatively explore the concept of In-Yer-Face Theatre, describing its significance and its relationship to New Writing, and to show how playwright Mark Ravenhill exemplifies some of the typical characteristics of 1990s British theatre.

Firstly, I'd like to stress the materialist aspect of the history of British theatre in the 1990s: at the end of the 1980s, Arts Council statistics showed that new plays formed less than ten per cent of the repertoire. By 1994–96, New Writing made up 20 per cent of staged work in subsidised theatres. What this means is that more new plays were put on than productions of Shakespeare and the classics. Since then, there's been a slight dip to about 16–17 per cent probably due to lack of money in regional theatres. Even more important has been the box office success of New Writing. In the late 1980s, it regularly attracted audiences of less than 50 per cent, by 1994 this figure was 53 per cent and by 1997 it was 57 per cent which meant that new plays were now outperforming adaptations, post-war revivals, translations, classics and even Shakespeare.[2] By 2001, it was clear that "theatre-going, still the most popular cultural activity, just ahead of visiting museums and galleries, hit a high of 24 per cent [of the adult population in Britain] in 1994–95 [when the new wave of young writers arrived], but declined to 22 per cent four years later."[3]

But as well as material changes, there was also a vital psychological change during this time. As a simple barometer of opinion, here are two quotations from Michael Billington, theatre critic of the Guardian newspaper. In 1991, he wrote: "New drama no longer occupies the central position it had in British theatre over the past thirty-five years." Five years later, in 1996, he'd changed his mind completely. "I cannot recall a time when there were so many exciting dramatists in the twentysomething age-group: what is more, they are speaking to audiences of their own generation."[4]

In other words, starting in about 1991 and 1992, there was a massive revival of New Writing in British theatre. A quick list of 20 new writers illustrates the variety and creativity of this era: Jez Butterworth, David Eldridge, David Greig, Nick Grosso, Zinnie Harris, David Harrower, Sarah Kane, Ayub Khan-Din, Martin McDonagh, Conor McPherson, Patrick Marber, Phyllis Nagy, Anthony Neilson, Joe Penhall, Rebecca Prichard, Mark Ravenhill, Philip Ridley, Shelagh Stephenson, Judy Upton and Naomi Wallace. It would be equally easy to come up with another 30 names,[5] and finding 100 new writers would not be too difficult. By any standards, these are impressive figures. One final statistic: a single theatre, the Soho Theatre in London, works with 200 writers every year – these kinds of numbers give some indication of the renaissance in New Writing.

But it was not just a case of numerical expansion. In terms of controversy, and media exposure, writers such as Sarah Kane and Mark Ravenhill have had a similar effect on British culture as John Osborne had in an earlier era, the 1950s and 1960s. Indeed, Ravenhill has enjoyed writing controversial articles for the newspapers. For example, in 1999 he argued that the original Angry Young Men – such as John Osborne, Arnold Wesker and John Arden – were 'straight boys' whose historic mission was to clear theatre of the "feyness and falseness" of gay writers such as Noël Coward and Terence Rattigan. Although the heady days of 1956, when *Look Back in Anger* opened, are usually seen in terms of class, with gritty kitchen-sink realists driving out "snobbish, dilettante and pampered" high-brows, what most commentators missed was the question of sexual orientation. This reinterpretation of the 1950s by a gay playwright was apt and allowed David Edgar to suggest that 'without Osborne we certainly wouldn't have had Ravenhill'.[6]

Controversy has certainly followed Ravenhill around. After the storyline he wrote for the third series of the BBC's cult soap opera, *This Life*, was dropped, and the series abandoned, there was wild media speculation that he'd killed off the main characters and introduced too many gay ones. All untrue. Then, in March 1998, the government's education minister David Blunkett denounced *Shopping and Fucking* as full of foul language and a waste of public money. Had he seen or read it? Apparently not. As director Max Stafford-Clark commented, 'It is shameful that there are puritans and philistines in the Labour Party who are just as damaging as those in the Conservative Party.' On one occasion, when Ravenhill appeared on a panel with David Hare to discuss new writing (London New Play Festival, May 1998), some journalists wanted to turn a perfectly amicable occasion into a battle between the old generation and the new. On another occasion, Ravenhill was attacked for refusing an invitation to a Buckingham Palace reception. In April 1997, at the Eighth Birmingham Theatre Conference, Ravenhill demonstrated his flair for publicity by appearing in an orange 'Girl Power' T-shirt. His Rule Number One is 'Don't be boring'. And what could be less boring than an in-yer-face antagonist?[7]

2. *What is In-Yer-Face Theatre?*

How do we make sense of the general renaissance in British New Writing? What does this explosion of creativity mean? The first step in understanding this phenomenon is to name it. I would argue in favour of the name In-Yer-Face Theatre, as opposed to, for example, 'New Brutalism' or the 'Blood and Sperm Generation', for the following reasons:

1) This name emphasises the sense of rupture with the past – it stresses what was new about the dramatic voices which were heard for the first time in the 1990s. After all, the concept of New Writing implies novelty rather than tradition.
2) This name also suggests what is particular about the experience of going to the theatre and watching extreme plays – the feeling that your personal space is threatened. In other words, it powerfully suggests the relationship between play and audience.
3) Finally, this name is absolutely full of resonance of the zeitgeist of the 1990s. It was often used about other cultural forms and thus it links theatre to the wider culture of that decade.

Basically, my argument is that although New Writing developed in the past ten years in a huge variety of ways, it was led by a small avant-garde group of in-yer-face writers. Although cultural critics have announced the death of the avant-garde on more than one occasion in the past 50 years, in theatre its recent re-emergence took a classical form: innovation, scandal and then retrenchment.

The phrase 'in-your-face' is defined by the *New Oxford English Dictionary* (1998) as something "blatantly aggressive or provocative, impossible to ignore or avoid". The *Collins English Dictionary* (1998) adds the adjective 'confrontational'. The phrase originated in American sports journalism during the mid-1970s, when it was an exclamation of derision or contempt, and gradually seeped into more mainstream slang during the 1980s and 1990s as an adjective meaning "aggressive, provocative, brash". It implies being forced to see something close up, and gives a sense of that violation of intimacy that some forms of extreme drama produce in the audience. It also suggests the crossing of normal boundaries. In short, it describes perfectly the kind of theatre that puts audiences in just such a situation.

More specifically, In-Yer-Face Theatre has certain clear characteristics:

1) It is a type of drama that uses explicit scenes of sex and violence to explore the extremes of human emotion. It is characterised by stage images that depict acts such as anal rape, child abuse, drug injection, cannibalism and vomiting. It also has a rawness of tone, a sense of life being lived on the edge.
2) It usually involves the breaking of taboos, insistently using the most vulgar language, sometimes blasphemy, sometimes pornography, and showing deeply private acts in public. These have the power to shock, and constitute an anthropology of transgression and the testing of the boundaries of acceptability.
3) Its basic aesthetic is that of experiential theatre. At its cruel best, it can be so intense that audiences feel – emotionally if not literally – that they have lived through the events shown on stage. This is partly due to the fact that young writers often had their work put on in small studio theatres, with audiences of 100 or so, where this intensity was easier to achieve. Instead of debating issues, In-Yer-Face Theatre imposes its actions and ideas on the audience.

In-Yer-Face Theatre is experiential theatre, and it works because it exploits two of the special characteristics of the medium: first, because it's a live experience, anything can happen. The paradox is that while the audience is watching in perfect safety, it feels as if it is in danger. Second, theatre in Britain is technically uncensored so everything is allowed. You can stage things that would be impossible to show on television or in the cinema – this gives writers the chance to explore the darkest sides of the human psyche without any compromise.

It's worth emphasising that In-Yer-Face Theatre is a question of sensibility rather than of showing any specific acts. It's crucial that while such plays might contain shocking scenes, the really disturbing thing about them is the bleakness, nihilism or despair of the emotions of their characters. In-Yer-Face Theatre is about human emotions, not just shock tactics.

To summarise: what the best young writers of the past ten years did was to transform the language of theatre, making it more direct, raw and explicit. They not only introduced a new dramatic vocabulary, they also pushed theatre into being more experiential, more aggressively aimed at making audiences feel and respond. What characterised the cutting-edge theatre of the 1990s was its intensity, its deliberate relentlessness and its ruthless commitment to extremes. Qualities such uncompromising, dangerous and confrontational became universally praiseworthy, and one of the playwrights they were used to describe is Mark Ravenhill.

3. Mark Ravenhill: In-Yer-Face and Beyond

No playwright likes being labelled, but it is quite clear that Mark Ravenhill is in many respects a quintessentially in-yer-face writer. His debut play, *Shopping and Fucking*, was first staged in September 1996 and immediately caused controversy because of its title. When it was accepted by Max Stafford-Clark's Out of Joint company, Sonia Friedman, the producer, was given legal advice that the title could not appear on posters or in adverts. Under a Victorian law – the Indecent Advertisements Act 1889, amended by the Indecent Displays (Control) Act 1981 – the word 'fuck' is banned from public display. Originally drafted to stamp out the explicit adverts that prostitutes put in shop windows, a law designed to curb a real-life activity was used to ban adverts for a play which represented, among other things, that activity. To solve the problem, the first posters for *Shopping and Fucking* used the image of a splintered fork to obscure the offending word. The next solution involved asterisks, so the title became 'Shopping and F***ing', and promotional postcards ironically advertised the play's West End transfer with a quote from the Evening Standard: "Entert***ing, Sh*cking & St*mulating."

When the play went on its national tour, in three towns, the local authority rejected even the asterisk version. So in Bracknell, Warwick and Newbury, citizens were encouraged to see a play advertised as 'Shopping and'. While metropolitan audiences are virtually unshockable, spectators in smaller cities were less blasé. In Swansea, in what Ravenhill calls the 'Welsh bible belt', a dozen Christians made a block booking and ten minutes into the show stood up and began singing hymns. Police had to be called. While such incidents helped make *Shopping and Fucking* notorious, and advertised the play far more effectively than any advert, they were rare. More common were heavy-handed jokes about alternative titles: 'Shopping and Shagging' or 'Shopping and Bonking'. In polite society, it was coyly called 'Shopping and Flower Arranging'.

First staged at the Royal Court, and subsequently revived in the West End and toured all over Britain and the world, *Shopping and Fucking* is clearly an example of In-Yer-Face Theatre. It's about three Generation Xers – Mark, Robbie and Lulu – who share a flat and try out various schemes to survive. Robbie works in a fast-food restaurant, Lulu auditions for a shopping channel, Mark goes to a detox centre to tackle his drug addiction. Asked by Brian – a sentimental gangster who cries when his son plays the cello – to sell drugs, they get into trouble when, in a moment of wild altruism, Robbie gives away 300 Ecstasy tablets. As Robbie and Lulu resort to selling telephone sex to raise the money to pay Brian, Mark meets Gary – a 14-year-old rentboy – and begins an affair with him. But Gary, who has been abused by his father, is seeking a 'good hurt' – and demands to be penetrated by a knife.

In performance, the shock elements of the play – Lulu removing her top while reciting Irina's speech from Chekhov's *Three Sisters*; Mark rising with blood on his mouth after licking Gary's anus; the anal rape scene with the knife – were balanced by the ironic quotation of postmodern ideas about grand narratives, and the use of stories to make sense of life. Certainly, the plot is deliberately unrealistic: it strains credibility to imagine that Lulu would attend a job interview with two stolen TV dinners concealed in her jacket; Robbie would have to be retarded to give away all 300 Ecstasy tablets; Brian's final decision to give the youngsters the money they owe him is sentimental if not ludicrous. But although the plot is full of such jokes, the strength of Ravenhill's writing is its snappy dialogues and its well-developed thematic coherence, its powerful metaphors of consumption and sexuality: Mark's shopping story is reprised when he retells a mutated version of it; Mark is thrown out of the clinic because he has 'lick and go' sex in a toilet, which is reflected in the gross toilet story about Diana and Fergie; Lulu's problem with sharing individual ready meals is mirrored by Gary's offer of pot noodles to Mark; Robbie gets sacked from his McJob after being attacked by a customer with a plastic fork, while Lulu witnesses an attack on a shop assistant with a real knife; Mark wants sex to be a simple transaction, but Gary wants it to hurt; the Rule Number One of drug dealing is mirrored by Brian's 'We need something [...] a set of rules'; Robbie's 'Fuck money' is challenged by Brian's 'Money is civilisation'. In a telling irony, Mark offers Gary a choice between being loved and being bought: Gary prefers to be bought, another echo of the play's shopping story. *Shopping and Fucking* may lack a naturalistic plot and well-rounded characters, but its strength is density of metaphor.

Above all, and despite its shock tactics, *Shopping and Fucking* is a political play. By showing the importance of telling stories and sharing food, Ravenhill stresses his characters' search for meaning and human contact. With vivid stage pictures, he shows how sex and intimacy can be subsumed by shopping and alienation. Capitalism, he argues, creates needs which it cannot satisfy. In the absence of the family, community or welfare, the characters are atomised individuals searching to make connections. So although the play presents a picture of the total domination of capitalism over all aspects of life, Mark, Robbie, Lulu and Gary are all shown as people who struggle to create genuinely human relations in a world where consumerism is eroticised and sexuality commodified.

Ravenhill's next two plays, *Faust Is Dead* (1997) and *Handbag* (1998), both directed by Nick Philippou and produced by the Actors Touring Company, were experiments in form that didn't quite work. *Faust Is Dead* was a two-hander about a postmodernist professor, Alain, and the son of a computer magnate, Pete. A sharp critique of the abandonment of intellectual responsibility by critical theorists, it was a rewriting of the Faust myth inspired by Lenau's 1836 version. Lack of money meant that in the first production, the character of Donny – a loser who can only feel alive by cutting himself – remained offstage because the company could only afford to pay two actors. In the rewritten version,[8] Donny is given a stage role which helps make him a much more emotionally significant presence. By contrast, *Handbag* is a small-cast play in which the actors set up resonances between the past and the present by doubling roles. Partly a prequel to Wilde's *Importance of Being Earnest*, and partly an acutely critical look at two contemporary gay couples – one male, one female – and their attempts to have a child by artificial insemination, the play also has its iconic victim, Phil. Like Gary or Donny, Phil – the underprivileged and confused youth – is the emotional focus of a cerebral play, which is full of jokes about gay lifestyle and Victorian social mores.

But if both *Faust Is Dead* and *Handbag* were experimental, and not completely successful, Ravenhill made a convincing return to form with *Some Explicit Polaroids* (Out of Joint, 1999), which further explored the territory he so excitingly surveyed in his first play. With a plot inspired by Toller's *Hoppla, wir leben!* (1927), the play begins with the release from prison of Nick, a militant left-wing activist who, 15 years previously, kidnapped and mutilated Jonathan, an industrialist. Nick's relationships with Helen, a former lover, and a set of youngsters come across as a journey of discovery as his traditional left-wing ideas are confounded by the grim facts of today's alienated pleasures, psychobabble and political loss of vision. At the same time, there is evidence of a new emotional maturity in Ravenhill's handling of the gay sex subplot, with its daring scene set in a hospital, where one young man masturbates his dead lover. *Some Explicit Polaroids* is Ravenhill's best work to date and thrillingly illustrates the idea that political theatre can be entertaining and humorous as well as committed and serious.

4. The bigger picture

Now I'd like to make a handful of points about how Mark Ravenhill fits into the wider significance of In-Yer-Face Theatre.

1) In-Yer-Face Theatre saved British theatre. Perhaps my most contentious argument is that if it had not been for a small avant-garde of young writers in the 1990s, New Writing in Britain would have gone into terminal decline. Theatre would have stagnated in a swamp of dull revivals of the classics and of Shakespeare; of adaptations of novels for the stage; of director's theatre and physical theatre – usually cheap imitations of what Continental European theatre is so good at. The great British tradition of New Writing – which puts the writer at the centre of the theatrical process – would have declined into a moribund state. In this context, Ravenhill has an importance which far exceeds the particular qualities of his writing, or the specific success of his plays. He is both a symbolic figure, who shows what is possible with the new sensibility, and a practical New Writing activist. As Literary Manager of Paines Plough in the late 1990s, he helped many other young writers and promoted the idea of New Writing.
2) In-Yer-Face Theatre is the drama of new laddism. Each historical era usually throws up a characteristic theme which sums up the essence of the zeitgeist. For the new wave sparked off by *Look Back in Anger*, this was a celebration and criticism of the Welfare State; by the time the generation of 1968 arrived, the theme changes into one of left-wing revolution and an urgent examination of its failure; by the 1980s, it was the turn of feminism and the discovery of marginal voices, usually gay and black drama.[9] By the 1990s, young writers were looking for an equally urgent preoccupation, an equally symbolic theme. They found it in the crisis of masculinity. In the 1990s, writers obsessively returned to stories which are not about the family, but about boys. In *Shopping and Fucking*, the anal rape of Gary is an example of an image often used in 1990s drama which symbolises the idea of masculinity in crisis. Men, who once were seen as active 'doers', are now represented as passive 'takers'; the penetrators are themselves symbolically penetrated. Ravenhill's play is also a typical example of what David Edgar classifies as 'the girl in a boys gang' play, with Lulu as the mother figure who holds the group together. Another aspect of this questioning of masculinity is the theme of the absent father: as Dan Rebellato points out, "The father that could have saved us has stepped aside, and we are left facing the father who will crush us."[10]
3) In-Yer-Face Theatre is a new sensibility. You can't buy an In-Yer-Face Theatre membership card – it's an aesthetic style, not a movement. Some writers write lots of in-yer-face plays; some use elements of this sensibility; others just write one in-yer-face play and then move on. But is it new? In some senses, no: think of Edward Bond's

Saved, Steven Berkoff's *East* or Howard Brenton's *Romans in Britain*. But, in the past, such plays were exceptions, now they have become the norm. What is new is the relentless quality of much 1990s writing, its overwhelming sense of a dark netherscape, the sheer insistence of its use of four-letter words. What's also new is the style in which the plays are written. If you look at the great plays of the 1970s and 1980s, they were often literary, with wordy, woolly and worthy speeches. By contrast, in most 1990s plays the speeches are much shorter, more telegraphic, more direct, more filmic even – the dialogues are much faster. In the 1990s, British New Writing threw off the dead hand of literature (in the sense of purely written work), and, through the use of an in-yer-face sensibility, created a new theatrical language. A good example is Ravenhill's work, not only because of its disturbing stage images – anal rape, oral sex, humiliating nudity, vomiting, urinating, drug injection – but also in its concise writing style and its open-ended dramatic structures. Instead of presenting audiences with a neat message, Ravenhill raises troubling questions.

4) In-Yer-Face Theatre is drama's answer to the fall of the Berlin Wall. One of the hardest questions is: why did this kind of drama arrive when it did? This is a very complex subject, but – to simplify – what happened was that changes in the wider world of politics and society (the end of Cold War, the decline in left-wing militancy, the petering out of doctrinaire feminism) all tended to free up theatrical imaginations. I'm not completely happy with the idea of 'Thatcher's Children', but there is an element of truth in the idea that a whole generation grew up in a context where there seemed to be no change possible – to which the only response, if you are critical of social conditions, is to do-it-yourself. In a sense, In-Yer-Face Theatre is do-it-yourself theatre. By the 1990s some key people – such as artistic directors Stephen Daldry (Royal Court), Dominic Dromgoole (the Bush) and Ian Brown (the Traverse) – realised that the only way to get things done was to use the resources you already had, to turn weakness into strength. So they gave young writers permission to journey to hell and report on what they found there. Dromgoole once told me: "In the 1980s, most theatres wanted well-meaning, well-reasoned, victim-based plays. (What Anthony Minghella once called 'mumble plays'.) But in the 1990s, theatres gave young writers freedom – no ideologies, no rules, no taste." As theatre shook off the style police, young writers embraced the opportunities offered to explore a new aesthetic. In this way, theatre became part of a general, autonomous do-it-yourself movement, in which artists no longer wait for state subsidy but create their work independently of subven-

tions. It is significant that Mark Ravenhill's earliest work – *Close to You* (1993) and *Fist* (1994) – was produced on shoestring budgets at underfunded venues.

5) In-Yer-Face Theatre is political theatre. In the past ten years, the death of political theatre has been prematurely announced on many occasions. Although it is true that the big state-of-the-nation play is almost extinct, the work of new writers is surely political even if the form they choose is plays about private passions. They explore personal pain rather than public politics, but it's worth stressing that most of them are passionately interested in staging critiques of modern social conditions, focusing on the problem of violence, the horror of abuse, the questioning of traditional notions of masculinity, the myth of post-feminism and the futility and injustice of consumerism. In a sense, these writers are firmly in the great tradition of romantic, sentimental and utopian rebels. They differ from phenomena such as Brit-art in that they are generally sceptical of postmodernism. Rather, they prefer old-fashioned ideas about political commitment and cultural provocation to new notions of irony, self-reflexivity and cynicism. In this context, Mark Ravenhill is a paradigm case: he is committed to left-wing ideas and highly critical of consumer capitalism, contemporary sexual mores and the effects of globalised media. While his plays are full of today's high-tech gadgets, they also argue powerfully for a return to the basic human values of community and personal relationships based on truth.

5. *Towards a critique of In-Yer-Face Theatre*

Finally, I would like to sketch out a few points which could serve as the beginnings of a thorough critique of In-Yer-Face Theatre, and to ask whether these criticisms apply to Mark Ravenhill:

1) Is In-Yer-Face Theatre just a case of cultural tourism? Harry Gibson, whose stage version of Irvine Welsh's iconic *Trainspotting* was a massive success, sees In-Yer-Face Theatre as a symptom of a modern malaise. He says, "The excess of the wild folk becomes a spectacle for the tame folk", a form of cultural tourism by which the privileged classes visit hellish ghettos in the safety of the theatre.[11] Indeed, Ravenhill has been accused of writing plays which are 'littered with lazy middle-class assumptions about the socially excluded'. His translation of Xavier Durringer's *A Desire To Kill on the Tip of the Tongue* (Edinburgh, 2001) was attacked for having "no feel for the language of the disadvantaged, disaffected white youth for whom he

is supposed to be writing".[12] On the other hand, his experiences of being gay and HIV positive give his portraits of the gay scene in *Some Explicit Polaroids* and *Mother Clap's Molly House* (National Theatre, 2001) a satirical edge and emotional charge which is deeply affecting.

2) Is In-Yer-Face Theatre a fashionable style, a new mannerism? I remember playwright David Edgar once saying that: "The bad side of the current boom in new work is the element of fashion – this leads some people to think that last year the in-thing was smack, and this year it's sodomy. This can lead to dangerous complacency." True, Ravenhill's signature stage images – anal sex, drug taking, the latest electronic gadgets – are certainly repetitive and mannered, but there is also evidence of development. While *Shopping and Fucking* and *Handbag* used anal sex as an image which represented the crisis of masculinity, *Mother Clap's Molly House* tries to show gay sex as joyful and funny. In his words, "Let's tear down this theatrical Berlin Wall, a wall that separates the horrific male rapes and the tender but sexless gay romances of the past ten years. And let's see men on the British stage having anal sex much as they do in life – frequently and for fun."[13]
3) Are the shock tactics of In-Yer-Face Theatre counterproductive? In 1998, Harry Eyres regretted how "sensation and nihilism stalk the stages", strutting their stuff in imitation of director Quentin Tarantino and artist Jeff Koons. "Sensationalism is predicated on insensitivity. The idea is that dulled audience response must be jerked into life by whatever violent means are necessary." But, he argued, "sensation merely entrenches the insensitivity it is supposed to challenge."[14] With Ravenhill, it is clear however that shock tactics always have a purpose – to focus the drama by bringing the characters into conflict.
4) Do in-yer-face plays lack heart? It is paradoxical that an era which flattered itself as being 'the caring decade' – as opposed to the 'greed is good' 1980s – produced a drama that often lacked compassion. Ravenhill's defence is simple: compassion is in the eye of the beholder, and it is not the role of the playwright to manipulate audience sympathies. He just has to present his play – it's up to the audience to find its own response.
5) Are in-yer-face plays any good? Peter Ansorge, an early critic of the new wave of the 1990s, argues that they do not constitute a new golden age because they are not as good as the first new wave of 1956.[15] Although it is easy to dismiss this point of view as hopelessly nostalgic, it does raise the question of how you judge plays which deliberately defy the naturalistic aesthetic which is traditionally the

means of judging new plays. Certainly, Ravenhill explicitly questions naturalism and his work is often experimental in form – but is it of any lasting value? It may be that one of Ravenhill's major strengths will turn out to be his biggest weakness: his unparalleled feeling for the zeitgeist could one day make him seem old-fashioned. On the other hand, his feeling for drama and staging conflict means that, at their best, his plays are good theatre: provocative, suggestive and culturally resonant.

6) Are in-yer-face plays too introverted? Adrienne Scullion argues that while many Scottish playwrights tackle the big issues, and are "vital in debating and describing our new social and cultural responsibilities", they have a "very different agenda to the fashion-victim, nihilistic 'shopping and fucking' introspection of London".[16] Certainly, there is evidence of a distinct regional divide, which mirrors political and cultural divisions, in British theatre. But is Ravenhill an example of 'introspective nihilism'? Certainly, he doesn't write large state-of-the-nation plays, but his work is of interest to much more than a metropolitan coterie, and, anyway, it shows signs of broadening out in its themes and political concerns.
7) Is the new drama reactionary? Political plays, as writer David Greig once pointed out, must contain a suggestion that change is possible. In a sense, they have to inspire audiences. In 1998, Michael Billington argued that even "the most visceral, popular plays of today imply that there is little hope of change: in Mark Ravenhill's *Shopping and Fucking* the 'money is civilisation' ethos murkily prevails". In Britain, Billington concluded, "We are living in an aggressively post-ideological age", and theatre offers only glimmers of hope.[17] While Ravenhill's work always offers a glimmer of hope of change, is this enough to justify his inclusion in the ranks of political and moral playwrights? I think that the answer is yes – if his plays demonstrate "the steady erosion of our common lives", they also "affirm what needs to be preserved", and this "sense of affirmation" is in the end more important, and more politically radical, than any shock tactics or scandal.[18]

6. Conclusion

Like many other young British writers of the 1990s, Mark Ravenhill has become a cultural export. His plays have been staged in Germany, and all over Europe and beyond. Inspired by him and similar imports, a group of German writers set up the short-lived TNT (Theatre of a New Type) in 1997 with the aim of creating a writer's theatre in Berlin. Two years later, the Taormina theatre festival awarded the Royal Court a major prize for giving a 'voice to a new generation of young writers whose moral anger, urban despair and political disillusion have sent shockwaves throughout the whole of Europe'. The advent of British New Writing encouraged a questioning of the European assumption that the director is God. Being led by writers, the British presence encouraged European writers to emulate them, and to value the word as much as the image. Finally, to complete this cultural circuit, the Royal Court has hosted translations of young German playwrights who have been influenced by British in-yer-face writers: for example, Marius von Mayenburg's *Fireface* and David Gieselmann's *Mr Kolpert* – which mixed the new 1990s sensibility with the wider traditions of European Absurdism – were staged by the Court in May 2000.

The opening of Ravenhill's *Mother Clap's Molly House*, a play with songs, at the National Theatre in September 2001 reminds us how far In-Yer-face Theatre has come since its inception at the start of the 1990s, with plays such as Philip Ridley's *Pitchfork Disney* and Anthony Neilson's *Penetrator*, through the heady days of scandal over Sarah Kane's *Blasted* and Ravenhill's *Shopping and Fucking*, down to the relative failure of Irvine Welsh's *You'll Have Had Your Hole*, and Kane's suicide in February 1999. Certainly one phase of the New Wave of the 1990s is over. The storming boys plays of the decade now seem already a bit dated, and an uncertain future beckons. With *Mother Clap's Molly House*, Ravenhill has reached a peak – he is no longer a fringe rebel, but a National Theatre playwright. His director is Nicholas Hytner, the next artistic director of this institution. Ravenhill has become a celebrity, and he is able to write for a large stage as well as for studio spaces. On the level of ideas, his work continues to push at boundaries and provoke debate. If his weak points – naive plotting, unsympathetic heroes, poor characterisation – raise questions about his genius, his stagecraft remains confident and boasts new ambitions. Whether he can continue to build on his success remains to be seen.

Notes

1 Edgar (1999: 28).
2 Reitz & Stahl (2001: 31). See also Arts Council of England (2000).
3 Kennedy (2001: 8).
4 Billington (1993: 360; 1996).
5 For example, Henry Adam, Samuel Adamson, Parv Bancil, Biyi Bandele, Simon Bent, Helen Blakeman, Simon Block, Simon Burke, Mike Cullen, Kate Dean, Hilary Fannin, David Farr, William Gaminara, Stephen Greenhorn, Karen Hope, Alex Jones, Charlotte Jones, Nicola McCartney, Linda McLean,

Gary Mitchell, Abi Morgan, Tamsin Oglesby, Michael Punter, Diane Samuels, Ed Thomas, Paul Tucker, Che Walker, Irvine Welsh, Sarah Woods and Michael Wynne. Most of these writers made their debuts in the 1990s, and the list does not include Irish and American writers who put on their first plays in the United Kingdom.
6 For Ravenhill, see chapter 5 in Sierz (2001). See also Gibbons (1999).
7 See Sierz (2001: 123, 150–152).
8 See Ravenhill (2001a: 95).
9 See Edgar (1999: 3–34). See also Stephenson & Langridge (1997: ix–xx).
10 Rebellato (2001: xiv).
11 Gibson (1999).
12 Hari (2000: 9).
13 Personal interview with the author, March 1997; see also Sierz (1997a), Ravenhill (2001b).
14 Eyres (1998).
15 See Ansorge.
16 Scullion (2000: 114–115).
17 Billington (1998).
18 Rebellato (2001: xix–xx).

Bibliography

Ansorge, Peter: *From Liverpool to Los Angeles. On Writing for Theatre, Film and Television*, London, 1997.
Arts Council of England: *'Annual 'Cork' Analysis'*, London, 2000.
Billington, Michael: *One Night Stands. A Critic's View of Modern British Theatre*, London, 1993.
–: "Fabulous five", *Guardian*, 13 March 1996.
–: "The Other Marx Brother", *Guardian*, 10 February 1998.
Bradwell, Mike (Ed.): *The Bush Theatre Book*, London, 1997.
Croall, Jonathan: *Inside the Molly House*, London, 2001.
Deeney, John (Ed.), *Writing Live. An Investigation of the Relationship Between Writing and Live Art*, London, 1998.
Dromgoole, Dominic: *The Full Room. An A–Z of Contemporary Playwriting*, London, 2000.
Edgar, David (Ed.): *State of Play. Playwrights on Playwriting,* London, 1999.
Eyres, Harry: "Sensation Stalks the Stage", *Spectator*, 9 May 1998.
Gibbons, Fiachra: "Angry Young Men Under Fire from Gay Writer", *Guardian*, 8 November 1999.
Gibson, Harry: "Rant". Letter to author, 9 April 1999.
Gottlieb, Vera & Colin Chambers (Eds.): *Theatre in a Cool Climate*, London, 1999.
Hari, Johann: "Diary", *New Statesman*, 27 August 2001, 9.
Kennedy, Maev: "Arts Audiences Dwindle Despite 'Extra' Cash", *Guardian*, 25 July 2001, 8.
Nightingale, Benedict: *The Future of Theatre*, London, 1998.
Ravenhill, Mark: *Plays 1 – Shopping and Fucking, Faust Is Dead, Handbag, Some Explicit Polaroids*. Ed. Dan Rebellato, London, 2001a.

–: “The Bottom Line”, *Guardian*, 20 June 2001b.
Rebellato, Dan: “Introduction”. – In Mark Ravenhill: *Plays 1*, London, 2001.
Reitz, Bernhard & Heiko Stahl (Eds.): *What Revels Are in Hand?*, CDE Studies 8, Trier, 2001.
Scullion, Adrienne: “Contemporary Scottish Women Playwrights”. – In Elaine Aston & Janelle Reinelt (Eds.): *The Cambridge Companion to Modern British Women Playwrights*, Cambridge, 2000, pp. 114–115.
Shellard, Dominic: *British Theatre Since the War*, New Haven, 1999.
Sierz, Aleks: “The Write Stuff”, *Independent*, 9 April 1997a.
–: “’About Now’ in Birmingham”, *New Theatre Quarterly* 51, August 1997b, 289–290.
–: “Cool Britannia? ‘In-Yer-Face’ Writing in the British Theatre Today”, *New Theatre Quarterly* 56, November 1998, 324–333.
–: “’In-Yer-Face Theatre’ Website”, *www.inyerface-theatre.com*, created 5 October 2000.
–: “Sources for the Study of Contemporary Theatre”, *Studies in Theatre and Performance* 20, no. 3, December 2000, 196–204.
–: *In-Yer-Face Theatre. British Drama Today*, London, 2001.
Stephenson, Heidi & Natasha Langridge (Eds.): *Rage and Reason. Women Playwrights on Playwriting*, London, 1997.
Wandor, Michelene: *Post-War British Drama. Looking Back in Gender*, London, 2001.

Graham Saunders, Bristol

The Apocalyptic Theatre of Sarah Kane

In this article I want to touch upon some of the aspects of Sarah Kane's legacy. By this I mean those features of her drama which mark out her importance as a writer, together with the role her work can provide in teaching practice, linking ideas and themes from past dramatic forms, texts and practitioners.

Sarah Kane's debut, *Blasted* on 12 January 1995, provides a fortuitous nexus for theatre historians. Just as the death of John Dryden in 1700 provides a useful literary demarcation between the Restoration and eighteenth century, so the death of John Osborne on Christmas Eve 1994 in retrospect marked a transition between the passing of one of the most influential post-war dramatists and the emergence of a new voice, whose work – even in her own lifetime – came to be recognised as one of the most original within British drama. It is now widely recognised that *Blasted* alone is a seminal play in recent British theatre history, Kane's plays continue to be performed throughout the world, and within many British universities she has become required reading on courses dealing with post-war drama.

However, in 1994 Osborne's passing somehow marked and confirmed what had been periodically commented upon throughout the 1990s – namely that new British drama was in decline. Whereas one of Dryden's last works, *The Secular Masque* (1700), openly welcomed in the new millennium and was critical of events in the past century – "Thy Lovers were all untrue / 'Tis well an old age is out / And time to begin a new" –,[1] the case was very different when it came to a critical assessment of British drama in the mid 1990s. Concerns were raised as to the quality and quantity of new writing reaching the stages, and indeed its whole relevance as a social and political force.

By not only inspiring and bringing forward a new generation of other young dramatists such as John Arden and Arnold Wesker, Osborne's *Look Back in Anger* (1956) had left an indelible impression on the cultural landscape. The figure of Jimmy Porter and his now famous diatribe about there being no "good brave causes left",[2] struck a chord amongst those who felt that Britain had somehow been cheated out of its aspiration for the 'New Jerusalem' promised immediately after the war.

A few critics vainly tried to cast about for similar maverick figures in contemporary culture as a replacement for the Osborne of the 1950s. Michael Ratcliffe, writing in the *Observer*,[3] put forward the American screen writer, film director and actor Quentin Tarantino as a possible candidate, but also conceded that the choice was a weak one owing to the amorality of Tarantino against the keenly directed sense of moral rage that pervaded Osborne's early work.

Yet, *Blasted* and *Look Back in Anger* in their own different ways served to reinvigorate the theatre once again as a place where new dissenting voices could be heard. Despite the vehement and almost unanimous critical opprobrium that greeted *Blasted*,[4] it at least proved that a play performed in a small studio theatre to an audience of not many more than a thousand people during its short British run, could unsettle sensibilities and even become a national news story about the depiction of violence on-stage. Moreover, *Blasted* provided a rare example of how the aberrant, through mass media notoriety, can suddenly find itself occupying, albeit for a short while at least, a prominent place in mainstream culture.

By the end of 1995 both *Blasted* and new writing in general had made British drama a talking point again, and over time *Blasted* has undergone a substantial critical revaluation; it is now acknowledged as an important work in several respects. Despite being described in early reviews as "no more than an artful chamber of horrors designed to shock and nothing more",[5] in retrospect it has been seen as an important piece of political drama. Despite the first half appearing to be a domestic exploration of Ian and Cate's sado-masochistic relationship, as *Blasted* unfolds, the personal relationships and the later arrival of the Soldier develop events into both a 'State of the nation' and 'State of Europe' play.

The dramatist Edward Bond, in an important early article on *Blasted*, saw in its imagery reminders of "Hiroshima, Nagasaki, Auschwitz, Dresden, Babi Yar",[6] while in an early letter of support, the Reverend Bob Vernon commented that its imagery spoke of urban deprivation: "My local shopping centre looks like Grozny, only two out of two dozen shops remain [...]. Some housing estates in our city look like war zones [...:] burnt out houses, glass and rubbish littered streets, [and] dazed, tranquilized people trying to survive".[7]

Blasted was also almost unique in its willingness to confront and dramatise at that time, aspects of the conflict in Yugoslavia and the atrocities associated with that particular civil war; it also raised the question, primarily through the character of Ian and his occupation as a tabloid journalist, of the passivity and culpability involved in allowing the war to continue which raged so near to the borders of other European nations. Kane commented in an interview on how the Bosnian conflict inspired the play:

> With *Blasted* I think that it was a direct response to material as it began to happen. I knew that I wanted to write a play about a man and a wo-

> man in a hotel room, and that there was a complete power imbalance which resulted in a rape. I started writing and one night I switched on the news […]. And there was a very old woman's face in Srebrenica just weeping and looking into the camera and saying – "please, please, somebody help us, because we need the UN to come here and help us." And I thought, "no one's going to do anything. How many times have I seen another old woman crying, from another town in Bosnia under siege and nobody does anything?" I thought, "this is absolutely terrible and I'm writing this ridiculous play about two people in a room – what does it matter? What's the point of carrying on? This is what I want to write about", yet somehow this story about the man and the woman is still attracting me. So I thought, "what could possibly be the connection between a common rape in a Leeds hotel room and what's happening in Bosnia"? And suddenly the penny dropped and I thought, "of course it's obvious – one is the seed and the other is the tree." I do think that the seeds of full-scale war can always be found in peace time civilisation. I think the wall between so called civilisation and what happened in Central Europe is very thin, and it can get torn down at any time. I then had to find a way of formally making that link.[8]

Blasted also seemed to be a lynch pin in the revival of fortunes in new writing, particularly by a group of young dramatists who, like Kane, received initial commissions for their work from the Royal Court. In retrospect its 1995 season was important for the number of significant new writers it brought forward such as Michael Wynne (*The Knocky*), Simon Block (*Not a Game for Boys*) and Joe Penhall (*Pale Horse*). Peter Ansorge, while sceptical about much of this new writing, was one of several critics who saw a new collective voice emerging, whereby, "the new regime at the Court [Stephen Daldry had been appointed Artistic Director in October 1993] has been cultivating a post-Thatcher brat-pack of writers in their early twenties who are undoubtedly in touch with the mood of young audiences".[9] Benedict Nightingale, in his book *The Future of Theatre*, summarised the main themes and concerns of this new generation of dramatists:

> Their characters drifted around weird cityscapes, where violence was a frequent threat and escape from feelings of entrapment mostly an illusion. But unlike their predecessors, these dramatists had no obvious ideology, no political credo, no social agenda. If their characters launched into generalisation, it was more likely to be about drugs or drink than the sins of the establishment. They observed the urban British quizzically, reported the contradictions they saw, and left the audience to reach its own conclusions.[10]

Although *Blasted* was initially credited as being the precursor that launched this group – variously known as 'the Britpack,' 'the New Brutalists' and 'the Theatre of Urban Ennui'[11] – these terms bedevilled Kane as a dramatist, whose work bore very little resemblance to this prevailing style of drama. Speaking in November 1998 she expressed these frustrations:

> *Blasted* was considered the beginning of a movement called 'New Brutalism' [...]. That is exactly the problem with movements, because they are exclusive rather than inclusive [...]. It is just a media label to refer to some things that might happen in a particular play. Actually it's not very helpful [...]. I do not consider myself a New Brutalist.[12]

In some quarters British critics slowly began to realise the schism that existed between Kane's work and much of the "limply ambitious [...] dialogue-driven"[13] drama of other contemporaries, alongside "her handling of image and metaphor [which] sets her apart from almost every other playwright of her generation".[14]

What then is Sarah Kane's role in pedagogy? What role can her drama occupy in the wider teaching of theatre, or does she in reality occupy no more than an interesting niche on university modules concerning themselves with the study of contemporary drama? Based on the use of her work in both seminars and practical workshops, it has been my experience that the material from Kane's plays furnishes profound insights not only into her own work, but also into other dramatists and theatre practitioners from earlier periods.

The main reason for this is the vital importance *theatre itself* occupies at the heart of Kane's writing. This might at first seem like a foolish statement, until one considers again the work of her contemporaries who were writing for the stage during the mid 1990s. Whereas in the past, dramatists wrote directly in response to the stage as a medium, or in the case of dramatists such as Osborne, Pinter and Ayckbourn, pursued early careers in the theatre before turning to writing, Kane's generation were more influenced by other cultural media. The dramatist Winsome Pinnock believed these new dramatists had "introduced a new theatre aesthetic of popular culture and in particular film, than [...] plays of the past".[15] Sheridan Morley observed that "the most influential director around has been neither Sam Mendes nor Stephen Daldry but Quentin Tarantino, who without leaving California has managed to condition a whole generation of young British playwrights".[16] The dramatist Charlotte Keatley saw such influences as both empty and disturbing: "The current vogue for American film criteria quite alarms me. All the plays seem to be called 'Sex and Violence' or something close to that. Plays like *Mojo*. Yes, so Jez Butterworth can write great, wacky dialogue, but it's yet again another play about a bunch of men doing nothing much".[17]

While Kane wrote the short screenplay *Skin* in 1995, otherwise she worked exclusively in theatre, and before her death expressed the wish that none of her work could ever be adapted for another medium. Speaking once in relation to *Cleansed* (1998), she saw it as belonging exclusively to live theatrical performance:

> I was having a particular sort of fit about all of this naturalistic rubbish which was being produced, and I decided I wanted to write a play that could never be turned into a film; it could never ever be shot for television; could never be turned into a novel; the only thing that could ever be done with it was that it could be staged. Now, you may say it can't be staged, but it can't be anything else either. It can only be done in a theatre. It may not be represented naturalistically. It's completely impossible to do *Cleansed* naturalistically. I wanted to write something that was totally theatrical.[18]

One of the starting points for an exploration of Kane's work is indeed its retreat from realism. Much of the early critical hostility from the British press over *Blasted* concerned itself not with the treatment of sex and violence, but the play's sudden switch in the second half from a realistic domestic setting with two people in a room, to a bewildering expressionistic landscape. This jolt in dramatic form was unnerving to many, who responded by accusing Kane of failing to control the play's structure. Jane Edwardes' comment was a typical response: "It would have helped to know how the characters are related to each other, where reality starts and fantasy begins, what war is being waged and why, and if we are really in Leeds".[19] Michael Billington, who despite subsequently withdrawing much of what he said in his first negative review of *Blasted*, still saw the sudden retreat from realism in the second half as an inherent weakness. Speaking in June 2000, Billington was still not convinced and felt that "the shock tactics she [Kane] used in the second half of the play demonstrated a lack of aesthetic control".[20]

Yet, the first half of *Blasted* is almost a textbook example of Ibsenite and Chekovian dramatic structure. Speech and action are related to character from the very opening stage directions: "**Ian** *comes in, throws a small pile of newspapers on the bed, goes straight to the mini-bar and pours himself a large gin*"(1:3).[21]

These actions immediately help to establish both his occupation as a journalist and his alcoholism. Moreover, Ian's first utterances, "I've shat in better places than this [...]. I stink," and "tip that wog when he brings up the sandwiches"(1.3), simultaneously reveal his cynicism, self-disgust and racism. Ian's later revelation about dying from a lung disease is also intimated early on when we hear him "*coughing terribly in the bathroom*"(1:4).

Cate's response to the hotel room is in stark contrast, and clearly shows right from the outset the differences in their personalities. She "*bounces on the bed* [...], *goes around the room, looking in every drawer, touching everything* [...], *smells the flowers and smiles*" (1:3–4), describing the room as "lovely"(1:4).

The use of props also holds symbolic significance, which is revealed as the action progresses. The items, "*a large double bed; a mini bar; champagne on ice; a large bouquet of flowers*" (1:3), become tangible ciphers that help to demonstrate seduction, sexual abuse, misplaced love and rejection. Often unity of action is achieved by these objects changing their appearance and function as the play progresses. For instance, the bouquet of flowers by scene two is "*ripped apart and scattered around the room*" (2:24), exposing the hollow gesture of Ian's love token to Cate.

The arrival of the Soldier and the explosion not only disrupt the structure of the hotel room, but the whole dramatic structure of the first two scenes. Kane felt it necessary to produce such extreme events in order to express the changes that have suddenly taken place to the world outside, beyond Ian and Cate's domestic relationship:

> I think that what happens in war is that suddenly, violently, without any warning whatsoever, people's lives are completely ripped to pieces. So I literally just picked a moment in the play. I thought, "I'll plant a bomb and blow the whole fucking thing up". I loved the idea of it as well, that you have a nice little box set in the studio theatre somewhere and you blow it up.[22]

By the time of *Cleansed* Kane had abandoned Naturalism entirely, and her last two plays, *Crave* (1998) and *4.48 Psychosis* (2000), largely dispensed with formal notions of character and narrative. These last plays, reminiscent of Samuel Beckett's later work, become far more introspective than *Blasted* and *Phaedra's Love* (1996), exploring individual mindscapes and concentrating upon themes such as loss, the nature of love – and of course suicide.

One area of Kane's work that arouses both interest and fierce debate amongst students is her depiction of gender. The dramatist David Edgar recognised that many of the new male dramatists emerging in the mid 1990s were writing about a shared theme – namely themselves – and the so called 'crisis of masculinity'. Edgar categorised drama from this period in the following way:

> Although I understand why writers resist the notion of being part of a movement, it seems to be unanswerable that the mid 1990s had an over-arching theme, embracing gay plays like Jonathan Harvey's *Beautiful Thing* and Kevin Elyot's *My Night with Reg,* boys' bonding plays

like Tim Firth's *Neville's Island* (and the boys' betting plays of Patrick Marber and William Gaminara), lads' plays like Jez Butterworth's *Mojo* and Simon Bent's *Goldhawk Road*, girls-in-a-boys'-gang plays like Irvine Welsh's *Trainspotting* and Mark Ravenhill's *Shopping and Fucking* (and indeed the subgenre of girls-in-and-out-of-a-boys'-bonding-play, of which genre Terry Johnson's *Dead Funny* remains the market leader). Whatever the distinctions between them, these plays address masculinity and its discontents as demonstrably as the plays of the early 1960's addressed class and those of the 1970's the failures of social democracy.[23]

The dramatist Phyllis Nagy found this vogue for plays about men an appalling development and was driven to comment that "if things carry on the way they are currently, with this 'laddism' […] then I for one, will stop writing plays".[24] Timberlake Wertenbaker similarly saw this new development of "male violence [and] homoerotica"[25] as both restrictive, reactionary, and generally unwelcoming to other women writers.

While Kane's work at least shares aspects of this theme, her treatment of diseased masculinity is startlingly different. The sexual politics in Kane's drama often revolve around women playing out intensely masochistic relationships to nihilistic, self-loathing male protagonists: Cate returns to Ian in *Blasted* despite having been raped by him; Phaedra's love for Hippolytus culminates in her suicide – an act which Hippolytus realises "is her present to me" (6.90); Tinker in *Cleansed* imprisons and tortures both Grace and the Woman, and in *Crave* the character C (who seems to be a young woman) seems unable to escape from the obsessive love of A, who appears to be both an older man and a paedophile.

The self-hatred within these men often manifests itself in symbolic medical pathology such as the loss of Ian's lung, which he describes as "this lump of rotting pork" (1:11), or the "inch of pleurococcus" that coats Hippolytus' tongue "like the top of wall" (5:85).

Men in Kane's plays often veer between intense expressions of love and aggression for the women trapped with them. From early on in *Blasted* Ian moves from abuse of Cate's brother – "Retard isn't he?" (1:5) – to Cate herself: "Your mother I feel sorry for. Two of you like it." He then immediately changes tactics to first show affection and then self-pity:

Ian You ever thought of getting married
Cate Who'd marry me?
Ian I would
Cate I couldn't
Ian You don't love me. I don't blame you, I wouldn't (1:6).

Yet, characters like Ian, Hippolytus and Tinker despite being monsters are also allowed to elicit an audience's sympathy. Partly this comes from their brutal honesty. Hippolytus for instance is ruthless at cutting through the romantic delusions of love that his stepmother holds for him:

Phaedra I wanted to see your face when you came.
Hippolytus Why?
Phaedra I'd like to see you lose yourself.
Hippolytus It's not a pleasant sight.
Phaedra Why, what do you look like?
Hippolytus Every other stupid fucker.
Phaedra I love you.
Hippolytus No.
Phaedra So much.
Hippolytus Don't even know me.
Phaedra I want you to make me come.
Hippolytus I'm not used to these post-coital chats. There's never anything to say. (4:82)

This brutal truthfulness, or total belief in a delusional goal is often what ultimately destroys Kane's characters. From Hippolytus' last words, "if there could have been more moments like this" (8:103), as "*a vulture descends and begins to eat his body*" to Grace's declaration to her dead brother, "love me or kill me, Graham" (6:120), or speaker A in *Crave* declaring, "Only love can save me and love has destroyed me" (175) – these extreme states and situations again remove Kane's drama – "whose imagery resembles the paintings of Hieronymus Bosch"[26] – from the largely socio-realist concerns of her contemporaries. This places her work far closer to the tradition of Elizabethan and Jacobean dramatists such as Marlowe and Webster, whose plays also concern themselves with overreachers and bitter nihilists such as Faustus and Bosola – who encounter and embrace violent catastrophe. This kinship with classical tragedy is an important strand running throughout Kane's work. Her rewriting of *Phaedra's Love*, using Seneca's version of the myth, is an obvious example, but Kane has also openly acknowledged her debt to Shakespeare's *King Lear* in *Blasted*,[27] and *Twelfth Night* in *Cleansed*. The latter is the most 'Jacobean' of Kane's plays, and one can detect in the writing the strong influences of John Webster's *The Duchess of Malfi*, and John Ford's *'Tis Pity She's a Whore*.[28]

This return to classical text by the modern dramatist is the subject of an essay by the dramatist Howard Barker. Kane has described Barker as "the Shakespeare of our Age",[29] and his plays and writings about theatre have in turn exerted an immense influence on her own dramatic practice. Barker argues that while much contemporary drama feels happy to embrace subject matter that could be called 'domestic tragedy' – for example child abuse, unemployment or drug addiction –, it is not comfortable in presenting dramatically the types of suffering that took place on the Elizabethan and Jacobean stage. Tragedy on the scale of Lear's madness or Faustus being dragged down to hell is no longer deemed a relevant way of commenting upon the human condition. Such drama has been consigned to the role of a theatrical artefact – held up as an epitome of 'culture', or a suitable subject for academic study.

Opposing this 'taming' of past tragic form, Howard Barker believes that "the secret of tragedy – its inviolable secret" is still to be found – albeit buried – in the "pleasures and dangers of the classical text, now consigned to the realms of cultural archaeology".[30] Contemporary drama which calls itself tragic to Barker is merely "a drama of accidents masquerading as tragedy", while "the tragedies of the 1960's were not tragedies but failures of the social services".[31] To Barker, tragedy is the dark anathema to "the rhetoric of access",[32] which he sees as a function of post-modern society, together with its "loathing of a secret".[33] Tragedy is an act of defiance to received notions of ideology, politics or religion:

> Tragedy is the most illegitimate of all art forms, the most devastating to social orders and consequently, the most de-civilizing, the darkest and yet simultaneously the most life-affirming, for precisely by standing so close to the rim of the abyss it delivers expression to the inexpressible, and stages emotions the so-called open society finds it impossible to contemplate.[34]

Not only do all of Kane's characters stand close to the 'rim of the abyss,' but they often launch themselves into the abyss itself. Barker believes that for an audience such a moment "liberates language from banality [and] returns poetry to speech", and in so doing "restores pain to the individual".[35] This restoration of tragedy is at odds with contemporary views of the form – where a car accident is deemed 'tragic' – as it exposes the contemporary audience to the unfamiliar emotions Barker speaks about. This is borne out to some extent by reports of the audience reaction to Kane's work: from the walk outs in *Blasted*,[36] to David Benedict's comment in his review of the British production of *Cleansed*: "For better or worse, the spell of most plays drifts off the moment you leave the theatre. Not Sarah Kane's *Cleansed*. Hard as you try, its compelling, horror-soaked atmosphere refuses to be shaken off. It clings to you like a shroud".[37]

Kane in turn recognised that her male anti-heroes came from completely different literary and dramatic traditions than the predominantly urban young men who occupied the work of contemporaries such as Nick Grosso, Mark Ravenhill and Judy Upton: "Probably all my characters in some way are completely Romantic. I think nihilism is the most extreme form of Romanticism. And that I think is where the plays get misunderstood. I think I'm a complete and utter Romantic, in the tradition of Keats and Wilfred Owen".[38]

While it's quite likely that Kane's comment is meant as a wry joke, it expresses much about both her own sensibility, and the behaviour of characters within her plays. In the case of Ian and Hippolytus for instance, this borrowing from Romanticism expresses itself in their ability to transgress norms of social behaviour – for which they pay a terrible price; while for female characters such as Phaedra and Grace their total immersion in obsessive love culminates in their destruction.

To illustrate the point more fully, this process of destruction and spiritual rebirth is an integral feature which takes place with both the eponymous 'hero' of Samuel Taylor Coleridge's poem *The Rime of the Ancient Mariner* (1798), and Ian in *Blasted.* Both Ian and the Mariner undergo "a form of purgatorial fire"[39] for transgressive acts. In answer to the question posed during an interview as to whether Ian is punished or redeemed at the end of the play, Kane responded, "both".[40] This dichotomy of states is explored in both poem and drama as the protagonists suffer for the consequences of their deeds through a series of stark and outlandish images: the Mariner witnesses Polar Spirits, and the corpses of his fellow sailors steering the ship while Ian is driven to eat the corpse of the buried infant. Walter Jackson Bate sees such bizarre images in relation to Coleridge's poem as "the condensed treatment of isolation and guilt [...] of the human mind",[41] and showing the theme of "man's trembling existence before the vast unknown".[42]

Paradoxically, figures such as Ian and the Mariner achieve heroic status through their acts of transgression:

> The Mariner has done a guilty thing, and he is certainly punished. Yet had he not done it, his sense of the universe (and ours through him) would be more limited. If he is a guilty man, he is also something of a hero simply because he has gone further in experience than others. In an admittedly qualified way, he is akin to the romantic heroes that were to become so common in nineteenth century writing – some of them Byronic, others patterned after Faust – who by violating laws acquire a depth of experience that others lack.[43]

Their ability to endure "the punishment of violation [which is] sinful, severe [and] sustained",[44] is also a form of rebirth which "involves the almost total destruction of the old self in order to make room for the new".[45] Coleridge uses this model of suffering and salvation through partial redemption to moralise – "He prayeth best, who loveth best" – and discloses to the reader that the Wedding Guest leaves the encounter "[a] sadder and a wiser man". *Blasted* avoids such an overt approach, and instead we witness the first tiny gesture of this process of spiritual rebirth through Ian's acknowledgement of "thank you" (5:61) at the end of the play, to the woman he has systematically abused.

This adherence to past forms in Kane's work, the links it creates to both classical and contemporary drama, as well as its own often startling originality ultimately dismiss the notion that she 'belongs' to the clique of young dramatists writing in the mid 1990s, but rather locates her drama within a larger framework, encompassing developments within both post-war British drama and the wider changes to the theatre taking place in Europe throughout the twentieth century. The premature death of Sarah Kane in February 1999 removed a strand of written drama that was boldly experimental, and it is somewhat depressing to note that almost all new writing since has retreated back to the comforts of socio-realism and the recurrent theme of urban disaffection. Like many of her characters, much of Kane's writing transgressed dramatic boundaries and was not afraid to take risks, or as Edward Bond concluded, in an obituary for *Theater der Zeit*, "her death is the first death of the twenty first century".[46]

Notes

1 Dryden (1987: 857).
2 Osborne (1964: 84).
3 Ratcliffe (1995: 14).
4 The following two extracts were typical of the extreme critical reaction to the play: "I do not think I've yet seen a play that can beat Sarah Kane's sustained onslaught on the sensibilities for sheer, unadulterated brutalism. Heaping shock upon shock, *Blasted* is a powerful experience in the same way that being mugged is a powerful experience" (Curtis 1995). Charles Spencer, writing in the *Daily Telegraph* commented, "The dramatist Sarah Kane (23) puts one in mind of the naughtiest girl in the class, trying to find just how far she can go with her outrageous behaviour before being sent to stand in the corridor […]. *Blasted* isn't just disgusting, it's pathetic. Miss Kane may kid herself that she has written a searing indictment of Britain today. What she has actually produced is a lazy, tawdry piece of work without an idea in its head beyond an adolescent desire to shock" (1995).
5 Curtis (1995).
6 Bond (1995: 22).
7 Vernon (1995: 18).
8 Rebellato (1998).
9 Ansorge (1997: 59).
10 Nightingale (1998: 19).
11 *Ibid.*
12 Rebellato (1998).
13 Benedict (1998).

14 *Ibid.*
15 Pinnock (1999: 28).
16 Morley (1995).
17 Langridge & Stephenson (1997: 73).
18 Rebellato (1998).
19 Edwardes (1995).
20 "Nightwaves" (2000).
21 Unless stated otherwise, all quotations from Sarah Kane's work comes from *The Complete Plays* (2001). A reference such as (4:53) refers to the scene followed by page number.
22 Rebellato (1998).
23 Edgar (1999: 27–28).
24 Langridge & Stephenson (1997: 28).
25 *Ibid.*, 137.
26 Benedict (1998).
27 "When I was writing *Blasted* there was some point at which I realized that there was a connection with *King Lear*. I thought I'm not only writing about fatherhood, but there's this scene where Ian goes mad and there's this Dover scene with Cate when she unloads the gun and is she going to give him the gun or not? And I thought the only thing I don't have in this play is blindness." (Rebellato 1998).
28 For instance, the line in *Cleansed* "love me or kill me, Graham" (6:120) is an almost direct borrowing from John Ford's early Caroline tragedy which also follows the passionate but incestuous love between a brother (Giovanni) and sister (Annabella):

Annabella: On my knees,
Brother, even by our mother's dust I charge you,
Do not betray me to your mirth or hate;
Love me or kill me, brother.
Giovanni: On my knees,
Sister, even by my mother's dust I charge you,
Do not betray me to your mirth or hate;
Love me, or kill me sister.

29 Rebellato (1999: 280–281).
30 Barker (1997: 173).
31 *Ibid.*, 18.
32 *Ibid.*, 172.
33 *Ibid.*, 171.
34 *Ibid.*, 172.
35 *Ibid.*, 18.
36 See for instance Bradberry & Doughty (1995: 3).
37 Benedict (1998).
38 Tabert (1998: 13).
39 Holmes (1982: 87).
40 Interview with author. Brixton, London, 12 June 1995.
41 Bate (1968: 62).
42 *Ibid.*, 60.
43 *Ibid.*, 57.

44 Jones & Tydeman (1973: 186).
45 *Ibid.*, 62–63.
46 Bond (1999).

Bibliography

Ansorge, Peter: *From Liverpool to Los Angeles. On Writing for Theatre, Film and Television*, London, 1997.

Barker, Howard: *Arguments for a Theatre*, third edition, Manchester, 1997.

Bate, Walter Jackson: *Coleridge*, New York, 1968.

Benedict, David: "Real Live Horror Show", *Independent*, 9 May 1998.

Bond, Edward: "A Blast at our Smug Theatre", *Guardian*, 28 January 1995, 22.

–: "Sarah Kane and Theatre", *Theater der Zeit*, May/June 1999.

Bradberry, Grace & Steve Doughty: "The Blasted Playwright is Lying Low", *Daily Mail*, 20 January 1995, 3.

Curtis, Nick: "Random Tour in a Chamber of Horrors", *Evening Standard*, 19 January 1995.

Dryden, John: "The Secular Masque". – In Keith Walker (Ed.): *John Dryden. A Critical Edition of the Major Works*, Oxford, 1987.

Edgar, David (Ed.): *State of Play. Issue 1: Playwrights on Playwriting*, London, 1999.

Edwardes, Jane: review of *Blasted*, *Time Out*, 25 January 1995.

Richard Holmes: *Coleridge*, Oxford, 1982.

Jones, Alan R. & William Tydeman (Eds.): *The Ancient Mariner and Other Poems. A Casebook*, Basingstoke, 1973.

Kane, Sarah: *The Complete Plays*, London, 2001.

Langridge, Natasha & Heidi Stephenson: *Rage and Reason. Women Playwrights on Playwriting*, London, 1997.

Morley, Sheridan: [no title], *International Herald Tribune*, 27 January 1995.

Nightingale, Benedict: *The Future of Theatre*, London, 1998.

"Nightwaves", BBC Radio 3. Broadcast 23 June 2000.

Osborne, John: *Look Back in Anger*, London, 1964.

Pinnock, Winsome: "Breaking Down the Door". – In Colin Chambers & Vera Gottlieb (Eds.) *Theatre in a Cool Climate*, Oxford, 1999.

Ratcliffe, Michael: "An Anarchist's Agenda", *Observer*, January 1995, 14.

Rebellato, Dan: "Brief Encounter Platform". Public Interview with Sarah Kane, Royal Holloway College, London, 3 November 1998.

–: "Sarah Kane. An Appreciation", *New Theatre Quarterly* 59 (1999), 280–281.

Spencer, Charles: review of *Blasted*, *Daily Telegraph*, 20 January 1995.

Tabert, Nils: "Gespräch mit Sarah Kane". – In Nils Tabert (Ed.): *Playspotting: Die Londoner Theaterszene der 90er*, Reinbeck, 1998, pp. 8–21.

Vernon, Bob: Letter to the Editor, *Guardian*, 23 January 1995, 18.

Michael Raab, Leipzig

'Post-feminist masculinity and all that shit'. Patrick Marber's *Closer* in London and Munich

When as a director or dramaturg you decide to do a play the first reading is of extreme importance. Either you have the gut feeling that the text is the right one at this moment for your theatre or you'd better stay clear of it, despite all later possible rationalisations. A good director tries to keep his first impressions at the back of his mind during the rehearsal process, because he knows that the audience will have only one chance to witness the play without the possibility to turn back the page or consult additional material. The same applies to the members of the cast, who all too often are in danger of bringing things to the foreground characters can't possibly know at a certain stage of their development. Obviously a production of Chekhov's *Three Sisters* could easily show already early on that these young women won't get anywhere, let alone to Moscow, but the impact on them and us in the last act is far greater if we have thought otherwise at least for a while. During the 1990s in my job as a dramaturg I read only two new English plays whose initial impact was an overwhelming one: Tom Stoppard's *Arcadia* and Patrick Marber's *Closer*. Stoppard's text shows the technical brilliance of a master craftsman, but its background in literary, social and gardening history is so specifically British that it faces many problems of cultural transfer. Fortunately this is less the case with *Closer*, which consequently (and in marked contrast to *Arcadia*) achieved production figures in the German-speaking theatre that are normally only possible with two-handers like David Mamet's *Oleanna* or Enda Walsh's *Disco Pigs*. *Closer*, whose title refers to Joy Division's second album, is that rare thing: a very good second play. Marber's 'début' *Dealer's Choice* about a group of male poker players in 1995 was promising but in its second half deflated the life-lies of its characters in an all-too-foreseeable manner. Still it transferred from the Royal National Theatre's Cottesloe auditorium to the West End. Two years later *Closer* made a similar progress with an intermediate stop at the Lyttelton. It ran for eight months at the Lyric Theatre in Shaftesbury Avenue. Productions in New York and in 30 other countries followed, bringing the play to Argentina and Australia as well as to Iceland and Israel.

German theatres have to plan their season in the main house as early as 18 months in advance, as subscribers want to know what they are going to see, so *carte blanche* for an exciting new work popping up rather late is only possible in the studio. When *Closer* was first presented in London on 22 May 1997 the 1997/8 season was completely scheduled in practically every German theatre. The Munich Kammerspiele have the advantage that it's very difficult to get a subscription there and spectators are known to pass them on in the family in their will. Trust in the programme is so big that the subscribers are prepared to buy a pig in a poke, and the management has the luxury of announcing its next premières at rather short notice. So, when in the autumn of 1997 we were able to field a very good cast for *Closer*, we scheduled an additional main house-production and secured the rights for the play's German-speaking première on the basis of the English text. This decision brought with it the considerable risk of not knowing what the translation would look like. In cases like that the theatre is completely dependent on the policy of the playwright's German agent and cannot – as for example in the Netherlands – commission its own version. We also had to find a director at very short notice, which proved difficult as they too usually plan at least for a season in advance, but we knew we might have to wait for quite a long time before a new play of that quality suitable for the main stage would again be available.

German theatre is extremely director-dominated, and directors tend to consider plays in terms of how much of their own vision and personality they can project into them. After all it will earn them high marks from the critics enhancing their chances for further employment or even leading to the artistic directorship of a theatre. Plays as tightly plotted as *Closer* are not particularly appealing to people who are keen to demonstrate their own uniqueness, if need be at the cost of a text. In their attempts to be original they are supported by the reviewers who all too often rather snobbishly refer to a very good production of a well-made play as 'merely solid'. At worst, a critic who is unable to differentiate properly between the work of writer, director, and actor might even insinuate that the result was mainly due to the company, imagining the director as not much more than a looker-on at rehearsals. No wonder directors who see it as their biggest achievement to disappear behind their work lead a tough existence in the German theatre. Rather than do a well-crafted new British play, their publicity-conscious colleagues take on the world-première of a half-baked new German text in the hope of getting the credit for having turned it into an at least bearable evening in the theatre. Or they might deconstruct a classic where there are no legal problems, because the author is no longer protected by copyright. For *Closer* we were fortunate to agree terms with a director from the same generation as Patrick Marber who is not desperately trying to score points in the arts columns with gratuitous effects imposed on a play. Christof Loy accepted to start rehearsing with just a weekend's break after a première in Basle. He had done an excellent production of Marivaux's *The Triumph of Love* in Stuttgart in 1996 and seemed the right choice for an author who, in a way similar to his French 18th-century colleague, casts a clinically precise look at social and erotic mores in the London of the 1990s.

In Marber's play four characters between 20 and 40 meet, fall in love in changing heterosexual constellations, betray each other and part again: a stripper (Alice), a photographer (Anna), a dermatologist (Larry) and a writer of obituaries for a daily paper (Dan). Except for Alice, Marber gives no reasons for the interest in each other or for the eventual rifts between the quartet: "Sexual attraction is as much a mystery here as it is in Jacobean drama".[1] For example Anna and Dan start kissing each other passionately out of the blue during a portrait session. In an interview with the *Sunday Times* Marber said:

> One of the starting points for the play was that I hadn't, since the film *Sex, Lies and Videotape*, seen anything that put my generation's romantic concerns in any kind of perspective. Soap does that to some extent, but soap is about working-class people and my plays are about middle- to lower-middle-class people. I just wanted to see something that expressed the conversations I was having – that my friends were having – that people in their thirties were all exploring. Sort of post-feminist masculinity ... and – oh, all that shit. [...] It was always part of the conception of the play that I would write about big ugly emotions contained within some, hopefully, formally beautiful structure. Which makes it crueller, I think.[2]

Accordingly a number of critics used metaphors and terms like 'quadrille' or 'square-dance' to describe the play, which covers four and a half years in twelve scenes and whose four characters never appear on stage together. The author sees Anna, Dan and Larry as "lookers" and Alice as "looked-at".[3] In the *Financial Times* Alistair Macaulay suggests:

> Marber has, I believe, drawn the dramatic idea of *Closer* from Racine's *Andromaque*. A loves B, B loves C, C loves D. However, when C decides to marry B, A's suffering is extreme. But whereas Racine's characters were royal, three of Marber's characters are middle-class, one working-class. Marber's drama is on a domestic scale, and yet he develops it with clinical precision, plotting his characters [...] with interconnections yet more intricate than Racine's.[4]

This seems persuasive as the dramatist directed Craig Raine's *1953* – which is itself a very free adaptation of Racine's tragedy transposing the action to Italy after the axis-powers' hypothetical victory in the Second World War – at the Almeida in 1996. But Michael Billington is also right when he states in a review of David Hare's *The Blue Room* that *Closer* "with its portrait of the spiritual solitude underlying modern sexual freedom" is even truer to the spirit of Schnitzler's *La Ronde* than Hare's updating of it to the London of the 1990s.[5]

Marber thinks his style of writing is strongly influenced by his previous career as a stand-up comedian: "There's no point setting up a joke for five minutes and then delivering a punchline because the audience will be at the bar. My dialogue probably reveals the paranoia of the stand-up: if you're not quick and interesting they will be gone".[6] *Closer* sometimes almost seems to move along in a staccato rhythm, for example when Dan interrogates Anna about her sleeping one last time with Larry, who otherwise would not have signed the divorce papers. Anna calls that "a mercy fuck … a sympathy fuck. Moral rape, everyone does it. It's kindness".[7]

Dan Did you enjoy it?
Anna No.
Dan So you hated every second of it? Did you … go down on him?
Beat.
Anna Yes.
Beat.
Dan Did you come?
Anna No.
Dan Did you fake it?
Anna Yes.
Dan Why?
Anna To make him think I enjoyed it, why do you think?
Dan If you were just his slag, why did you give him the pleasure of thinking you'd enjoyed it?
Anna I don't know, I just did.
Dan You fake it with me?
Anna Yes, yes I do. I fake one in three, all right?
Dan Really?
Anna I haven't counted.
Dan Tell me the truth.
Anna Occasionally … I have faked it. It's not important. You don't *make* me come. I come, you're … in the area … providing … valiant assistance.
Dan You make *me* come.
Anna You're a man, you'd come if the tooth fairy winked at you. (73–74)

The language of *Closer* has a topical quality, yet is never naturalistic, but extremely condensed and sprinkled with very funny one-liners. It was no coincidence that more than one critic felt reminded of Noël Coward's *Private Lives*. To find a German equivalent for Marber's racy dialogue is no easy task, and when we received the translation a few days before the first read-through we particularly had a problem with the way Alice was supposed to speak. The dramatist deliberately lets open the background of this character who perpetually redefines herself. She appropriates a Victorian biography found on G. F. Watts' memorial in Postman's Park for her own means, including the name, and gives a number of contradictory reasons for a scar on her leg. Until the very end of the play she remains a mystery. In the original text Alice from her appearance and her accent seems to come straight out of the gutter, but uses strangely obsolete terms like 'codswallop', which the translator changed into 'Psychoschrott'. Despite the well-known fact that nothing dates as fast as yesterday's youth slang 'very good' became 'echt geil'. The character throughout appeared dumber than Marber wishes her to be, for instance when she explicitly refers to a statue as 'a Minotaur' and in German is expected to say ''n Stier' or when 'a lonely old bastard' turns into 'ein einsamer alter Witschi', whatever that may be. To be fair, normally a translator would have had more time before handing over his version and under less pressure perhaps relations between him and the theatre might have remained more cordial, but when the whole tone of a character differs from the original it is far more arduous to find a common ground than when it comes to simply correcting the odd lexicographical error. With just seven weeks of rehearsal time we had to set a specific date after which it would have been too confusing for the cast to relearn their lines, which resulted in some uneasy textual compromises. An emergency meeting between translator, agent, director and dramaturg on neutral ground in a Mannheim hotel lobby led to absurd exchanges. When we questioned whether 'Look at your little eyes' in German should really be 'Sehen Sie mal Ihre Mausaugen', the answer was: "If you don't fancy my 'Mausaugen' at least you have to say 'Äugelein', because that sounds more poetical", which is exactly the kind of spinsterishness Marber did not want. When this debate continued via fax and telephone, the director finally tore the cable out of the rehearsal room wall, and we decided to take the risk of having a miffed translator attend the première and complain about changes afterwards. That's exactly what happened but was made bearable for both sides by the production's almost unanimous success with audiences and critics and the author's endorsement.

There were additional losses in two other areas: stage design and acting style. Whilst the aesthetics of the English theatre are often decades behind developments on the continent, Vicki Mortimer's set for Patrick Marber's own production looked as simple as it was effective, and the few pieces of furniture and props which were needed increasingly accumulated at the back of a basically empty playing space. In Munich, unfortunately, we overdid things a bit to the effect that with the same budget one could have produced a Wagner opera in Mainz or Münster. Huge towers covered with ugly black rubber were lugged around by a small army of stagehands without making a significant difference when the curtain opened again. In these matters the final word is with director and designer, who objected to any scaling down of their concept. A further difference to British procedures concerned the work of director and cast. In England it is common practice for an actor to count the number of laughs he can get when first reading a text. With Laurence Olivier this was the case even when he played King Lear. If a line falls flat during a performance you know immediately that your timing was wrong. German theatre practitioners dislike terms like gag, laugh or curtain line. Christof Loy objected to "this kind of technical language" and maintained his way of directing was "an atmospherical one". And the cast sometimes took refuge in claims like: "If I feel uneasy, I'd rather let the laugh go and stay true to my character instead" – as if the two things were incompatible. A diligent search for hidden subtexts leads to impressive results with classical plays or work from the turn of the 19th to the 20th century, which in Britain, due to short rehearsal periods of between four and six weeks, often appear more arranged than directed. With a new text this method can become counterproductive when the line 'I was looking for a cigarette' may be just a simple statement not becoming more substantial by ominous pauses. English actors and actresses all too often have to cope with what Harriet Walter calls 'Chief Blockers':

> Briefly, their system might be:
>
> | | | |
> |---|---|---|
> | DAY ONE | *a.m.* | read-through and design model |
> | | *lunch* | |
> | | *p.m.* | block Act One |
> | DAY TWO | *a.m.* | finish blocking Act One |
> | | *lunch* | |
> | | *p.m.* | block Act Two |
>
> DAY THREE ... well, you can carry on.
>
> Weeks two, three and four will be more of the same, going over and over the plan fixed in the first week, until the actors are perfectly drilled. Extra time will be given to set pieces like balls or battles, and actors will be reluctantly surrendered for occasional wardrobe fittings or publicity interviews. In the last week, the director will put on his (seldom her) field-marshal's cap and oversee technical rehearsals. All that then remains is to keep an eye on the shape and speed of the show ('*Faster and louder, please*'), a rallying of the troops on the opening night and Bob's your uncle. I exaggerate, but only a bit.

> Given that the Chief Blocker seldom acknowledges the existence of acting process, it is not surprising that the highest praise an actor will confer on them is, 'At least he/she leaves you alone.' I suppose unhelpful hands off are better than unhelpful hands on, but most bad acting habits set in because the actor has been forced to work in isolation, and breaking those habits takes a lot of ... Trust and Time.[8]

Nevertheless, despite occasional polemical outbursts like Simon Callow's book *Being an Actor,*[9] the English theatre is far less director-dominated than ours. Adolf Dresen, himself a director, relates how an English colleague described the difference between English and German actors to him: "The director rings to say that he's held up by traffic congestion. What do the English do? They start rehearsing on their own. What do the Germans do? They go home".[10] Christof Loy does not belong to the animal trainer category of directors. His production received rave reviews and was even voted the best of the year by one of the Munich papers. Why was it still unable to stand up to Marber's own?

Due to the more elaborate scene changes, the slower playing, and quite a few artificial pauses too many, the Munich version lasted half an hour longer than the London one, a substantial difference even when one takes into account that English is more concise than German. This is not an isolated observation: Almost exactly the same time difference occurred between Terry Johnson's own production of *Dead Funny* and Klaus Weise's German première in Oberhausen. The more leisurely pace leads the audience to contemplate rather the *how* than the *what* and *why* of an evening in the theatre. Adolf Dresen argues:

> We got an estranged theatre which constitutes a hermetically sealed world. It gets its satisfaction from itself, only laughs about its own jokes. When I saw Ken Loach's film *Riff-Raff* I asked myself which German actor would still be capable to play something like that. Loach's brigade of bricklayers was so real that I immediately thought: How often were the actors forced to work on a building site during a period of unemployment? This was not only a question of authenticity. Most of all down to the tips of their toes you felt the film crew's solidarity with the underprivileged and from this solidarity all real art profits. In Germany on the contrary we have the waffling around of those who judge different 'aesthetics' and praise the revelations of the 'avantgarde'.[11]

Dresen's younger colleague Michael Funke is of the same opinion:

> The practice of production becomes more culinary all the time. The German theatre always tries to find interesting translations. We are world champions when it comes to translating the translation of the

translation. That's why many productions function only via their aesthetics and only the aesthetics are discussed in a highly intellectual way.[12]

Needless to say that this is only of marginal interest for the vast majority of spectators.

About the wave of new British plays in the second half of the 1990s often referred to as 'in-yer-face theatre', Aleks Sierz says:

> They pushed the theatre into being more experiential, more aggressively aimed at making audiences feel and respond. Of course, all theatre has designs on the feelings of its audience – what characterized in-yer-face theatre was its intensity, its deliberate relentlessness and its ruthless commitment to extremes.[13]

Of all the texts Sierz discusses in his book, *Closer* is formally far and away the most polished and accomplished. Still when reading it for the first time I felt as if I just had been hit in the stomach by particular lines, asked myself whether the characters really did just say that to each other and promptly reread exchanges like the one immediately before the interval, which for Marber leads up to "the verbally most brutal moment"[14] of his play:

Larry Did you touch yourself while he fucked you?
Anna Yes.
Larry You wank for him?
Anna Sometimes.
Larry And he does?
Anna We do everything that people who have sex do.
Larry You enjoy sucking him off?
Anna Yes.
Larry You like his cock?
Anna I love it.
Larry You like him coming in your face?
Anna Yes.
Larry What does it taste like?
Anna IT TASTES LIKE YOU BUT SWEETER.
Larry THAT'S THE SPIRIT. THANK YOU. THANK YOU FOR YOUR HONESTY. NOW FUCK OFF AND DIE, YOU FUCKED-UP SLAG.

Blackout. (55–56)

Neil Norman was honest enough to write about this passage in the *Evening Standard*: "I wanted to shout 'No. No. You don't *need* to know this!' knowing full well that should I ever be in the same position I would behave in exactly the same way. Every man recognises the truth of this moment, the masochistic need to feel the pain of the betrayal *in the details*; if not, how can he then act the wounded party and recapture the higher moral ground?"[15] – an insight into the male psyche Marber shares with Robert Altman, who includes a very similar scene in his film *Short Cuts*. Yet Marber never uses obscene language for simple shock value. It always says something about the psychological situation of his characters. The *Evening Standard*'s Nick Curtis is right to point out that of the play's many four letter words "'love' is undoubtedly the most brutal".[16] Liza Walker, the original Alice, "found that couples either tended to get 'really huggy' after the show or 'move further away from each other'".[17] When journalist Ben Smith went, "he made the 'huge mistake' of taking his girlfriend. Squirming in his seat, he felt as if someone had 'found my secret diary'. After the show, apparently, she asked him questions such as: 'So, do you really think about ex-girlfriends when you wank rather than about me?'",[18] thereby validating Marber's line for Larry: "If women saw one minute of our home movies, the shit that slops through our minds every day … they'd string us up by our balls, they really would." (92) The audience reaction *Closer* initially attained seems to have been similar to the hysteria generated by the first production of Schiller's *Die Räuber* in Mannheim: "Some people broke down, sobbed openly, ran for the exit; others cuddled during the interval and one couple allegedly had sex in a theatre box".[19]

The energy generated by the production certainly had something to do with the way it was pieced together. For his first play *Dealer's Choice* Marber had already used the National Theatre's Studio. It was almost completely developed there with the help of the original cast. The Studio, which has no equivalent in the German theatre, is based next to the Old Vic near Waterloo Station. The building was provided rent-free by the Canadian impresario Ed Mirvish as long as he still owned the adjacent theatre. When that came up for sale in 1998, the National was able to buy the annex with the help of lottery money and sponsorship. Donations make up the budget of £ 300.000 per year. The Studio's brief is training for the National's company but it is also open for members of other theatres for projects and workshops. An important aspect of its work is helping young authors. There are ten commissions for a play every year. The dramatists are paid £ 1.500 and have six months to write the piece. Even more coveted is the cooperation 'on attachment': Twelve authors work on this basis for two months respectively and receive £ 2.000. They are given a room, can work with actors on their texts, discuss it with dramaturgs from the National and the Studio's staff, but do not necessarily have to deliver a finished work. The important 1994/95 season of premières at the Royal Court Theatre Upstairs, which meant the breakthrough for Sarah

Kane, Joe Penhall, Judy Upton, Nick Grosso and Judith Johnson, was co-produced by the Studio. Martin McDonagh benefited greatly from his time there, and Patrick Marber is its biggest success story:

> [With *Dealer's Choice*] I went to the Studio with an idea for a play about poker, got the actors to improvise, then I went away and wrote the play. With *Closer*, the play was kind of fully formed in my head and I used the Studio to get nearer to what it was. I needed actors to help me get to what I saw.[20]

The first draft was written in just one week, which must have added to the play's incredible drive, but the author-director changed a lot later on: "At least a third of *Closer* was rewritten in rehearsals, because of what the actors brought to it".[21] One can hardly imagine a method better suited to make the cast identify with a work they perform. Even the recast version I saw in the West End was characterised by an enormous commitment of the four actors and actresses. After all, they too and not only the audiences must have had the feeling that the play deals with emotions they know about very well themselves. Despite the highly formal structure of the text they still managed to give the impression that they had just strayed in from the street and talked without any recourse to a misunderstood naturalism in heightened everyday language. This directness and authenticity brought people to the theatre in London whom you'd otherwise rather see in the cinema or at a rock concert. In Munich we lost part of the street-cred and one had the overall impression that the play was rather treated as a piece of literature interpreted on a high artistic level. The production served the play's intricate form well, but the language occasionally appeared stilted in comparison with the original, which generally was characterised by far more emotional grit. A woman seeing the production for the second time still told me that *Closer* was the first new play in ten years which she felt had anything to do with her own life.

Patrick Marber is equally removed from a theatre mainly appealing to an elitist minority (as it is propagated in Germany by the dramatist Botho Strauß or the philosopher Peter Sloterdijk) as from opportunist attempts to criticise the new media by using them on stage. In the theatre it is completely superfluous to parody talkshows or soap operas, because they do that unwittingly already on their own. Marber's justly celebrated internet scene in *Closer* is not only a fashion statement – 'Look, how much we theatre people know what's hip at the moment' – as is often the case with the use of TV-screens or projections on stage. The scene is extremely funny and tells the audience a lot about the characters as Dan pretends to be Anna and fools the chatroom novice Larry into a rendezvous with her, thereby unintentionally triggering off their subsequent falling in love. Marber was the first to use this kind of verbal cyber-sex in a play and the scene is a guaranteed success even in otherwise rather lacklustre productions. Lacklustre you certainly couldn't call the Munich version. The author himself rated it highly, thought it "gratifying to see the play performed with such grace and commitment" and saw it being true to his credo "I'd prefer elegance and lightness to Sturm & Drang anyday!"[22] Despite all the hassle with the translation I did not regret working on the German première of such an important piece of new writing as *Closer*. When I occasionally revisited the production later in its run I still, nevertheless, yearned for those punches in the stomach experienced at the first reading.

Patrick Marber found it difficult to write a follow-up to *Closer*. Talk of a big Jonsonian city comedy set in today's London came to nothing. When *Howard Katz* premièred at the Cottesloe in June 2001 it did not receive the critical acclaim heaped on the previous play. Between writing assignments Marber also works as a director and has done productions at the National (Dennis Potter's *Blue Remembered Hills*), the Almeida (Craig Raine's *1953*), the Comedy (Harold Pinter's *The Caretaker*) and the Royal Court (David Mamet's *The Old Neighbourhood*). His interest in Mamet is no coincidence as the American's style of writing dialogue influenced his own. So it was particularly apt that Marber had his comeback as a performer not as a stand-up comedian but in Mamet's *Speed the Plow* in 1999 at the New Ambassadors Theatre. *Howard Katz* also owes a structural debt to Mamet's *Edmond*. Despite its mixed reception Marber does not have to worry about his position as an author. And he can be sure that if a British literary manager in 2050 tries to find a play on the question of how relationships worked in the London of the 1990s, he'll propose a revival of *Closer*. A dramaturg in Berlin or Hamburg will have to look for a longer time and still not find anything apart from cerebral trifles. This is a poor testimony for the highly subsidised German theatre.

Notes

1 Aleks Sierz: *In-Yer-Face Theatre. British Drama Today*, London, 2000, p. 194.
2 Tom Shone: "Close and Personal", *The Sunday Times*, Culture supplement, 26 October 1997, 17.
3 Quoted in Sierz, *In-Yer-Face Theatre*, p. 188.
4 *The Financial Times*, 2 April 1998, reprinted in *Theatre Record*, 26 March – 8 April 1998, 420.
5 *The Guardian*, 23 September 1998, reprinted in *Theatre Record*, 10–23 September 1998, 1236.
6 Sally Greene: "Enter Genius, from Left", *Independent on Sunday*, 15 March 1998.

7 Patrick Marber: *Closer*, London, 1997, p. 72. All further references to the play will be included in the text.
8 Harriet Walter: *Other People's Shoes. Thoughts on Acting*, London, 1999, pp. 54–55.
9 Simon Callow: *Being an Actor*, London, 1984.
10 Hans-Dieter Schütt: *Hinterm Vorhang das Meer. Landkarte der neuen Theaterwelt*, Berlin, 2001, pp. 29–30.
11 *Ibid.*, 40–41.
12 *Ibid.*, 136.
13 Sierz, *In-Yer-Face Theatre*, p. xiii.
14 Interview with the author, 4 February 1998.
15 *Evening Standard*, 2 April 1998, reprinted in *Theatre Record*, 26 March–8 April 1998, 422, emphasis in the text.
16 *Evening Standard*, 30 May 1997, reprinted in *Theatre Record*, 21 May–3 June 1997, 677.
17 Sierz, *In-Yer-Face Theatre*, p. 190.
18 *Ibid.*
19 *Ibid.*, 187.
20 "Patrick Marber Talks to Richard Eyre". – In *Closer* [Programme of the National Theatre production], p. 6.
21 Sierz, *In-Yer-Face Theatre*, p. 191.
22 Letter to the author, 21 September 1998.

Raimund Borgmeier, Giessen

'Convergences of different threads'.[1] Tom Stoppard's *The Invention of Love* (1997)

I.

In an early interview, Tom Stoppard once remarked: "Quite frankly, I have great difficulty seeing connections between any of my plays [...]."[2] Yet some critics do not agree with Stoppard in this respect and rightly see fundamental connections and correspondences in his dramatic oeuvre. Paul Delaney states: "The entire canon of Stoppard's major plays demonstrates such a consistency, a consistency which has been largely ignored by most observers."[3]

This also applies to Stoppard's latest play, *The Invention of Love*, which was premiered in 1997 at the Royal National Theatre with Richard Eyre as director and, after a most successful season – it received, among other honours, the Evening Standard Award for Best Play 1997 –, was transferred to the West End. It deals, first and foremost, with the life of the poet A.E. Housman, the author of *A Shropshire Lad*, who was also regarded as the greatest classical scholar of his time. With this, Stoppard clearly leaves the domain of the sciences, in which his two previous plays *Hapgood* (1988) and *Arcadia* (1993) had been set,[4] and moves into new territory. At the same time, however, he picks up threads from his previous writings; the play shows all the features that have made Stoppard so popular as a playwright both with critics and audiences, and the song of praise sung by the *Sunday Times* does not seem undeserved: "*The Invention of Love* is wonderful: it amazes you by its dazzling interweaving of narrative, argument and mood. It is spellbinding: it holds you fast in its mood of melancholy and generous exhilaration."[5]

Stoppard's turning to new territory is not so sudden and abrupt as it might perhaps seem. Stoppard has often emphasised the emergence of a certain play from his own personal interests. Once, an interviewer asked him: "How do you go about writing a play? Do you do a lot of research before you start to write or is it an idea that you have and try and work out?"[6] He answered: "It's an idea. I don't really, on the whole, write plays which require research. I mean, some of them look as though they require research, but they're written out of my own interests."[7] In the case of *The Invention of Love*, such an interest can be concretely traced. As early as 1994, Stoppard explained:

> My life is sectioned off into hot flushes, pursuits of this or that. Rather in the same way as a year ago [1993] or more, a fairly quiescent interest in or sympathy towards Roman poetry and literature of antiquity suddenly had its turn. I think it turned into something more obsessive through reading about A.E. Housman, again somebody I had read for years on and off.[8]

This interest grew into Stoppard's new play.

The Invention of Love represents the decisive phases of Housman's life in two acts, principally in accordance with biographical facts. In Act I, we see him as a young scholarship student coming to the University of Oxford, which, then, was a place of fascinating arguments. Ruskin and Pater are arguing about life and art, and also, the young Oscar Wilde makes his provoking contributions to intellectual culture. At the same time, there is a controversial discussion going on about the value and meaning of classical heritage. Against this backcloth, Housman has to find his own way. Personally, he is moved by strong feelings for his fellow student Moses Jackson, a scientist and enthusiastic sportsman, feelings which this man cannot in any way reciprocate or even understand. Academically and intellectually, young Housman sees himself above all confronted with the question of whether he should rather become a poet or a scholar. He feels particularly repelled by the academic teaching practice, as he finds it, and he proudly decides to determine his own course of studies and its contents – as a biographer describes it: "One lecture of Jowett's was enough to make him [Housman] abandon the course in disgust at the Professor's disregard for minutiae, and in general he found the temptation irresistible to anticipate his degree and embark upon the work of a qualified scholar."[9] The result is disastrous: mysteriously for everybody, the highly gifted student fails the final examination.

Act II shows Housman after the examinational fiasco, first in the country, in conversation with his sister, who tells him about the reaction of the family to the hope-bearer's failure, and then in London. There, like Moses Jackson, he takes a job in the patent office and shares a flat with Jackson and his philological college friend Pollard, who works in the British Library. Jackson, endowed with little sensitivity, is still completely in the dark about his friend's feelings. It is not until one day a casual remark made by his girlfriend leads to an open exchange of views that he understands the true situation, which now becomes unbearable, and so Housman announces that he will move out immediately. Work in the patent office leaves Housman time for other activities; in the evening, he works in the British Museum, and over the course of some years, he publishes scholarly works of his own and makes himself a name as an eminent classical scholar. In spite of the merciless and almost rude way in which he deals with other scholars in his writings, he is acknowledged by his peers, and in the end, even manages to obtain the chair of Latin at University College, London. At that time, London is, as we learn, also the scene of journalistic and political machinations and quarrels, which, amongst other things, leads to Oscar Wilde being convicted of homosexuality. Housman's own homosexual feelings for his friend Mo, however, are never realised, but find their expression only in his poems, which are repeatedly quoted by himself and other characters in several passages towards the end of Stoppard's play.

If it is to be understood by the audience as a biographical representation, it has to follow the main lines of chronology. Thus Stoppard's play is basically chronological, though it is by no means – as can be expected from Stoppard – a 'well-made-play'. One may feel reminded of what the author once said about his work as a playwright in general: "[T]he only useful metaphor I can think of for the way I write my plays is convergences of different threads. Perhaps carpet-making would suggest something similar."[10] Various different plot strands and thematic warps are tied together. Motifs and key terms, but also the different characters suddenly re-emerge again and again. Particularly the depiction of the contemporary cultural background of Oxford in Act I and London in Act II is continuously interwoven with the personal plot around Housman. This makes the play interesting for the spectator, who is surprised time and time again by sudden turns, and it creates the impression of contingency and profusion.

II.

In addition to this, *The Invention of Love* is in principle a 'memory play'. Stoppard observes the chronology and, at the same time, rolls it up from the rear by introducing at the beginning of the play Housman aged 77 at the end of his life. In contrast to *Travesties*, where the memory figure appears as one character with two faces ('*Henry Carr*, appears as a very old man and also as his youthful self' according to the list of characters), this time the protagonist is split into two characters: "AEH, A.E. Housman, aged 77" and "Housman, aged from 18 to 26" (9), played by two different actors.

Again and again, there are passages in which AEH reminds himself and us that, strictly speaking, he is at the end of his life in the undignified situation of a patient in an old people's home. "I may as well wet the bed, the night nurse will change the sheets and tuck me up without reproach. They are very kind to me here in the Evelyn Nursing Home" (28–29), he remarks early in the play. Later, he does not want a conversation that is important to him to be interrupted by the sheets being changed, and he says testily: “Not now, nurse, let him finish” (37). In the subsequent, somewhat complicated lecture, he interrupts himself with the ironic remark: “I think it must be time for my tablet, it orders my tenses.” (39) Towards the end of Act I, he suddenly asks the prosaic question: “Is there a chamberpot under this seat?” (44) When, in one of the last sequences of Act II, his sister Kate appears once more and teases him playfully that he is the “[s]ame old Alfred”, he promises, in the same tone, to reform, and says (before dealing with his reputation for censoriousness and misanthropy at his final place of action, Cambridge): “But I intend to change. The day nurse will get the benefit of my transformation into ‘a character’, the wag of the Evelyn.” (90) Also at the very end of the play, on the penultimate page of the printed text, AEH once again draws attention to the fact that principally, the whole action takes place in the memory of an old man: “Which goes to show, I know what I’m doing even when I don’t know I’m doing it, in the busy hours between the tucking up and the wakey-wakey thermometer faintly antiseptic under the tongue from its dainty gauze-stoppered vase on the bedside cabinet.” (101)

As in this instance, the memory-passages invariably contain humour and irony. They contribute to show that even in such a severe personality as that of the poet and leading classical scholar Housman there is a human factor, which is of great importance. Above all, however, Stoppard as a writer, who has been convincingly connected with post-modernism,[11] achieves alienation by this strategy. By not just working along a historical line, he brings about a state of potential simultaneity and actuality, which has a strong impact on the spectator. Stoppard creates a kind of artistic balance-sheet of a life.

The memory-passages can also be understood in the light of what Richard Corballis in his study *Stoppard. The Mystery and the Clockwork* views as a central principle of Stoppard’s plays; he points out: “Specifically I contend that in all Stoppard’s work an abstract, artificial view of the world (‘A’) is pitted against the flux of reality (‘B’), and the audience is invited to eschew the ‘clockwork’ of the former in favour of the ‘mystery’ of the latter.”[12] The memory-passages underline “the flux of reality”, and this constituent seems highly necessary in order to counteract the fact that, with a protagonist like Housman, the element of the “abstract, artificial” is very pronounced. In this way, Stoppard also shows himself as a writer who writes for the stage.

III.

The Invention of Love confirms what critics have stated about Stoppard's previous plays: "Stoppard has 'never written anything for discussion' (*TLS*). His plays are written for, and shaped by, the theater".[13] And the playwright himself early on decidedly underscored that his works are meant for the stage: "Plays are events rather than texts. They're written to happen, not to be read".[14] As the above-quoted press reaction shows, this is true of *The Invention of Love* to a high degree. It is a play which is not easy to read but which creates great fascination when produced on the stage. As in his previous plays, Stoppard manages to transfer unwieldy themes and subjects into concrete terms and bring them visually into the theatre. From the very beginning, the spectator finds himself enthralled by what is going on on the stage.

When the curtain rises, an impressive opening scene presents itself to the audience: on the stage, they see, with upsurging mists, a river on which a boat with a ferryman slowly approaches; on the bank, a formally dressed old man is waiting for the boat's arrival. As it turns out, we are in the underworld, and AEH, old Housman, apparently after his death, is waiting for Charon to take him across the Styx. This scenic image imprints itself forcibly on the spectator's memory, and it is taken up several times in the course of the play.

Stoppard here follows a strategy that proved successful in earlier plays. In an interview in 1983, he was already reminded by the interviewer: "In one of our previous conversations, you said that your plays start with an image, usually visual."[15] And one critic can summarise: "Stoppard's habit of fore-shadowing his themes in virtually self-contained tableaux attached to the front of the plays also indicates a strong sense of overall design."[16]

If one wants to interpret the impressive opening image here thematically, the boat trip – and this is after all the traditionally predominant meaning of boat and ship metaphors – certainly has something to do with human life and its passage. Housman's life, which we see in decisive phases in this play, also has, amongst other things, exemplary significance. The Horace poem IV,7, "Diffugere nives", which is mentioned several times in the play, deals with exactly this theme: in contrast to nature, which is renewed in the course of the seasons, human life is unique and unrepeatable. Death means a definite ending, and a dead man cannot be brought back from the other world to life either by his own outstanding gifts and qualities or the efforts of loving friends. Therefore it is important to use life in the best way possible.

In Stoppard's play, however, the passage over the Styx is not only a serious matter. Charon, in his dry manner, makes a number of disclosures about the inhabitants of the underworld and proves himself an obtuse, forgetful old man when AEH, driven by his thirst for knowledge, tries to elicit from him further textual passages of Aeschylus' lost play *Myrmidones* (cf. 27–28).

Boat trips on other levels of reality, which are also represented on the stage, continue the motif in a comical way and contribute to the complexity of the dramatic texture. As early as the second sequence of the play, Charon has comic competition from the three young men Housman, Pollard, and Jackson, who appear on the scene in a boat. There is a comic parallelism when young Housman, reproached for laziness, boasts of his rowing performance with the rhetorical question: "[W]ho brought you up from Hades?" (4) In this case, though, Hades is obviously a place on the river Thames near Oxford.

The young men have on board a dog, whose comic significance Stoppard underlines in a stage direction in the printed text: "*The dog is played realistically by a toy (stuffed) dog*" (*ibid.*). This and young Housman's remark, "to say nothing of the dog", is to be understood as an ironic reference to the famous comical novel by Jerome K. Jerome *Three Men in a Boat (To Say Nothing of the Dog)* (1889), whose adaptation in a television film Stoppard carried out in 1975.[17] In Act II of Stoppard's play, these three men, Jerome with his two friends, are actually rowing onto the stage. They talk with ironic disapproval about Oscar Wilde, who is imprisoned in the gaol of Reading, where they are passing, for homosexuality, and about Housman, whom they suspect of the same attitude: "He's a Latin prof. [...] But of the Greek persuasion" (86). To prevent us from misunderstanding the casual, leisurely tone of these men, at the end of the play, AEH as narrator points out to us that this Jerome has triggered off the fatal chain of events which led to Wilde's questionable conviction (cf. 101).

Shortly before this hint, the three young Oxford undergraduates are also seen once more in a boat on the stage. This time, Pollard answers Housman's question concerning the destiny of the boat trip ("Where are we going?") with significant ambiguity: "Hades" (100). Earlier, we saw Wilde leave the scene in a boat: "*The Boatman poles Wilde away*" (97). And in the last dramatic sequence, before the final speech of the 'narrator', AEH, once again the ferryman of the underworld takes action: "*Dimly, Charon is seen poling Wilde across the Styx*" (102). The dramatic image of the boat trip, accordingly, serves as a definite bracket that holds Stoppard's play together, and it is significant that this happens on different levels.

IV.

The orientation of the play towards the theatre manifests itself particularly in the fundamental significance of the dialogical principle. The author himself emphasised this many years ago when he said: "I write plays because writing dialogue is the only respectable way of contradicting yourself. I'm the kind of person who embarks on an endless leapfrog down the great moral issues. I put a position, rebut it, refute the rebuttal, and rebut the refutation. Forever. Endlessly."[18]

Even if this may seem slightly exaggerated, critics have confirmed it by attesting Stoppard "his unwillingness to take sides"[19] and by stating besides that "his plays tend to build upon a series of juxtapositions".[20]

The main contrast in *The Invention of Love* lies in the protagonist himself. He not only meets Stoppard's "fondness for eccentrics"[21] but even unites two seemingly incompatible persons in himself: "A poet and a scholar" (2) is what Charon at the beginning says he is told to carry, and he adds: "It sounded like two different people" (*ibid.*). Indeed, the two fields of activity in which Housman excels seem to be mutually incompatible: writing lyrical poems, where empathy and feelings matter, and textual criticism, searching for the best textual version and finally establishing a reliable text, where sober reason counts.

To make this contrast dramatically understandable, the playwright has to externalise it. Stoppard achieves this here in two ways: on the one hand, by introducing, as mentioned, the protagonist both as a young man ('Housman') and at the end of his life ('AEH'); and on the other hand, by making Oscar Wilde, to a large extent, take over the part of the poet. It is no coincidence that Charon, who is still waiting for the poet at the beginning, finally carries Wilde over the Styx.

Daniel Mendelsohn, in his intelligent review of the play under the title "The Tale of Two Housmans" goes so far as to say that

> the real hero of *The Invention of Love* isn't Housman at all, but a contemporary of his who cut a far more dashing figure, someone who was, if anything, the Anti-Housman – in nearly every way, his temperamental, creative, and intellectual opposite; someone who, after being gossiped about, invoked, admired from a distance, and quoted throughout Stoppard's play, finally appears at its close for a climactic showdown: Oscar Wilde.[22]

It is certainly true that Wilde represents the successful poet in the play and that Stoppard's admiration for Wilde, well-known since *Travesties* at the latest, is unmistakable in Wilde's triumphal catalogue of achievements at the end (which is also quoted by Mendelsohn):

> I made my life into my art and it was an unqualified success [...]. I awoke the imagination of the century. I banged Ruskin's and Pater's heads together, and from the moral severity of one and the aesthetic soul of the other I made art a philosophy that can look the twentieth century in the eye. [...] I lived at the turning point of the world where everything was waking up new – the New Drama, the New Novel, New Journalism, New Paganism, even the New Woman. (96–97)

Wilde closes with the question "Where were you when all this was happening?" (97), and AEH answers: "At home" (*ibid.*). Here the audience, indeed, laughs at Housman's expense, as Mendelsohn observes. But this does not necessarily happen "at the price of intellectual fairness", as the critic maintains.[23] Mendelsohn simplifies matters when he states somewhat angrily: "[T]he whole point of *The Invention of Love* is to make Housman into the (unattractive) representative of timid, thwarted, dry-as-dust 'scholarship' and 'science', so that Wilde can become the heroic and tragic representative of 'poetry' and 'emotion'".[24] Wilde has less the dramatic function to degrade Housman than rather, on the contrary, to stress the poetic potential that is in Housman, too. Like Wilde, Housman is a poet. So it seems characteristic that in Stoppard's play, it is no other than Wilde who recites a poem from Housman's *A Shropshire Lad* at great length (cf. 92–93) and who finally reminds the other: "You didn't mention your poems. How can you be unhappy when you know who wrote them? They are all that will still matter" (97).

V.

With *The Real Thing* (1982), love has become a central theme for Stoppard, as he himself declares in an interview.[25] That this is also the case here, is made apparent by the title. This title bears significance for both parts of Housman's personality. First, *The Invention of Love* in the sense of literary history happens in ancient Rome. In an early sequence of the play, Housman quotes four lines from Catullus' poem 5 ("Vivamus, mea Lesbia, atque amemus") in English translation (cf. 12), and his fellow student Pollard comments:

> Like everything else, like clocks and trousers and algebra, the love poem had to be invented. After millenniums of sex and centuries of poetry, the love poem as understood by Shakespeare and Donne, and by Oxford undergraduates – the true-life confessions of the poet in love, immortalizing the mistress, who is actually the cause of the poem – that was invented in Rome in the first century before Christ. (13)

Towards the close of the play, we are also told that the real inventor of the love elegy was Cornelius Gallus. Of him, though, only one single line is extant. Yet Virgil, as AEH reminds us, has erected a monument to him (cf. 98–99).

This eminently concerns Housman as a philologist, but love is also decisive for the poet. First and foremost, Housman's poetry can be viewed as a sublimation of his unhappy love for Moses Jackson. To lovers, as to the poet, it is not facts that count, but essential truth. As Wilde says in his final conversation with AEH: "Truth is [...] the work of the imagination" (93). The image that a lover forms of a beloved person is, above all, an invented one. Again, Wilde expresses this with the words: "We would never love anybody if we could see past our invention" (95). So, in the end, it does not seem to matter much that Housman's great love remains unhappy and unsuccessful in real life. That does not mean that for this reason Stoppard's play must become a tragedy. The invention of love reaches its goal in poetry, and there it finds its lasting fulfilment. It is here where love, which, according to Sophocles is "like the ice held in the hand by children" (43), becomes real.

While this is true of any kind of love, Stoppard's play also takes up the topic of homosexuality in the specific context of the late Victorian period. Both Housman and Wilde have a homosexual disposition and suffer tremendously as a result of this. Housman finds no fulfilment in reality, so he feels to a great extent, he has to lead a personal life of withdrawal and renunciation. Wilde is even judicially prosecuted, has to suffer a prison sentence for his homosexuality and is ruined in social circles.

Stoppard gives us a demonstration of the general climate of opinion in the late Victorian period, in which homosexuality is almost a fashionable phenomenon for the so-called "Aesthetes", but is otherwise resolutely rejected and verbally branded as "beastliness" (7) or "buggery" (17). We learn that the British Law to which Wilde falls victim, takes advantage of this general opinion; however, in reality it is contrived by clever political strategists to achieve their own purposes (cf. 61). The very way one deals with the phenomenon linguistically shows the wide-spread insecurity and rejection. Moses Jackson says in the decisive talk with Housman: "Rosa said you're sweet on me" (74). Jerome speaks with contemptuous irony of "the Greek persuasion" (86). And even the seemingly neutral and acceptable term "homosexuals" is not approved of by AEH, who considers it a "barbarity" and rejects it for reasons of linguistic aesthetics: "It's half Greek and half Latin!" (91)

At any rate, one has to come to terms with the problem that classical antiquity, so highly esteemed in Oxford and in the educational life of the time, had a fundamentally different view on the matter. Jowett, master of Balliol and resolute champion of morals and decency at the university, remarks with cynical openness: "A Platonic enthusiasm as far as Plato was concerned meant an enthusiasm of the kind that would empty the public schools and fill the prisons where it is not nipped in the bud" (21). In order not to irritate the undergraduates, the classical texts are simply altered, as young Housman says in a conversation with old AEH in Act I: "In the translation of Tibullus in my College library, the *he* loved by the poet is turned into a *she*" (40, emphasis in the text).

To Housman, however, classical antiquity with its attitude to homosexuality furnishes ideal patterns of conception. He views a correspondence to his own relationship with the beloved Moses Jackson in the Horace-poem IV, 1, "Intermissa, Venus, diu", where the poet complains that he must fall in love once more, this time with beautiful Ligurinus after he saw him running across the Field of Mars. In five places in Stoppard's play (42, 49, 66, 69, 76) Mo is talked about as Housman's Ligurinus or the name 'Ligurinus' is mentioned.

Also the other poem by Horace (IV, 7), which, as mentioned, deals with the uniqueness and unrepeatability of life, provides Housman with a conceptual model for love between men, i.e. the mythical heroes Theseus and Pirithous. So Stoppard has Housman exclaim enthusiastically in Act II: "Theseus and Pirithous. They were kings [...]. They weren't sweet on each other. They loved each other, as men loved each other in the heroic age, in virtue, paired together in legend and poetry as the pattern of comradeship, the chivalric ideal of virtue in the ancient world." (76)[26] The heroes of Chaeronea, too, are mentioned several times in this sense, e.g. before the end of Act I: "[T]here was such an army, a hundred and fifty pairs of lovers, the Sacred Band of Theban youths, and they were never beaten till Greek liberty died for good at the battle of Chaeronea." (42) But this heroic age is definitely over. AEH has nothing left but the (unintentionally comic) complaint: "Oh, Mo! Mo! I would have died for you but I never had the luck!" (5) As in the case of other important themes and motifs of the play, Stoppard stresses the great significance of this exclamation by the means of recurrence (cf. 46, 100).

The Invention of Love once more proves, like the previous plays, Stoppard's incomparable mastery of bringing unwieldy material that seems to be basically unsuitable for dramatical presentation successfully onto the stage. He dares, for instance, to declaim lengthy quotations from Latin literature in the original to a modern-day audience – and, as the reception in the theatres demonstrates, is successful in doing so.

Almost the same is true of the representation of textual criticism, an essential field of Housman's successful activities, which is hardly understandable for non-experts and whose significance for producing a reliable text seems difficult to comprehend. With the concrete example of a line from Catullus' longest poem, "The Marriage of Peleus and Thetis" (64,

324), Stoppard shows us how textual criticism works and what it achieves. The line read in the corrupt tradition: "Emathiae tutamen opis, carissime nato," and it is corrected into: "Emathiae tutamen, Opis carissime nato" (37). Though only one comma is put in a different place and one word is capitalised, the sense is completely different and much more convincing. This is demonstrated to us in the longest sequence of Act I, when the old AEH meets his younger self ("Housman") and talks with him about his interests and plans for his life. Even if the spectator who does not know much Latin cannot follow the demonstration in detail, he certainly understands the general sense. At the same time, through this meeting, which would not be possible in real life, the sequence has an underlying surreal tension, and we easily understand that the young Housman will not, of course, heed the advice of his older self, "You had better be a poet" (*ibid.*), but will also continue working as a scholar. Old AEH himself, after all, is not consistent; for his definitions of textual criticism not only show expert knowledge but also a high degree of enthusiasm: "Textual criticism is a science whose subject is literature" (38), and: "Textual criticism is the crown and summit of scholarship" (*ibid.*).

Later on in the play, we are also offered a modern example of the tasks of textual criticism. The sentence "the papers have been hashing it up" through incorrect transmission becomes "hushing it up" (67), which others understand as "mashing it up" or "washing it up" (68). It is now the task of the textual critic to find out the true, authentic version and carry it through.

Housman and Pollard, both philologically educated and interested, demonstrate this to Housman's colleague Chamberlain in a conversation in Act II. In this play, too, Stoppard's characters are the bearers of certain functions and, therefore, according to one critic, "deliberately two-dimensional".[27] It is confirmed what the author, with his characteristic irony principally says about the characters in his plays:

> In general terms, I'm not a playwright who is interested in character with a capital K and psychology with a capital S. I'm a playwright interested in ideas and forced to invent characters to express those ideas. All my people speak the same way, with the same cadences and sentence structures. They speak as I do.[28]

Last but not least, one of the ideas and themes which the play deals with in the context of Housman and his life is also the issue of the importance of classical education. The orthodox position is more than clearly held by the old Oxford don Jowett, who goes about to enlighten the young undergraduate Housman with the rhetorical question: "If you cannot write Latin and Greek verse how can you hope to be of any use in the world?" (23–24) Accordingly, the young Pollard formulates the educational maxim: "We study the ancient authors to draw lessons for our age" (46). When Housman, whose rude manner in scholarly debates appears several times in the play, rejects this categorically ("That's all humbug."), Pollard tries again and gives the pragmatic answer: "We study the ancient authors to get a First and a life of learned ease" (*ibid.*). That this is borne out, to some extent, by the real life of the time, is underlined in another passage, when Housman's new job in the patent office is talked about and Moses Jackson says: "It's true, then – a classical education fits a fellow for anything" (53).

The protagonist has a different opinion. For him, "[t]he ideas and moral influence of the ancient philosophers" are "[h]umbug" (31). According to him, the ancient writers have merely a relative importance: "The only reason to consider what the ancient philosophers meant about anything is if it's relevant to settling corrupt or disputed passages in the text. With the poets there may be other reasons for reading them; I wouldn't discount it" (*ibid.*). It is surprising to find AEH here as an advocate of progress. Similarly, he says earlier on with reference to a young scientist: "[H]e knows more than the ancient philosophers" (31).

Yet there are other passages where progress is rather given a question mark. In this sense, Housman sceptically comments on one essential achievement of modern times: "When you consider the ocean of bilge brought forth by the invention of printing, it does make you wonder about this boon of civilization" (73). Even more negative towards progress is Ruskin's attitude: "Mechanical advance is the slack taken up of our failing humanity. Hell is very likely to be modernization infinitely extended" (14). But Ruskin's turning to the past, significant for "Oxford in the Golden Age" (102) and for the mental climate of the Victorian age, is also presented in a satirical light, particularly in the song from *Patience* by Gilbert and Sullivan sung at the beginning of Act II:

> 'Though the philistines may jostle,
> you may rank as an apostle
> in the high aesthetic band,
> if you walk down Picadilly
> with a poppy or a lily
> in your medieval hand …' (52)

Subsequent to this song, there is a conversation between Housman and Jackson, who have apparently just seen a theatre performance of Gilbert and Sullivan. While Housman finds the show "quite jolly", Jackson is totally enthusiastic and talks about "[a] landmark" (*ibid.*). It turns out, however, that he doesn't mean the performance or the work they have seen but the fact that the theatre, the Savoy, has been equipped with electrical lighting in place of the gas lighting used before. "Electricity is going to change everything" (53), Jackson dreams with unchecked enthusiasm.

This is not only a continuation of the theme of progress, but at the same time, Stoppard again takes up the central theme of the 'invention' of love. Jackson, who also at the very end, once remarks that he never took to all that philological, literary stuff, "all that *veni, vidi, vici* ..." (101), is obviously a rather superficial person. He is not really worthy of the love Housman feels for him. Love is based on the imagination, and so an invention of love takes place.

It is remarkable how Stoppard here, and throughout the play, manages to tie together the different thematic and plot strands. The image of carpet-making, suggested by himself, gives a very appropriate description of the play's texture.

VI.

This is also connected with the basically comic orientation of the play. Though Housman's life story might have rather provided the material for a tragedy, Stoppard's play is clearly a comedy. Stoppard's "penchant for puns"[29] manifests itself right at the opening when the protagonist interprets the underworld ferryman's cry, "Belay the painter!" – i.e. 'tie the boat-rope to a post (to secure it)!' – in the sense of Ruskin's lecture, which he attended in his first semester at Oxford: "Painters belayed [i.e. artists waylaid/criticised] on every side." (1) Another example is to be found later when the philologist Ellis calls the poet Propertius "[t]he greatest of the Roman love eligists, and the most corrupt" (26). Housman's meaningful repetition of "corrupt" makes the pun clear to the less attentive spectator as well.

Especially in the beginning, the audience is adapted to the comic tenor of the play by humorous elements at different levels. The old and somewhat clumsy ferryman apparently has misunderstood the instruction he received, "[a] poet and a scholar" (2), and erroneously waits for a second passenger. In his subsequent self-introduction, AEH shows his dry sense of humour saying: "In Greek I am, as it were, an amateur, and know hardly more than the professors" (3). The underworld corresponds, in a comical way, to the upper world, when the ferryman reassuringly warns him about the hell-hound: "You will see a three-headed dog when we've crossed over. If you don't take any notice of him he won't take any notice of you" (33–34). But instead of the hell-hound there is next, together with the three young men in a boat, "*a toy (stuffed) dog*" (4).

Later in the play, Jowett gives a comical description of his Plato translation:

> In my translation of the Phaedrus it required all my ingenuity to rephrase his description of paederastia into the affectionate regard as exists between an Englishman and his wife. Plato would have made the transposition himself if he had had the good fortune to be a Balliol man. (21)

In a discussion about morals and decency in Act II, Harris observes with dry sarcasm: "Traditionally, Parliament has always been the protector of the British virgin, but usually on a first come first served basis" (60). After that, he and his journalist colleagues discuss whether one of them really ate a mouse and how he did it.

The list of examples of comic elements at different levels could be easily enlarged. So in this aspect, too, it becomes manifest what one critic says about Stoppard's dramatic art at the end of his study: "With Post-Modern sensibility, Tom Stoppard openly strives to amuse his audience and considers entertainment an integral feature of his craftsmanship, to be achieved through the expert management of the full range of the elements of stagecraft."[30]

Notes

1 Quoted in Blüggel (1992: 216).
2 Quoted in Hu (1988: 9).
3 Delaney (1990: 8).
4 See Reitz (1990: 125–137) and Reitz (1995: 165–177).
5 Stoppard (1998: quoted on the reverse side of the cover). This edition is used for all subsequent quotations.
6 Jenkins (1990: 17).
7 *Ibid.*
8 Gussow (1995: 85).
9 Scott-Kilvert (1955: 9).
10 Blüggel (1992: 216–217).
11 Cf. Blüggel (1992: 121 *et passim*).
12 Corballis (1984: 15).
13 Jenkins (1990: 2).
14 Gussow (1995: 37).
15 *Ibid.*, 40.
16 Corballis (1984: 153–154).
17 Cf. Page (1986: 78).
18 Gussow (1995: 3).
19 Jenkins (1987: 175).
20 Corballis (1984: 154).
21 Jenkins, (1987: 175).
22 Mendelsohn (2000: 3).
23 *Ibid.*, 8.
24 *Ibid.*

25 Gussow (1995: 62).
26 Other instances where Theseus and Pirithous are named are on pp. 5, 39, 44, 75.
27 Corballis (1984: 155).
28 Gussow (1995: 35).
29 Delaney (1990: 3).
30 Hu (1988: 227).

Bibliography

Blüggel, Beate: *Tom Stoppard – Metadrama und Postmoderne*, Frankfurt a.M. *et al.*, 1992.
Corballis, Richard: *Stoppard. The Mystery and the Clockwork*, Oxford & New York, 1984.
Delaney, Paul: *Tom Stoppard. The Moral Vision of the Major Plays*, London, 1990.
Gussow, Mel: *Conversations with Stoppard*, London, 1995.
Hu, Stephen: *Tom Stoppard's Stagecraft*, New York *et al.*, 1988.
Jenkins, Anthony: *The Theatre of Tom Stoppard*, Cambridge *et al.*, 1987.
–: *Critical Essays on Tom Stoppard*, Boston, 1990.
Mendelsohn, Daniel: "The Tale of Two Housmans", *The New York Review of Books*, 10 August 2000.
Page, Malcolm: *File on Stoppard*, London & New York, 1986.
Reitz, Bernhard: "'The act of observing determines the reality' – Die Darstellungskonventionen des *thriller* und die Rolle des Zuschauers in Tom Stoppards *Hapgood*". – In B. R. & Hubert Zapf (Eds.): *British Drama in the 1980s. New Perspectives* [= *anglistik & englischunterricht* 41], Heidelberg, 1990, pp. 125–137.
–: "Beyond Newton's Universe – Science and Art in Tom Stoppard's Arcadia". – In B. R. (Ed.): *Drama and Reality*, Contemporary Drama in English 3, 1995, pp. 165–177.
Scott-Kilvert, Ian: *A.E. Housman*, London, 1955.
Stoppard, Tom: *The Invention of Love*, second edition, London, 1998.

Bernhard Reitz, Mainz

'I just wouldn't want to be at the other end of his anger'. Harold Pinter's Political Plays of the Nineties

I.

Sir Harold Pinter's official homepage, *www.haroldpinter.org*, is headed by a quotation which Pinter scholars have been familiar with since the early days of Pinter's career as a playwright: "There are no hard distinctions between what is real and what is unreal, nor between what is true and what is false. A thing is not necessarily either true or false; it can be both true and false."[1] First expressed in 1958, this statement was also part of a programme note provided by Pinter for the double-bill *The Room* and *The Dumb Waiter* which was staged at the Royal Court Theatre in 1960. Pinter expanded his ideas in "Between the Lines", a speech he gave at the National Student Drama Festival in Bristol in 1962.[2] Fourteen years later, this speech, though now with the revised title "Writing for the Theatre", became the introduction to the first volume of Pinter's collected plays.[3]

"Writing for the Theatre" still remains the most definitive comment Pinter ever made on his craft, and because of this it is worthwhile to recall at least the immediate context of the lines quoted above:

> We don't carry labels on our chests, and even though they are continually fixed to us by others, they convince nobody. The desire for verification on the part of all of us, with regard to our own experience and the experience of others is understandable but cannot always be satisfied. *I suggest there can be no hard distinctions between what is real and what is unreal, nor between what is true and what is false. A thing is not necessarily either true or false; it can be both true and false.* A character on the stage who can present no convincing argument or information as to his past experience, his present behaviour or his aspirations, nor give a comprehensive analysis of his motives is as legitimate and as worthy of attention as one who, alarmingly, can do all these things. The more acute the experience the less articulate the expression. (11, my emphasis)

For many of those who had puzzled over the 'true' identity of Stanley or Davies as well as over Pinter's seemingly inconclusive plots since Pinter's early career, the radical refutation of the aesthetic pretensions of the well-made play to realism provided for a deeper understanding of his work. Indeed, why should a protagonist who evades the challenge to voice his innermost convictions, and whose 'true' identity is not unquestionably and definitively revealed in a last-act resolution, be conceived of as being less 'real'? "Writing for the Theatre" emphasised the ambiguity of character and plot as an, if not *the* central constitutive element of Pinter's plays. "Language", Pinter wrote in "Writing for the Theatre", "is a highly ambiguous business" (13).

By challenging the established conventions of stage realism, "Writing for the Theatre" also underscored that theatre is, first and foremost, play and playing. Subsequently, even scholars like John Russell Taylor, who had argued with reference to *The Caretaker* in favour of Pinter's "closer and closer approach to realism",[4] readjusted their approaches. The debate about the possible extent and the forms of realism in Pinter's work receded behind the analysis of the "battles for position" and the "memory games" as which these battles were to be increasingly enacted in full-length plays such as *Old Times* and *No Man's Land.* However, Harold Pinter himself was to shake off the notion that the ideas expressed in "Writing for the Theatre" had provided a lasting framework for the understanding of his plays. In the Thessaloniki degree speech he quoted himself only to modify his position decisively. After the introduction cited above, Pinter continued:

> I believe that these assertions still make sense and do still apply to the exploration of reality through art. So as a writer I stand by them but as a citizen I cannot. As a citizen I must ask: What is true? What is false?
>
> There are certain facts which more or less everyone knows to be true but which few people actually talk about, although there is, I believe, a growing surge in the world, an oceanic nausea, if you like, to which more and more people subscribe.
>
> What is the relationship of military might to "market forces"?[5]

Having redefined the theme of his acceptance speech thus, Pinter dropped the issue of art and reality and elucidated to an increasingly uncomfortable audience the 'true' nature of US imperialism, the blatant assertion of American power in the attacks on Serbia and Iraq – "illegal, immoral, illegitimate acts" –, and he concluded with an appeal to resist the "vast, brutal malignant machine" of US aggression because in his view it pushes the world towards a nuclear catastrophe.[6]

This shift from art to politics, which is integral to the degree speech, also characterises Pinter's homepage as a whole. The official internet source provides biographical and bibliographical information about Pinter. However, significantly more space is given to the playwright's ongoing political commitment in speeches, interviews, as well as in his letters to papers and journals. Pinter's right to be highly opinionated about political issues both international and domestic cannot be questioned. Nor can he be criticised for taking advantage of his fame as an outstanding contemporary literary figure. In the more recent history of British drama, playwrights of distinction have always participated in political debates and not only through their plays. John Osborne was notorious for his often unsought comments on British and international politics, and during the Vietnam War, John Arden returned from a visit to the United States as a consecutively militant opponent of US imperialism. Edward Bond has agitated violently against what he believes to be a self-complacent, irrational capitalist society. Likewise, David Hare and Howard Brenton, who spearheaded the theatres' resistance to Thatcherite politics, were always ready to voice their disapproval via other media as well. What Brenton said about Nato's intervention in Serbia in *Collateral Damage* differs only in degree from the convictions expressed by Pinter in Thessaloniki.

The issue is not that Harold Pinter, after having passed for decades as a politically uncommitted playwright has, from the eighties onwards and with seemingly ever increasing vehemence, outed himself as being poignantly opinionated about politics. However, from a scholarly point of view, the degree speech at Thessaloniki raises more than one question about Pinter's work since the 1980s. Central to these is the question of whether the linguistically somewhat sloppy distinction between "true facts" which one is supposed to be aware of in "real life", and the presupposition that in art there "are no hard distinctions between what is real and what is unreal, nor between what is true and what is false", can be made at all. Pinter claims that he can differentiate between his identity as a writer and his role as a citizen, that political commitment and artistic, aesthetic convictions can be more or less neatly separated. This paper will focus on whether this claim is validated by his plays.

II.

In July 2001, the New York Lincoln Center honoured Harold Pinter with a festival as part of its annual festival. Nine of Pinter's plays were performed. Among them was a revival of his very first, *The Room*, as well as his most recent, *Celebration*, in a double-bill from the Almeida Theatre which Pinter himself directed. Dublin's Gate Theatre presented *The Homecoming*, and Pinter acted in a performance of *One For the Road*. The Royal Court Theatre contributed its most recent double-bill, consisting of *Mountain Language* (1988) and *Ashes to Ashes* (1996), which had premièred only days before. Although a festival is largely dependent on available productions, the selection, on which Pinter seemingly had some influence, clearly aimed at being representative. It should be noted, however, that no less than three of Pinter's overtly 'political' plays were included. All performances had been sold out long before the festival, and with the exception of the Royal Court's production they all received favourable reviews. However, during the performance of *Mountain Language* and *Ashes to Ashes* members of the audience rose and left.[7] Pinter seems to have anticipated such reactions. In an interview with Mel Gussow before the festival, he recalled a woman who, after the first New York performance of *Ashes to Ashes*, is reported to have said, "And he has the brass to call this a play".[8]

Although no-one walked out during the preview which I attended at the Royal Court before the plays were taken to New York, the London reviews of Katie Mitchell's production did to some extent foreshadow the reaction of the American audience.[9] While most reviewers conceded that the combination of *Mountain Language* and *Ashes to Ashes* – the plays were performed without interval – created a short, but very intense and haunting experience, they also voiced their disappointment with Pinter's achievement as a playwright. Starting with a reference to Mitchell's casting, Robert Hewison wrote in the *Sunday Times*:

> To have the most articulate victim in *Mountain Language*, Anastasia Hille, and the most brutal soldier, Neil Dudgeon, as female and male in a rhetorical game of sexual ping pong [in *Ashes to Ashes*], implies that the personal is also the political. However, Pinter parodies himself. Linen-skirted woman and brown-shirted man run through the familiar Pinter tropes: sexual menace, questionable memories, the twisted common phrase, the Pinter pause, the restated repetition, the arch phrase and the meaningful ellipsis are all here. In 60 minutes, Pinter at his best, and worst.[10]

A much harsher verdict came from Charles Spencer in the *Daily Telegraph*. Obviously enraged that Pinter did not tie Rebecca's recollections of the Holocaust explicitly to Nazi-Germany – at one point in the dialogue Rebecca talks about having watched in Dorset how "a whole crowd of people" was driven into the sea by "guides": "The tide covered them slowly"[11] – Spencer commented on *Ashes to Ashes*: "[T]he play is marred by Pinter's insistence that all this could be happening in Britain today. The woman describes people being marched into the sea by 'guides' in Dorset. Come off it, Harold! One feels like screaming. Is Lyme Regis notorious for its death camps?"[12] In comparison a much more moderate and balanced evaluation of the two plays came from Benedict Nightingale, who stated with reference to *Mountain Language*:

> There's a place for plays like this – a strong one, given the predicament of the Kurds both in 1988 and now – but nobody could claim that *Mountain Language* is on an artistic par with the sort of work Pinter writes uniquely well. Indeed, the main challenge he's faced in the past quarter century has been to reconcile his sly, subtle strengths with his urge to express his political outrage.[13]

In view of Spencer's outcry against *Ashes to Ashes* and Nightingale's sympathetic understanding for Pinter having taken up the cause of the Kurds in *Mountain Language* it could be argued that in the nineties Pinter has had to cope with the same type of biased criticism which Edward Bond had to stand up to in the sixties. One of the few who defended *Saved* against its hostile reviewers at that time was Alan Brien, the theatre critic of the *Sunday Telegraph*:

> It appears that the British audiences and critics can stomach unlimited helpings of torture, sadism, perversion, murder and bestiality when perpetrated by foreigners upon foreigners [...]. But when Edward Bond [...] shows us London youths, here and now, beating and defiling a bastard baby [...], then a cry goes up to ban and boycott such criminal libels on our national character.[14]

However, it would not be fair to Pinter's critics to dismiss their reservations against the political plays as resulting from an ideological disagreement only. Even if, as evidenced in the quarrel about Howard Brenton's *The Romans in Britain* in 1980, reviewing can occasionally become highly politicised, both Pinter's political plays as well as his much more radical political statements so far have been dealt with respectfully by reviewers and commentators alike, and because of this Spencer's "Come off it, Harold!" provides the exception, not the norm. Neither is it justified to assume that these reservations result from nothing else but the disappointment that the political plays are not as 'Pinteresque', as doubly-refractive and as oscillating as, for example, *The Caretaker* and *The Homecoming*, or as the 'memory games' which were to follow them. The reproach that Pinter is not "at his best" in his political plays cannot be discarded offhandedly as the sloth of critics who are supposedly unwilling to acknowledge that a playwright is entitled to deviate from what is expected of him.

If one is prepared to concede that behind the reservations about Pinter's political plays there is neither an ideological bias nor an intellectual immobility on the side of the critics, then it is necessary to scrutinise exactly how the political plays are inferior to the acclaimed masterworks. The direction in which an answer could possibly be found is indicated by Nightingale's statement that not only in the late eighties and the nineties, but for the past quarter of a century Pinter has faced the challenge of reconciling "his sly, subtle strengths with his urge to express his political outrage". This however, implies a comparative structural analysis of the political plays and those plays which have been labelled as typically 'Pinteresque'.

III.

In terms of referentiality, *Mountain Language* and *Ashes to Ashes* are the most explicit of Pinter's political plays. Unlike Arnold Wesker or the meanwhile nearly forgotten Bernard Kops, both of them playwrights of Pinter's generation who, like him, had grown up in London's East End, Pinter was for a long time very wary of thematising Jewish identity and history. References, such as the choice of names,[15] were casual if not deliberately covered. However, *Ashes to Ashes* leaves no doubt that the past which is uncovered during the 'interrogation' of the female protagonist is the Holocaust. Rebecca has survived it, but the name Pinter has given her also suggests that which she is now incapable of after all she has gone through: in Hebrew, 'Rebecca' means 'to relate' and 'to unite'.

In *Ashes to Ashes* the term 'Holocaust' is never used, and in the confrontation between the women who are waiting and the prison guards in *Mountain Language* neither the Turks nor the Kurds are ever mentioned. However, Pinter himself has conceded that the play was inspired by a visit to Turkey which Arthur Miller and he had been on in 1985 through their function as vice-presidents of the English and American PEN. During five days they talked to Turkish and Kurdish writers and protested against the ongoing human rights abuses. In an interview with Radio 3, Arthur Miller has recalled how, towards the end of their visit, Pinter exploded at a dinner party given in their honour by the American ambassador. When the lady editor of the largest Turkish newspaper accused Miller and Pinter of having come to Turkey for their own publicity only, "Harold blew his stack and said 'I throw that back in your face'".[16] Although Miller then felt obliged to calm the situation by giving an impromptu speech, his recollection is full of admiration for Pinter's spirited breach of dinner etiquette: "As it worked out, we were a good pair because he exploded and I imploded. We were the bad guy and the good guy. […] But I thought Harold behaved marvellously as he always does. I just wouldn't want to be at the other end of his anger, that was all."[17]

Because of their historical and geographical references, *Ashes to Ashes* and *Mountain Language* are the plays most often referred to when 'political' Pinter is discussed. Equally politically committed plays such as *One for the Road* (1984), *Party Time* (1991) or the short pieces *Precisely* (1983) and *The New World Order* (1991), which preceded *Party Time*, do not include such references, but their statements are no less clear. With the advantage of hindsight, it could even be argued that Pinter, far from turning 'political' as late as the eighties, began his career as a politically committed playwright. In *The Room* and *The Birthday Party*, mysterious intruders invade homes and turn seemingly peaceful domestic encounters into interrogation scenes. When, in 1960, Pinter was asked how these mysterious intruders were to be interpreted by audiences, he replied that from his point of view protagonists such as Goldberg and McCann, who take Stanley away after having questioned him all night, had nothing unusual whatsoever about them: "[It] has been happening in Europe in the last twenty years. Not only in the last twenty years, the last two to three hundred".[18]

Pinter's comment does not devaluate the existential readings of the early plays which critics, for lack of a more precise term, initially had labelled 'comedies of menace'. However, Pinter leaves no doubt either that these plays have a political dimension as well and should not be mistaken for mere escapist exercises of the sort of which many reviewers and critics at the time believed the so-called Theatre of the Absurd to consist. The proximity of Pinter's very early work to politically committed drama, albeit intentionally veiled, is even further enhanced by a play which Pinter had kept in his desk for more than two decades. In 1980 he published *The Hothouse* with an introductory "Author's Note":

> I wrote *The Hothouse* in the winter of 1958. I put it aside for further deliberation and made no attempt to have it produced at the time. I then went on to write *The Caretaker*. In 1979 I re-read *The Hothouse* and decided it was worth presenting on the stage. I made few cuts but no changes.[19]

In *The Hothouse* we witness a power-struggle, a 'battle for position' between Roote and his secretary or deputy Gibbs. Roote runs an institution where the inmates are called 'patients', but they are locked away in cells. Since Roote is addressed by his staff as 'Colonel', and since the institution is under the authority of an unspecified 'ministry' which has no resemblance whatsoever to the National Health Service, the impression is gained that the 'institution' is very similar to the totalitarian psychiatric prison-hospital which Tom Stoppard put on stage in *Every Good Boy Deserves Favour* in 1978.

Throughout the two acts, the power-struggle between Roote and Gibbs is waged verbally, and all the "Pinter tropes" mentioned by Hewison are employed. However, the play does not conclude with an open ending. In a dumb show the audience witnesses the 'patients' emerge from their cells at night, and the final interview at the ministry reveals that Roote and all his loyal staff have been killed. Gibbs, most likely the instigator of the revolt, claims to have restored order, and he is rewarded with Roote's position.

Although *The Hothouse* was written more than two decades before Pinter's reviewers began to reconsider him as a political playwright, several of what were to become the constitutive markers of Pinter's political plays were already present. *The Hothouse* anticipates the prison as the location of the political plays to come. While in *No Man's Land* (1975), where the rooms are locked at night, it is uncertain whether the location is Hirst's expensive home or a sanatorium for the affluent, in *One For the Road* there can be no doubt that the interrogation takes place in a prison. Likewise, in *The New World Order* a prison is the most likely setting for the interrogation of the blindfolded man and in *Mountain Language* the prison scenery is explicit and referred to in the stage directions. Nor does *Ashes to Ashes* leave any doubt that Rebecca had been sent to a concentration camp. The concentration camp is not the location of the play's "time present", but it establishes the context of the memories which Devlin tries to unravel.

This move from private homes to institutions or, even more explicitly, prisons and concentration camps, is structurally important. When a home is the battleground in Pinter's plays, and the dramatic conflict is launched through the intrusion of a 'catalytic stranger', there is no pre-established hierarchy, and the course which the battles for position take, does, as evidenced by *The Caretaker*, *The Homecoming* and the 'memory games', depend on the protagonists' ability to hold their ground, especially in linguistically complex encounters.[20] However, a prison as a location changes the initial character constellation decisively. Pinter's prisons are political prisons, and the crimes which the inmates are accused of are so-called political crimes. Because of this, audiences have no choice but to see the inmates of Pinter's prisons *a priori* as victims who have a claim on their sympathy, and the interrogators, guards and executioners *a priori* as despicable handymen of inhumane political systems which have no qualms about torturing and executing opponents. In *One For the Road*, the suggestively named Victor, who has been imprisoned together with his wife and son, may because of his steadfastness be considered to be the moral victor. However, up to the very end when he has to learn from a casual remark that his little son Nicky has been killed – "He [Nicky] *was* a little prick"[21] – he and his family are shown as victims. They were never a match for their merciless interrogator Nicholas, who has his precocious little namesake executed as a warning, so that Nicky's parents will refrain from further political activity.

As evidenced by *Saved*, *The Bundle* and *The Woman*, in the plays of Edward Bond the killing of babies and children is the ultimate proof that the perpetrators are representatives of a society which has lost both its humanity and its rationality. The very same notion is enhanced by the murder of Nicky and by Rebecca's recollection of how her baby, which she had tried to hide, was torn from her arms – an experience so traumatic that she can survive only by denying to herself that she ever had a child: "I don't know of any baby", she insists repeatedly at the end of the play.[22]

In the political plays the victimisation of Pinter's protagonists is further enhanced by other dramatic means. Already in *The Hothouse*, the 'patients' are not referred to by name but by numbers, and beyond their gender the patients 6459 and 6457, who are mentioned throughout the play, are never identified.[23] However, the importance of names as identity constituents is thematised in *Mountain Language*. There, an elderly woman who while waiting outside the prison, has been bitten by a Doberman Pincher, is denied medical aid and compensation because she cannot give the name of the dog:

> *Officer*: Every dog has a *name*! They answer to their name. They are given a name by their parents and that is their name, that is their *name*! Before they bite, they *state* their name. It's a formal procedure. They state their name and then they bite. What was his name? If you tell me one of our dogs bit this woman without giving his name I will have that dog shot![24]

Beyond expressing the irrationality of the system he serves, the officer makes it clear that any acceptance of an individual presupposes a name. With the exception of the Hooded Man, who in a dream-like sequence is addressed by his wife Sara Johnson, the Young Woman, as 'Charley', and an anonymous 'Joseph Dokes' who is mentioned at the end of the play, none of the protagonists in *Mountain Language* is given a name. The oppressors are distinguished by their military rank only, and the oppressed by gender and age. On the one hand, this anonymity underscores the societal representativeness of both groups. On the other hand, however, the officer's speech leaves no doubt in its specific context that the oppressors are unwilling to accept the oppressed as human beings. The victims are forbidden to speak their language, which is another important identity constituent, and in their enforced anonymity they rank below the Doberman Pinchers, which boast an established genealogy.

The callousness with which human lives can be reduced to the anonymity of numbers is most explicit in Pinter's very short one-act play *Precisely*. The beginning of the dialogue between Stephen and Roger, "[*t*]*wo men at a table with drinks*",[25] gives the impression of an ongoing business transaction in the range of 'twenty million'; no currency specified. But after eighteen of the less than seventy lines it becomes clear that the 'business' which Stephen and Roger are discussing is a large-scale purge, that they are talking about human lives and not about money. Roger dreams of an even larger purge, "almost the whole population", and he pleads, "Another two million. And I'll buy you another drink. Another two for another drink", but Stephen, who apparently is of superior rank, fixes the figure at "[t]wenty million dead, precisely" (220).

How Pinter's political plays visualise victimisation as commodification is also exemplified by *The New World Order*. There, the nameless blindfolded man who before his incarceration had "never stopped questioning received ideas" (276), and his equally nameless wife, who is next in line for interrogation, are helpless objects in the hands of their torturers. The blindfolded man never speaks, nor is he ever spoken to. Des and Lionel, the two inquisitors, who claim that they are "keeping the world clean for democracy" (275), are long past acknowledging the humanity of their victims. Whether a male victim should be referred to in grammatically correct terms as 'a prick' or 'a cunt', is for Des and Lionel just a linguistic quibble.

The coarse language of Des and Lionel underscores that in Pinter's political plays the commodification of the victims has a sexual dimension as well. It becomes most apparent in his delineation of the female protagonists, and it is also foreshadowed in *The Hothouse*. There, Roote's mistress Miss Cutts attempts to stabilise her position in the ongoing power-struggle by offering herself to Gibbs as well, but she fails to secure her life. In *One For the Road*, the sexual commodification becomes much more explicit. Nicholas taunts Victor with seemingly intimate knowledge about Victor's wife Gila,[26] and when he later interrogates Gila, who appears before him bruised and in torn clothes, his question "Have they been raping you?"[27] is not a question at all but a statement of facts. He calls Gila a 'fuckpig', and his insistence on being told how often she has been raped is but another means of humiliating her.

The notion that next to innocent children women are the most likely 'collateral' victims of likewise despotic and cynical systems is further confirmed in *Mountain Language*. The guards are impervious to bribes, but apparently not impervious to the perception that "intellectual arses wobble the best".[28] At the end of the third short scene of *Mountain Language*, when Sara Johnson learns that the prison is visited weekly – "except when it rains" – by the administrator Joseph Dokes, she asks the sergeant: "Can I fuck him? If I fuck him, will everything be all right?" Reassuringly, the sergeant replies, "Sure. No problem."[29] Sara's self-humiliation out of despair is the coda to the suffering of the Elderly Woman; the mother who is allowed to see her tortured son, but is not allowed to talk to him.

In *Ashes to Ashes* the sexual commodification of Pinter's female victims becomes even more crucial. Only during the very first lines of the play, when Rebecca describes how her 'lover', while standing over her, made her first kiss his fist and then lick his palm before he puts his hand around her throat,[30] there is the possible assumption that Rebecca and Devlin might be but another of Pinter's couples who are about to give their relationship some extra thrill. The more Rebecca reveals about her 'lover', the clearer it becomes that this man was the commanding officer of a concentration camp: "he ran a really tight ship, he said".[31] Apparently Rebecca only survived because this officer chose her as his mistress, and in the light of this, the sado-masochistic encounters she recalls gain a very different quality. The aura of the frivolous dissipates quickly when it becomes apparent that Rebecca was not only in the hands of a man who, as far as her life was concerned, was literally 'master next to God', but that this 'lover' also was the same man who had torn her baby from her arms at the railway station.

Structurally, *Ashes to Ashes* and *Old Times* share so many similarities that it is difficult to believe they are unintentional. Both plays begin with males, respectively named Devlin and Deeley, who persistently attempt to explore their partner's past. In both plays, the women resist this curiosity about their past lives. However, while Kate in *Old Times* is evasive only where Deeley suspects a more than friendly relationship with her former roommate Anna, Rebecca denounces Devlin's heightened interest in her bodily reactions to the hand at her throat as outrightly pornographic: "I think you're a fuckpig."[32] In both plays either factual or imagined visits to a cinema complicate the plot, and a line-by-line comparison would reveal further cross-references such as the use of popular music-hall melodies.

Pinter has given *Ashes to Ashes* a self-referential beginning, but he was also careful not to overstretch the parallels. In *Old Times*, the appearance of Anna puts an end to Deeley's clumsy interrogation. What follows is a clash of invented memories through which both Deeley and Anna attempt to substantiate their claims on Kate. Aptly named, Kate is to be subdued, to be tamed and made subservient by the identity-concepts created for her. This, however, does not happen. By weaving the fictions invented about her into a metafiction which effectively synthesises and refutes both Deeley's and Anna's claim on her at the same time, Kate secures her independence. For how long though, is not clear, because the ending of the play, where the protagonists take up positions on stage which are a variation of the beginning, suggests that the 'battle for positions' will continue.[33]

In *Ashes to Ashes*, there is no catalytic stranger such as Anna who establishes the rules for a memory game. Devlin and Rebecca are locked in an increasingly merciless struggle in which Devlin attempts to gain control over Rebecca's past. He feels "compelled to ask [...] questions" and demands "a concrete image" of the initially mysterious lover.[34] Whenever Rebecca attempts to evade his inquiries, Devlin doggedly returns to his subject, and he becomes more and more nagging in his questions. The climax of their confrontation is reached when Devlin, very much like Deeley increasingly enraged about his inability to master-mind the conversation, grabs Rebecca's neck and demands from her a repetition of her sexual encounters with her lover. At this point, Rebecca, who has shifted from first-person recollections to a seemingly detached third-person description of a deportation scene, returns to the first-person narrative and recounts to the echo of her own voice how her baby was taken from her.

Billington's suggestion that Rebecca, rather than relating a personal experience, "by an imaginative transference becomes that woman evocative of refugees the world over", and Devlin likewise a somehow archetypal sadistic and Fascistic lover,[35] cannot be completely refuted, but it is not supported by the structure of the play. The change from the first-person recollection to the third-person description reflects Devlin's increasing pressure upon Rebecca's intimacy and memory. Like the unnamed woman in Beckett's *Not I* (1973), Rebecca uses the third person as a means of soothing, if not neutralising pain, but fails in upholding that barrier because of the intensity of the experience.

The political plays discussed so far may give the impression that Pinter's focus is solely on the relationships between the inquisitors and their victims. However, in at least two plays, *Party Time* and his most recent *Celebration*, Pinter evokes the societal context for the violations of human rights shown in the interrogation scenes. *Party Time* opens as a gathering of apparently well-to-do citizens at which the men talk about status symbols and the women about looks, love, and sex. A favourite topic is the 'new club', and only passingly is it mentioned that apparently one member of this party set-up is missing. However, the innocent question of the not-too-bright Dusty is met with a sharp retort by the host: "Nobody is discussing this. Nobody's discussing it, sweetie. Do you follow me? Nothing's happened to Jimmy. And if you're not a good girl I'll spank you."[36] Shortly afterwards, the audience learns from a newly arrived guest that there are roadblocks outside and that with the exception of soldiers nobody is to be seen. At the end of the party Gavin, the host, informs his guests that there has been a round-up while they had been celebrating. It is at this point that Jimmy enters the stage, but he is not a belated guest. Jimmy speaks from a prison cell:

> I had a name. It was Jimmy. People called me Jimmy. That was my name. […] What am I? Sometimes a door bangs, I hear voices, then it stops. It all stops. It all closes. It closes down. It shuts. It all shuts. It all shuts down. It shuts. I see nothing at any time any more. I sit sucking the dark.[37]

In *Party Time*, the members of the 'new club', mostly *nouveaux riches* according to what they have to say, tolerate if not support a purge which stabilises their status, and they condone the accompanying violations of human rights, even if one of their circle is among the victims. *Celebration* does not expand significantly that disillusioned vision of contemporary society. At a posh Italian restaurant, which in the course of the play is upgraded from the "most expensive fucking restaurant in town" to the "best in the world", six guests celebrate their inflated egos with "the best of the best" the place has to offer.[38] They are wheedled by the owners and disturbed only by a waiter who repeatedly tries to interest them in his grandfather, a man who apparently knew all the great 20th-century writers, politicians, and movie stars personally, if not intimately. However, none of the names ring a bell with the guests. They are cocooned in their affluent present, and if that present has a past at all, it does not extend beyond sexual encounters more or less fondly remembered.

Celebration is even more a caricature of a high-level consumer society than *Party Time*. Both plays stage protagonists who show no trace of societal responsibility whatsoever. Nor do they have any historical consciousness. Motivated by self-interest and self-esteem only, they acquiesce to whatever outrage perpetrated, as long as they themselves are spared. By deliberately looking away, they provide for the vacuum of moral responsibility within which the likes of Nicholas, Roger and Stephen, or Des and Lionel can pursue their perverted dreams of order and stability.

In their unshakeable and blatantly self-assured devotion to their cause, Pinter's inquisitors are fundamentalists. However, the scope of Pinter's political plays since the late eighties gives cause to suspect that the creator of these zealots of law and order has adopted an increasingly fundamentalist perspective himself. Not only in the repetitive political statements but by means of his plays as well, Pinter accuses the Western, in his view US-dominated societies of tolerating or belittling any violation of human rights whatsoever as long as it is not perpetrated by an ideological opponent. His plays are a warning that such a licentiousness will, if it has not already, eventually undermine the moral standards of all these societies.

This encompassing perspective explains Pinter's refusal to give his political plays an explicit historical or geographical reference. There is evidence that *Ashes to Ashes* was at least in parts inspired by a biography of Albert Speer.[39] However, Pinter was neither set upon sustaining the memory of the Holocaust as such, nor can he be suspected, as Charles Spencer did, of insinuating that Britain is the next most likely location for the erection of concentration camps. *Ashes to Ashes* is a reminder that wherever the respect for human lives and personal integrity has ceased – Devlin's attitude towards Rebecca is a crucial point –, concentration camps can become, and as recent history has shown not only in former Yugoslavia, will become reality again. *Mountain Language* simply underscores that the first among the victims will most likely be those who belong to an ethnic or a religious minority, and because of this the pairing of the two plays in a double-bill is convincing.

In Friedrich Schiller's terms, Pinter's political plays turn the theatre into a 'moral institution'. His humanistic concern and commitment are beyond doubt and deserve respect. They have also bridged the gap between him and those playwrights who, like Arden or Bond, not only voiced their political commitment much earlier but who also insisted on Pinter being irresponsibly uncommitted. However, it cannot be overlooked that in his political plays Pinter has sacrificed the complexity with which he invested his most ambiguous and mysterious characters from *The Birthday Party* onward, to the clarity of his message. The protagonists of *Party Time* and *Celebration* are one-dimensional, if not cardboard figures. They define themselves within three or five lines, and thereafter they are stuck with the role which has been imposed upon them – Dusty in *Party Time* and the likewise promiscuous and cunning Suki in *Celebration* are outstanding examples.

Compared to these one-dimensional protagonists, the relationship between Pinter's inquisitors and their victims is, as described above, somewhat more complex. However, there too the intellectually participating audience which Pinter's battles for position presuppose, is neutralised because – with the partial exception of *Ashes to Ashes* – the battle is reduced to witnessing the linguistic deconstruction and parallel physical and/or psychic destruction of pre-defined victims. The "shared common ground" which Pinter's political plays evoke, is not the "quicksand" any longer, as he previously described reality in "Writing for the Theatre" (12) – a quicksand, in which right and wrong have no stable foundation –, but rather a clear-cut moral opposition which is imposed on the audience with the rise of the curtain. Neither self-referentiality nor the repeated "Pinter tropes" can conceal that in his political plays Pinter has decided to waive for good the reservations he once voiced about political commitment for both playwrights and citizens. In "Writing for the Theatre" he said:

> There is certainly a good deal of prophecy indulged in by playwrights these days, in their plays and out of them. Warnings, sermons, admonitions, ideological exhortations, moral judgements, defined problems with built-in solutions; all can camp under the banner of prophecy. The attitude behind this sort of thing might be summed up in one phrase: '*I'm* telling *you*!' […] Beware of the writer who puts forward his concern for you to embrace, who leaves you in no doubt of his worthiness, his usefulness, his altruism, who declares that his heart is in the right place, and ensures that it can be seen in full view, a pulsating mass

> where his characters ought to be. What is presented, so much of the time, as a body of active and positive thought is in fact a body lost in a prison of empty definition and cliché. (12–13)

In view of the full text of "Writing for the Theatre", both the heading of the official Pinter homepage as well as the beginning of the Thessaloniki degree speech have an exculpatory ring.

Notes

1 Pinter (2000a).
2 Pinter (1962: 25).
3 Pinter (1976: 9–16). Subsequent page references to this edition will be included in the text.
4 Taylor (1974: 335).
5 Pinter (2000a).
6 *Ibid.*
7 Cf. Lueken (2001: 43).
8 Cf. Mel Gussow's interview with Harold Pinter (Gussow 2001: 4. The page reference is to the *New York Times* premium archive, www.nytimes.com).
9 For the reviews cf. *Theatre Record*, 807–812.
10 *Ibid.*, 811.
11 Pinter (1998: 416).
12 *Theatre Record*, 807.
13 *Ibid.*, 811.
14 Cf. Browne, Terry: *Playwright's Theatre*, London, 1975, p. 63.
15 The possible Jewish identity of Goldberg in *The Birthday Party* puzzled quite a number of critics. In comparison, the referentiality of 'Ruth' in *The Homecoming* is much more obvious. 'Ruth' translates as 'friend' and thus fits her role in the play. Moreover, in the Old Testament, Ruth is the widow of a Judean emigrant who in accordance with the levirate marries her brother-in-law.
16 Cf. Billington (1997: 298).
17 *Ibid.*
18 Interview with the BBC, 3 March 1960. Cf. Innes (1992: 282).
19 Pinter (1980: 6).
20 The exception, of course, is *The Caretaker*.
21 Pinter (1998: 247, my emphasis).
22 *Ibid.*, 432–433.
23 Pinter employs a variant of this in *Victoria Station*, where the taxi driver who is exposed to the whims of the controller is always addressed by his number 274 only.
24 Pinter (1998: 253–254).
25 *Ibid.*, 215. Further references to this edition of *Precisely* will be included in the text.
26 *Ibid.*, 230–231.
27 *Ibid.*, 243.
28 *Ibid.*, 257.

29 *Ibid.*, 264.
30 *Ibid.*, 395–397.
31 *Ibid.*, 405.
32 *Ibid.*, 398.
33 Cf. Reitz (1993: 345–346 and 1986: 61–78).
34 Pinter (1998: 399–400).
35 Billington (1997: 380).
36 Pinter (1998: 284).
37 *Ibid.,* 313–314.
38 Pinter (2000b: 18, 67, and 62).
39 Cf. Billington (1997: 374–375 and 384).

Bibliography

Billington, Michael: *The Life and Work of Harold Pinter*, London, 1997.
Browne, Terry: *Playwright's Theatre*, London, 1975.
Gussow, Mel: "Notes on Pinter, Given by Pinter", The New York Times, 15 July 2001.
Innes, Christopher: *Modern Drama 1890–1990*, Cambridge, 1992.
Pinter, Harold: "Between the Lines", *The Sunday Times*, 4 March 1962, 25.
–: *Plays 1*, London, 1976.
–: *The Hothouse*, London, 1980.
–: *Plays 4*, expanded edition, London, 1998.
–: "Degree Speech to the Aristotle University of Thessaloniki April 18th 2000", www.haroldpinter.org/home/thessa.html [2000a].
–: *Celebration & The Room*, London, 2000b.
Lueken, Verena: "Ein Fehdehandschuh liegt zwischen den Sätzen", *Frankfurter Allgemeine Zeitung* 182, 8 August 2001, 43.
Reitz, Bernhard: "Nachwort". – In Harold Pinter: *Old Times*. Ed. Bernhard Reitz, Stuttgart, 1986, pp. 61–78.
–: *The Stamp of Humanity. Individuum, Identität, Gesellschaft und die Entwicklung des englischen Dramas nach 1956*, Trier, 1993.
Taylor, John Russell: *Anger and After*, third edition, London, 1974.
Theatre Record 21, 2001, Issue 13.

Heiner Zimmermann, Heidelberg

Howard Barker in the Nineties

1. The Outsider

In the last decade Howard Barker, who belongs to the same generation as Caryl Churchill, David Edgar, David Hare and Howard Brenton, has become an outsider in the English theatrical establishment. Over the last three years, 27 of his works have been staged in six different languages in 17 countries, including New Zealand, Canada, and Slovenia, whilst Britain has seen only four productions of his plays. None of his plays has ever been shown in the National Theatre.[1]

With his six collections of verse from *Don't Exaggerate* (1985) to *The Tortmann Diaries* (1996) he is the poet among contemporary British playwrights. Can the development of his reputation therefore be taken as a test of how much room there is for poetry in British theatre? He is a painter whose expressionist drawings reduce forms and movements to their essence. In the last decade he also distinguished himself as the director of his plays. He has, moreover, expounded his theory of the theatre in a collection of essays, *Arguments for a Theatre*.[2] Recently John Calder published the fifth volume of his collected plays, which by now number more than forty. Many of them have been translated into several European languages. The dialogue of academic scholars, actors, theatre directors and translators with his work fills several book-length studies and special Barker issues of theatre reviews.[3]

2. The Reversal

The history of the reception of his drama, which began in the early seventies, is marked by a breach. The rupture of his love affair with the Royal Shakespeare Company over the production of *The Bite of the Night* in 1986 epitomises his final break with the theatre of commitment and the birth of his radically new 'Theatre of Catastrophe'. This entailed the desertion of a part of the devoted crowd of his leftist followers and put an end to the Barker festivals, which had testified to the extraordinary popularity of his work in the British theatre.[4] Problems started as early as the beginning of the eighties, when the Royal Shakespeare Company refused to produce *Crimes in Hot Countries* (1983) although they had commissioned it, because it did not fit into any of the usual categories such as political satire or history play. The Royal Court under Gaskill and Stafford-Clark was, however, also increasingly disconcerted by Barker's new work, which had left the dramaturgical traditions of Stanislavsky and Brecht far behind. *Downchild* (1985) was the last of his series of epic diagnoses of the state of the nation highlighting the underbelly of the glamorous façade of the public political spectacle. As the theatres which had so far produced his plays believed that they had to conform to the prevailing traditional stage realism for reasons of box office returns, they became reticent to stage the new Barker plays. This provoked, however, a unique phenomenon in modern theatrical history: In 1988, a group of actors who were committed to his work from earlier Joint Stock productions founded the Wrestling School. The ensemble dedicated itself to developing performance techniques adapted to his demanding, unconventional new texts. Ian McDiarmid, the actor and director, put his extraordinary talent at the service of Barker's work, offering the Almeida Theatre as a venue. Kenny Ireland directed numerous Wrestling School productions at the Leicester Haymarket Theatre and abroad. The actors' company has remained the most important interpreter of Barker's work in the United Kingdom up to the present.[5]

3. *The Critique of Satire*

Barker was the first of his generation of political playwrights, who, well before the fall of the Berlin wall, re-defined the possibilities of opposition through art after the loss of the authority of socialism and of Christian humanist morality, which was ignored by his peers. In spite of his audience success, he was disillusioned by ten years of writing political satires. He could no longer believe in the subversive power of the Brechtian Theatre of Enlightenment, which, in its English version, told its audiences what to think and whose attacks on the establishment consolidated its identity instead of provoking change. In his view, political satire undemocratically elevated the dramatist to the position of "The One Who Knows" and humiliated the audience into the position of those who are ignorant.[6] He consequently declared the dramatist's ignorance as the first principle of his theatre, extolling imagination instead of cognition. He moreover denounced political satire's distinction between good and bad as superficial and despised it for rehearsing moral platitudes about which there was already general consent.[7] He doubted that the theatre had ever raised consciousness or changed the perception of reality of a substantial part of any society or rendered any society more just.

Impressed by poststructuralist philosophy and Francois Lyotard's declaration of the end of grand narratives as well as Foucault's critique of reason and enlightenment, he revised the principles of his dramatic art. In a volte-face, he also worked at the deconstruction of the ideology of reason and at the liberation of repressed desire, instinct and passion in the theatre. The historian with a degree from Sussex University was convinced that art could not be excluded from the general historical process of continuous destruction and renewal. A new situation asked for a new art.[8] He expressed this in his television drama *Pity in History* (1982) through the image of 16th-century Puritan iconoclasm. In this play, a sculptor's apprentice attempts to emancipate himself from the influence of his master. He smashes the monuments carved by his teacher, who does not oppose this. The chaos of debris produced by the destruction of tradition constitutes the quarry for the creation of the new art, which is inspired by the beauty of the fragments of the old. Barker thus epitomised his demolition of the traditional model of drama and his revival of discarded dramatic conventions for his new ends.[9] To the musical and political satire, which in his eyes dominated the stage, he opposed a Theatre of Catastrophe, which tried to restore tragedy to the postmodern stage.

The reversal was foreshadowed by the reckless self-fulfilment of the individual in Barker's early plays such as *Cheek* (1970) or *Claw* (1975), whose protagonists violated all moral norms created by reason and ended tragically. Also his later satires exhibited egotism unrestrained by the fetters of conscience or any feeling of guilt and thus constituted his first attempts at an archaeology of the self repressed by morality and civilisation. In most of his epic anatomies of the state of the nation, the satirist's hate was also directed against all compromise and reconciliation. *The Hang of the Goal* (1978), *Victory* (1983) and *The Castle* (1985)[10] were milestones on his way to a new theatre whose overwhelming success still attested to his audience appeal.

Reflections on the nature and possibilities of a new art preoccupied him not only in the essays, interviews and lectures collected in *Arguments for a Theatre*, but also in his plays. They show his wish to bridge the gap of non-understanding, which separated him from a part of his audience and critics. In the prologues to several plays, he tried to prepare his audience for the unaccustomed spectacle which awaited them. The procedure does not lack irony, as the speaker of the second prologue in the *Last Supper* (1988) discovers when he realises that he is doing exactly what he announces the play will not do: "**The play contains no information** / Aren't you tired of journalists? [...] No one will hold your hand tonight / Nor oil you with humour [...] When the poem became easy it also became poor / When art became mechanised it became an addiction / I lecture! / Oh, I lecture you! (*A terrible storm of laughter*)".[11] In *The Bite of the Night*

(1986) Macluby, the soap boiler, evokes an audience who has discarded conventional expectations and attitudes: "**It is not true that everyone wants to be / Entertained / Some want the pain of unknowing**".[12]

4. The Theatre of Catastrophe

Barker's Theatre of Catastrophe, which he endeavoured to establish as his new trade mark, is characterised by its opposition to the Brechtian Theatre of Enlightenment, and by its affinity with early Greek tragedy as he sees it as well as with certain aspects of Artaud's Theatre of Cruelty. It destroys fundamental parts of the traditional model of drama and makes metaphorical use of historical material.

Refusing any justification through utility either by moral didacticism (*docere*) or by entertainment (*delectare*), his theatre claims a right to an existence of its own. He attempts to explore what the Theatre of Enlightenment represses or ignores. His Theatre of Catastrophe puts to the test the traditional humanist values, which are endorsed by Brecht's British followers. The purposefully unconventional or immoral actions of his characters uncover contradictions between will and desire, between reason and the unconscious, and explore the contradictions inherent in moral principles. Contrary to Brechtian theatre his characters put the individual's desires, the individual's claim to self-fulfilment above the welfare of society.

5. The Appropriation of Tragedy

The Theatre of Catastrophe attempts to restore to the stage tragedy and the experience of suffering and pain which modern theatre had banned.[13] It intends to rediscover the dignity, the meaningfulness and beauty of pain and suffering. By designating Greek tragedy as its model, Barker appropriated its authority for his new theatre. Catastrophe and the suffering caused by it were for him the essence of tragedy. Whereas in Greek drama 'catastrophe' meant the turn of the action either to a good or fatal ending,[14] in Barker's theatre it signifies a historic event which has shattered the political, cultural, and moral order and entails the protagonists' 'utter transformation', impelling them to disregard the laws of reason and of ethical norms.[15] In his 'theatre of moral speculation', it is thus also the process of exploration and realisation of the self beyond the limits of rationalism and morality, a process which is willed by its subject. In the amoral state of catastrophe, the principle of justice is suspended. Barker even finds this situation in classical tragedy, since, in his opinion, it discloses that the gods are amoral and capable of malice just as it reveals man's uncivilised self.[16] He also justifies his representation of pain for its own sake and his belief in its beauty by referring to classical tragedy: "The Greeks understood the pleasures hidden in the spectacle of pain as well as its place in life, its supreme irrationality".[17]

Barker sees in classical tragedy, just as in his own "theatre without conscience", "the refusal of the individual to leave the personality unexcavated, the eruption of will into areas of social piety".[18] In contrast to his protagonists, however, the tragic hero suffers because he cannot control the consequences of his actions. Destiny inflicts on him an excess of pain, which exposes the limits of reason and justice. His final destruction signifies the restoration of justice. Barker ignores this, pretending that Greek tragedy has no moral implication.[19] His protagonists refuse all reconciliation with order and morality. Following their desires, they remorselessly transgress all ethical norms. They want to acquire forbidden knowledge beyond the limits of what is known. Their endeavour is consequently contrary to *diánoia*, the tragic hero's act of cognition which has moral consequences. Barker's "theatre of moral experimentation" takes the modern breakdown of the moral consensus to extremes in order to re-assess the traditional ethical standards which society has outlived and to test the consequences of repressed thought.[20] It explores the meaning of evil as well as the dialectics of good and bad, showing that the one creates the other. It reveals the negative side of virtue and the positive side of vice, thus dismantling the bipolar opposition of good and evil and erasing the dividing line between both. The suppression of pity is shown to be a prerequisite for survival, e.g. in *The Possibilities* (1987), and pain is presented as a key to knowledge. As catastrophe, with the obliteration of the barriers of morality, brings the annihilation of ideology, Lvov, the egomaniac protagonist of *The Last Supper* (1988) believes: "Only catastrophe can keep us clean" (23). Catastrophe in Barker's plays is not only the precondition for reconstruction and a new life; in his eyes, its spectacle of pain also possesses a subversive beauty.

6. *The Action*

The action in the Theatre of Catastrophe has nothing to do with the mimesis of reality in classical drama. It imagines an alternative life without the norms of reason and morality. As Barker, in line with postmodern philosophy, no longer believes in human essence, his characters lack a stable identity. Since they follow only their instincts and desires, their behaviour becomes unpredictable. Their actions consequently never build up a causally connected chain of events, but remain incoherent. Barker's plays correspondingly lack the linear narrative of a story. Disruptions fragment their sequence of episodes. The Theatre of Catastrophe ignores the laws of probability. It represents what is improbable and hence surprises. It confronts its audience with ambiguity and irreconcilable contradictions. In *The Bite of the Night* the second prologue therefore warns the spectators: "*Clarity / Meaning / Logic / And Consistency / None of it / None* [...] *No ideology on the cheap*".[21]

7. The Use of History

In most of his plays, Barker uses historical events as starting points for rewriting the historians' official version and presenting an alternative, imaginary version, which never happened. The restoration of the monarchy in England in the 17th century, for instance, provides the frame for *Victory* (1981). The action of *The Europeans* (1993) is situated in Vienna after the siege of the Turks in 1683, and *Hated Nightfall* (1994) imagines a version of the death of the Romanovs in the Russian Revolution of 1918. History provides Barker with situations of political, social and cultural upheaval, usually war, or revolution, which provoke his characters' inner catastrophe, the overthrow of their rationality and the transgression of moral norms as they follow their instincts and desires.[22]

The inevitable bias of all historiography is demonstrated by the example of reporting on war in *The Power of the Dog.* Even photographs at their best only show a subjective section of reality and at their worst they are fakes. In the same play a project of a 'wholefilm', which is to juxtapose projections of a bourgeois and a Marxist, a political and a personal perspective on the same events, does not comprise the whole of reality and is therefore abandoned. Barker consequently exhibits in his plays the fictional character of his version of history. He understands his use of history as metaphor and a projection of the present. In this sense, he can describe the action of *The Castle* (1985), which takes place in the period of the crusades, as "entirely free of history".[23]

His plays reject the traditional attempt to interpret the present through history or to control the future by means of reconstructing historical reality as a succession of causal relationships. They destroy the myths of the teleology of history and of historical progress. In *The Bite of the Night* alternative explanations of the Trojan War are played off against one another in Macluby's Prologue to the second act, when he concludes, "**No more causes of war will do**" (40, emphasis in the text). Barker believes that desire, lust, power, passion, instinct, and violence, which know neither reason nor morality, are the driving forces of history, which is, consequently, an irredeemable chaos, the eternal war of everybody against everybody. In

The Power of the Dog history, with reference to Psalm 22, is compared to "a mad dog" (23), for, as Lvov believes in *The Last Supper* (1988): "The perfectly human is as near to inhumanity as you should want" (22). Reason has never been able to control instinct, desire or anxiety. Thus, they determine the course of history, which cannot be tamed. The only history worth writing therefore is "the history of emotions looking for a politics of the emotions", as did the Oxford historian Theodore Zeldin.[24]

The representation of the history of the human instincts, passions and desires repressed by civilisation is, however, also the history of the disciplining and maiming of the human body through its subjection to the norms of society.[25] The human body becomes the battlefield of history. The comedian McGroot in *The Power of the Dog* accordingly defines history as "a woman bein' raped by ten soldiers in a village in Manchuria".[26] From the beginning of Barker's career the body as the source of desire, lust, and pain is the focus of his plays. The desecration of the regicide Bradshaw's exhumed corpse, and his widow's struggle to collect its scattered parts in order to bury them, form the backbone of *Victory* (1984). In *The Castle*, the witch, Skinner, who castrated and killed the builder of the fortress, is chained to his decaying corpse, which she has to drag around with her until the end of the play. Helen's body as the object of male desire is the origin of the Trojan War in *The Bite of the Night*. Different types of society try to control her by controlling her body, which leads to her increasing mutilation. As she is gradually reduced to a trunk, she becomes a puppet manipulated by man (44). It is even planned to boil her down to distil her fragrance. In the last scene there remains only a torso, which is interred by the male protagonist.

If Barker in the subtitle of *The Power of the Dog* defines the play as 'anti-history', he means without doubt that it focuses on the irrationality of the events from the Second World War which it evokes. But his plays also refer to narratives which are repressed by official historiography and to which this term therefore applies equally well, such as those of the vanquished, the women, the minorities, the individual. In *The Bite of the Night* Savage, the Professor of classics, attempts to write the history of Troy which Homer omitted. His *Ruinad* is to describe the heroic life of the defeated in the rubble of the war (34). Katrin, the protagonist of *The Europeans* (1993), forces the official historians to inscribe the female discourse of her mutilated and raped body into the official male record of the victory over the Turks. For this reason she also stages the birth of the child of her collective rape as a public spectacle. The historical model of Galactia, the protagonist of *Scenes from an Execution* (1984, staged 1990), is the Renaissance woman painter, Artemisia Gentillesci, whose extraordinary work was, until recently, excluded from the male record of the history of art.

In contrast to the Theatre of Enlightenment Barker does not appeal to the spectators' faculty of ratiocination and moral judgement, but addresses his audience at a level "beneath the consciously moral".[27] He suspends the laws of reason and morality, categorically rejecting all social responsibility. To Brecht's "theatre of daylight, clarity, and dubious truths" he opposed his "theatre of obscurity",[28] a black box where imagination, desire and passions are liberated, where the criminal act is freely permitted because imagination needs darkness to unfold and flees from daylight.[29] In the dark, moreover, the audience is atomised, their solidarity broken and the individuals are unhampered in their reaction by the neighbour's controlling gaze. Only thus can Barker free his spectators' contradictory feelings. Instead of instructing his audience, he leads them into moral conflicts. As in a laboratory, his theatre freely explores transgression, chaos and pain to provoke in its audience "the ecstasy of moral uncertainty".[30] His protagonists' improbable irrational actions and their terrible transgressions prevent the audience's identification with them, their empathy or pity for their suffering.[31] The characters expose the spectators to feelings, thoughts and desires which they repress and hide from themselves. Their emotional reaction is torn between shame, consternation, disgust, bewilderment, protest and fascination as their repressed desires, concealed imaginations and dreams are shown up and the parts of their personality which they deny or conceal are exposed. Confronted with situations on the stage in which the distinction between good and evil is no longer possible, their moral convictions are confused and they are bewildered and lost. They are, moreover, overwhelmed by the plethora of what they experience.[32] The fundamental destabilisation of the self aimed at by the Theatre of Catastrophe is obviously opposed to the Aristotelian idea of *kátharsis*, the purging of the spectators' fascination with fear and the terrible, as well as of their inclination to lament.[33] Barker ignores this and emphasises that classical tragedy, by its representation of terror and the assertion of the self over the collective arouses fascination as well as repulsion. Unlike Aristotle he believes that "tragedy asserts nothing in its own defence – not its therapeutic essences, its cathartic effects of social behaviour, nothing Aristotelian at all".[34] He hopes, however, that his audience's moral confusion will force them to examine their ethical standards and judge for themselves instead of receiving a message. Barker's rejection of catharsis, his emphasis on the pre-moral condition of Greek tragedy, on its insight that existence is horrifying, contradictory and painful, his focus on the individual desire to discover his/her true self coincide, however, with Nietzsche's constructions of classical tragedy in *The Birth of Tragedy*. He follows the German philosopher in his censure of rationalism, which pretends to be able to overcome the contradictions causing the pain, suffering and meaninglessness of existence revealed by tragedy. Barker's recourse to tragedy thus is part of a radical critique of Enlightenment, which was started by Nietzsche and was taken up by postmodernist philosophy.

His appropriation of Michel Foucault, however, appears to be contradictory. He follows Foucault when he denounces the current society's "neurotic demand for the illumination of all dark places".[35] But he also sees in the Roman-Catholic confessional an emblem of his own "theatre of secrets and darkness" as it grants privacy to self-exposure, which brings to the surface "the normally *unspoken*, the counter discourse, the private".[36]

9. Post-modern or Avant-garde?

At first sight Barker's 'anti-humanist theatre', which deconstructs the discourse of rationality, seems to be a genuine offspring of postmodernism.[37] Its action is fragmented and establishes no linear sequence of time, it shuns the mimesis of reality, remains self-reflexive and its characters lack identity. This impression is, however, contradicted by the dramatist's characterisation of his texts as avant-garde theatre and elitist, by his condemnation of popular mass culture as shallow and obfuscatory – an attitude incompatible with the postmodern integration of 'high' and 'popular' culture. Barker's theatre is in fact avant-garde in the original sense of the production of an imaginary reality, which has never existed before.[38] Like the avant-garde theatre it wants to perplex its audience. By waking its audience from the sleep of reason, the Theatre of Catastrophe believes itself to be radically political in the same sense as Derrida considers his concept of deconstruction to be political. The focus of Barker's theatre on catastrophe, pain and suffering has little in common with the playful elusiveness of postmodernist collage and parody and the exhibiting of intertextual references. Barker wants it to be a sort of inversion of Brechtian enlightenment and yet it continues the project of enlightenment in so far as he confronts his audiences with parts of their self which are hidden away in their unconscious. Thus, these irrational aspects are brought into the view of reason even if only to show its limits. Barker's cult of the individual as well as his unlimited belief in language are equally untainted by the spirit of postmodernism. Like Artaud he attempts to liberate and discover the unconscious created by the individual's subjection to the symbolical order of language and the social norm, which divided the subject. Through the archaeology of the self, their attempts at self-discovery, Barker's protagonists try to recover their self of the imaginary phase,[39] which existed before their socialisation and the original repression (*Urverdrän-*

gung) when body and mind, passion and reason were still united. While Artaud tried to open access to the unconscious part of the self through the destruction of the order of language as well as by non-linguistic means of trance and ecstasy, Barker has an unlimited trust in the power of language and linguistic expression.[40] He believes that language can serve as the key to what is repressed by its own ideological order. His characters ignore the ideological prison of language, which precedes the individual. They count on metaphor and poetic language and try to liberate the unconscious through vehement rhetorical outbursts and ecstatic declamations. They are not afraid of thus subjecting the hidden self, the inarticulate area that is not yet charted by the power of rationality and social norms.[41] Barker's aesthetic of explicitness ignores the allusion to the 'unsayable', to what cannot be represented. It reveres the radical openness, the shamelessness of beauty. As this contradicts the traditional conception of the aesthetic value of elliptic and condensed language, Barker confronts his actors with the difficulty of inventing new convincing modes of expression.

At the beginning of the nineties, two texts by Barker dating back to 1984, *Scenes from an Execution* (1990)[42] and *The Europeans* (1993), were performed for the first time on stage. *The Europeans* had been refused by the Royal Shakespeare Company despite having been commissioned by them in 1984. This meant that Barker's attempt to clarify – also in his plays – his conception of the theatre and its role in contemporary society was carried over into the nineties.

10. The Nineties

In the Viennese Imperial Academy of Art in *The Europeans* (shown in Act One, Scene Eight) Emperor Leopold sets the critics the task of defining "the principles of a new art" because after the defeat of the Ottoman Empire "the stir of Europe from its sleep commands a terrible and unrelenting movement of the soul".[43] Starhemberg, the glorious leader of the Austrian army, becomes the author's mouthpiece, for the general's concepts in fact rehearse the tenets of the Theatre of Catastrophe: "I need an art which will recall pain [...]. I need an art that will plummet through the floor of consciousness and free the unborn self [...]. I need an art that will shatter the mirror in which we pose. I want to make a new man and a new woman but only from the pieces of the old" (31). As it rises from the rubble of tradition after its destruction, his new art is equally the product of war. The new man/woman it creates is fashioned from the debris of the old whose self-deception it has shattered. It has nothing to do with the rococo and jazz asked for by the Empress, nor with Starhemberg's memory that "[d]uring the war, while the ground rose under the shellfire [...] and everything was racing from itself, the eye from the socket and the arm from the joint, you heard in the fractional silences a singing record going round, deep in a cellar, and the lips of the soon-to-be-dead were mouthing sentiments of banal happiness" (31–32).

11. The Artist as Painter

As in *The Europeans,* the artist in Barker's plays is always a painter, and the topic of art is evoked from the perspective of visual art.[44] In *Scenes from an Exhibition*, the painter, Galactia, painfully learns the limits of the critical potential of art. A painting of the battle of Lepanto, commissioned by the doge of Venice, becomes the centre of the conflict in *Scenes* between the artist and the state, because the female artist, who is modelled on the Renaissance painter Artemisia Gentillesci, instead of celebrating the glory of the Venetian victory, exposes the horrors of war. Her critique of the official militarism and racism in her picture is defused by the state. The establishment appropriates the picture by focusing on its aesthetic value as a major work of art. The artist's fame finally drives her into collusion with the state whose patriarchal hierarchy and ideological transformation of violence and war into patriotism and bravery she attacked.

Barker's anti-pastoral, *Ego in Arcadia* (1992), inverts Poussin's warning in his famous painting 'Et in arcadia ego' that even in the pastoral idyll death is present. Barker's play imagines a sort of hell, where everybody desperately suffers from unrequited love, but where, similar to Sartre's *Huis clos*, nobody can die – unless they can give an adequate, melancholy expression to their pain. Poussin is one of the inmates of this 'purgatory à la Barker'. The opera libretto, *Terrible Mouth* (1992), was inspired by a self-portrait of Francesco Goya. In his glance and grin in the painting Barker recognises a repudiation of the satirical spirit of Enlightenment which informs his 'Caprichos' and 'Desastres de la guerra', and the moralist's fascination and collusion with the horrors he denounces.[45] In spite of Goya's famous dictum 'The sleep of reason brings forth monsters', Barker believes that the painter was not only repulsed but also fascinated by these monsters who still exert the same fascination on the observer today. Goya, the play's protagonist, correspondingly becomes the collusive voyeur, who eagerly draws the atrocious rape of his beloved mistress and patroness, the Duchess of Alba.

The 'pre-text' of *Judith* (1995) is equally a famous painting by Artemisia Gentillesci, which depicts the slaying of Holofernes.[46] *Ursula* (1998) was sparked off by the picture of the 'Massacre of the Virgin Martyrs' by Lucas Cranach the Elder. The end of the Wrestling School's production of *Und* (1999), which the author himself directed, was commented on by a projection of Jacob van Ruisdael's painting 'The Jewish Cemetery'.

12. Anti-history or the History of Emotions

As in the preceding decade, Barker's Theatre of Catastrophe of the nineties confronted its audiences with historical situations of upheaval, which overturn all moral norms and lead to moral and emotional confusion or to the radical reactions of his protagonists, who refuse to conform to the principles of reason. Katrin and Starhemberg in *The Europeans* relentlessly reject all collaboration with the imperial policy of reconciliation and refuse to play the role of the suffering victim or the conquering hero. The greater part of Barker's plays of the nineties such as *Judith*, *Hated Nightfall* or *Und*, on the contrary, are connected by their focus on the ambiguous relationship between executioner and victim and on the two political ideologies which determined the history of the 20th century. The victim's collusion with his/her hangman induces the erasure of the role dichotomy or even the inversion of both roles.

In *Hated Nightfall* (1994), Barker evokes the killing of the imperial family of the Romanovs during the Russian revolution at Ekaterinburg in 1918. The outward circumstances of *Und* suggest that it takes place in the 'Reichskristallnacht'. The monologue investigates the self-deception of an aristocratic Jewish woman who, in colluding with her future executioner, avoids confronting her impending arrest. The historical setting of *A Hard Heart*, a beleaguered city perhaps during the Peloponnesian War, of the medieval legend of Ursula or of the story of Judith's rescue of Jerusalem (by seducing and slaying Holofernes) from the Apocrypha of the Old Testament are more vague.

13. Hated Nightfall

Hated Nightfall was probably sparked off by the discovery of the remains of the Romanovs. The two unidentified bodies from Ekaterinburg became the protagonists of Barker's play. It is another of Barker's dreams of absolute freedom and reckless individualism and implies a radical critique of communism and its idea of revolution. Dancer, the central character, is the former tutor and appointed henchman of the Romanov family. Accomplishing this task becomes for him a quest for his true self and for the meaning of his acts. He is "fifty and absolute"[47] and a law onto himself (9), trying to maintain his individuality against an ideology which negates the individual. In a Nietzschean manner, he casts off the fetters of morality in order to explore his unknown self and to 'become who he is'. Anxious to remain autonomous in his decisions, he kills the Revolutionary Committee's emissaries, who urge him to proceed with the liquidation, as well as the sentimental functionary who, overwhelmed by pity, offers to let the victims escape. Dancer's awe of the symbolic, historic act of executing the Tsar family contrasts with the facile banality of his unscrupulous murder of the Party emissaries. He is, however, incapable of removing their bodies. Even these deeds cannot be obliterated. His Hamlet-like hesitations lead to a more and more tangled and intimate relationship between him and his prospective victims. They reveal a maze of contradictory desires and emotions and the pressure of ideology. Dancer discovers not only that he entertains an "obscure feeling of devotion" (11) for the imperial family, but also a fundamental desire for love: "[A]ll I want is love [...], it is the single and obsessive object of my life" (19). The executioner's affection for his victim and the victim's affection for the executioner become the leitmotif of the play. As early as the first scene, Dancer and the Tsar are locked in a dance of death as the latter tries to throttle the tutor. Later Dancer's killing of the Party functionaries is carried out in a deadly embrace with them. From the play's beginning Dancer shows an erotic obsession with the Tsarina, Caroline, which at first only finds an outlet in the form of voyeurism. Dancer, who dreams of "an immaculate moment of love" (21), later, however, dares to kiss the Empress, who permanently sleeps in order to escape from the unbearable threat of execution. The anguished and bewildered imperial family's morals gradually dissolve under the strain of the catastrophic situation. They try to save themselves by seducing their executioner. The Tsar offers him money in exchange for his liberty, which Dancer declines as "his passion has no price" (28). After the Princess, the Empress also offers herself to the tutor, which for a moment provokes him to fantasies of a romance in Venice, Paris, or Nice. For an instant, the Tsarina, who never experienced real passion, even really desires her relentless lover and executioner. Ultimately Dancer however does not dream of fulfilment but of *Liebestod*. The executioner becomes the victim as a functionary arrests him in the name of the Revolutionary Committee. He hails the woman as his bride: "My bride has arrived" (43). The banquet he prepares in the second part of the play celebrates the ritual of his wedding with a sacrificial death, the inevitable consequence of his revolution of the individual. The ritual unites him with the Romanovs, who are, like him, the victims of the new order of communism. The Tsar family finally declare their love for Dancer, who like Gloucester in *King Lear* is blinded because he has offended against the official ideology. For he wanted the revolution which frees the individual and exclaims: "Throw open the windows of the soul! Let the winds of civil disorder and the rhetoric of lawyers whirl the pages of the antique books, sheets in the gutter, splintering crucifixes underneath your boots" (33). He declares his love of chaos: "Chaos / I like it / Chaos / How it suits me / It's my medium" (31). The designated "doorman of the century" (18) therefore disowns the role of making history and insists, "I am the antithesis of History which has manacled their souls" (46) – which is exactly what the author wants his play to be.[48] Both the representative of imperial absolutism and the Party emissary, the victim and his executioner, on the other hand, share the belief that order and the rejection of chaos are the foundation of society and the state.[49] They consequently want to eliminate Dancer, who opposes imperial rule as much as the submission to Party discipline and its enforcement like a religious dogma by cleansing society of dissenters. In the nineties, Barker thus resumes the critique of Stalinism, which he started in *Claw* (1975), from the perspective of his exploration of the individual's instincts and passions.

Hated Nightfall was called "Barker's most accessible play in years" by Michael Billington,[50] a fact which the author emphatically denied. Compared with *The Bite of the Night*, however, the play's dramaturgical design is conventional. The anonymous centre of power, which exercises control through phone calls and messengers, is a well-worn theatrical device. The repetition of the emissaries' interventions and their killing by Dancer turns pathos into bathos. Neo-expressionist stage symbolism overemphasises the portentous meaning of actions such as the Prince's pouring of a dark, blood-like liquid from a watering can over the wedding cake at the end of the play. The chorus emerging from trap doors in order to lend a voice to Party ideology, just like the protagonist's blinding at the end, are laborious attempts to revive stage conventions of the classical tragedy.

14. Und

Und is, like *Judith*, a piece of poetic chamber music, another dance of death, which locks victim and executioner in a lethal erotic embrace. For in this monodrama the Jewish victim's soliloquy is constantly addressed to her absent fascist lover. The protagonist, Und, relates all the increasingly threatening happenings of the play to him although they could be performed by any Nazi hooligan. He becomes the screen of her projections, which are desperate attempts to cope with an unprecedented situation.

Her stream of consciousness reveals her state of mind. The mirror on the stage, which reflects her face, thus making it visible for the audience, leaves no doubt that this is a confrontation with herself, a scrutiny of the self in the extremity of catastrophe. The speaker's unusual name Und – the German word for 'and' – refers to the protagonist's dual nature: she is an aristocrat and a Jew. Only after some time does she involuntarily confess the latter fact: “I’m not an aristocrat I’m a Jew”.[51] Her name also suggests her terrible insignificance as an individual.

Und is waiting for an admirer. As she intimates through casual remarks such as “he gathers Jews” (211) or “The Jews exhaust him probably” (214), he is a Nazi. What begins as the preparation of tea for two, a meeting of lovers, turns into the nightmare of a pogrom, the siege of her house with circumstances recalling the ‘Reichskristallnacht’. This is indicated by a climax of more and more threatening events from the tempestuous ringing of the door bell to the smashing of windows with bricks, arson, stifling smoke and brutal hammering at the door.

The description of her lover as a man who has braved death undaunted, confronted “hoops of tungsten razor sharp” and “clouds of toxin” (212) and who admired the beauty of the spectacle of battle and bombardment, expresses her reverence for this model of masculinity and vigour. She repeats parts of the portrait like a refrain during her soliloquy. Und’s impossible fascination with the enemy, a functionary from the highest ranks in the Nazi hierarchy, is rooted in her aristocratic self. In her eyes, it is the attraction of two superior minds to each other. Her aristocratic ideal of virility coincides with fascist ideology. As an aristocrat, she is convinced of her superiority by birth, a concept similar to the idea of the master race in Nazi ideology. She regularly interrupts her soliloquy to give orders to her servants. The traditional aristocratic attitude of superiority to the norms of morality and social conventions makes her tolerant of Nazi terror and violence even when they are directed against herself. She is aware that aristocratic self-fulfilment was to a large extent founded on the transgression against moral law. Despite the empirical evidence of barbarous outbreaks of brutal violence she still extols

> the deliberation of a disciplined and beautiful mind which was able to contemplate its own extinction walking walking walking into the mouth of death as if in summer streets he saw a café with a green tin table and passing between trams dreamed a coffee dreamed a cigarette just such an attitude of mind characterises the way in which those bricks are thrown (218).

She pretends that her lover has as exquisite manners as she herself. She is impressed by his authority and extols his composure many times. His contempt of death and thus of life becomes a model for her in her extremity. To the terror of interminable bell ringing, hammering at her door and the smashing of her windows with bricks she responds with a perfectly composed and elegantly written letter of apology, which she has delivered to her invisible partner on a silver tray. When the answer only contains the word 'Jew' she recognises in the exchange "[t]he strange communication of distinguished minds" (228). She employs all her refined knowledge of the subtleties of social convention and etiquette to transform in her thoughts the brutality of the attacks on her house into well-mannered acts. Even towards the end she still talks about "the ineffable / Refinement / Of his ringing" (230).

All along, she keeps up the pretence of the initial situation. She remembers her wish to seduce him. In her discourse, she even transforms the aggressions she suffers into erotic gestures. She compares his ringing to a kiss and pretends that "[t]he siege is desire / Desire / Expressed / As / Rage" (216).

Up to the last instant, she vacillates between sudden glimpses of the truth and desperate attempts at self-delusion in order to protect herself from an unbearable reality. By excusing her lover, she attempts to preserve her self-esteem. Her transformation of the brutal instincts and anarchic violence unleashed by fascism into order, self-discipline and virility ironically exposes the working of Nazi ideology. Her collusion with her torturer also originates in incredulity with regard to events of unprecedented inhumanity. This is another reason for the incredible "patience of the Jews" which Und evokes (215).

Her ordeal leads her into a state of increasing psychic and physical dissolution and humiliation. She is abandoned by her servants, stifled by smoke, undressed because of the heat, drenched by sordid liquid and so exhausted that she finally cries. When she is sent tea and flowers on the ominous trays which link her with the world outside, she once more believes in the invisible man's love in spite of all. But when she is finally sent a symbolic heap of earth, she can no longer fend off the insight that her idyll is over and that "[t]his man intends to murder me" (234). Her disillusionment signifies her death for she now admits that meeting him will be meeting her death. Anticipating this she at last decides to open the door with the words "I died on seeing / On seeing died / Let him in" (238).

No historic victim-executioner relationship has been as intensely analysed as that between the Jew and the Nazi fascist. Therefore, Barker's reflection on the seductiveness of fascism cannot discover anything new,[52] nor does his exposure of Jewish collusion provide a new insight into the abysses of human nature. By focusing on a Jewish victim who is fascinated by her Nazi torturer and shares his ideals of masculinity and superiority, the play suggests a common ground between aristocratic beliefs and ideals and the Jewish belief in being the chosen people on the one hand and fascist racism on the other. This certainly goes against the grain of the traditional audience expectation and distribution of sympathy. In showing the protagonist's rhetorical transformation of brutal terrorism and anarchic violence into virility, courage and order, the play moreover deconstructs the glossy surface of official Nazi ideology. It thus could be said to bear a political message – an idea the author would probably hate.

15. Barker's Influence

In comparison with some of his earlier plays such as *The Bite of the Night* or *The Last Supper,* the form of *Und* is relatively conventional. Nevertheless, it can be maintained that Barker's destruction of the traditional concept of drama in the eighties prepared the ground for the non-mimetic texts which emerged in the British theatre of the nineties. His repudiation of social realism, the fragmented action, the unpredictable characters and their rejection of rationality and morality in his plays never ceased to provoke the critics. His plays, however, were still based on characters, dialogues and conflicts, still distinguished between the spoken text and stage directions, between what is to be acted and what to be narrated on stage. Not so the radically epic, post-dramatic texts by younger playwrights such as Martin Crimp's *Attempts on her Life* (1997) or Sarah Kane's *Cleansed* (1998), *Crave* (1998) and *4.48 Psychosis* (2000), which lacked the features that constitute traditional drama. And yet they were enthusiastically acclaimed by large audiences.

Although the intention behind Sarah Kane's first plays was satirical enlightenment and not the bewildering deconstruction of moral values and rationality as in the Theatre of Catastrophe, certain aspects of her dramaturgy strongly recall Barker's plays. Her texts similarly explore human passions, drives and instincts, which are freed from the fetters of rationality and morality. Moreover, representations of physical and psychic pain in *Blasted* or *Cleansed* are as relentless as in Barker's plays. Kane too, enquires into the relationship between the desires, sexuality and aggression of individuals in the domestic sphere and the horrors of war. Like Barker, she returns to the model of tragedy, similarly excluding catharsis (*Phaedra's Love*). She also explores the ambiguities of the relationship between torturer and tortured in *Blasted* (Ian – Cate) and in *Cleansed* (Tinker – Grace; Tinker – Carl and Rod), which happens to be located in a university just as *The Bite of the Night*. In *Cleansed* she investigates the loss of the self, the loss of dignity caused by the catastrophe of love. Both in Barker's and in Kane's plays the human body becomes a central means of dramatic expression. Thus, the progressive mutilation of Carl as punishment, depriving him of all means of the bodily expression of his homosexual love in *Cleansed*, recalls the social chastisement of Helen in *The Bite of the Night*, in which her body is gradually reduced to a torso. That these parallels are not entirely fortuitous is supported by the fact that when asked in an interview for the authors who had the greatest influence on her work, Kane named Harold Pinter, Howard Barker and Edward Bond.[53] Dan Rebellato reports that during her studies in Bristol she performed in Barker's *Victory*,[54] playing the role of Bradshaw, the regicide's widow, who attempts to recover the parts of her husband which were disinterred and desecrated by the Royalists. According to Rebellato she also wished to play the character of Skinner, the uncompromising feminist witch in *The Castle*, who, demonised and tortured, finally conquers the key to the centre of male power.

As Sarah Kane's admiration of Barker's work illustrates, box office success is not an adequate measure of the influence of a dramatist's work. Barker's dwindling presence in the British theatre, mentioned at the beginning of this essay, says nothing about the reputation of his work amongst actors and academics. The Wrestling School's annual production of a new play is ritually welcomed by a group of fervent connoisseurs and commands the respect of the more enlightened critics. Moreover, the renown of his work abroad considerably augmented during the nineties, an increase evident in the growing number of productions of his works on the European continent, the organisation of Barker festivals and his invitation to symposia. Just to name a few instances: in connection with the production of *Scenes from an Execution* he was the guest of honour of the Esslinger Theatertage in 1994. English productions of *The Castle*, *Judith* and *Hated Nightfall* were invited to Berlin, Paris, Lille and Copenhagen in 1995. In May 1998 the Kunsten Festival des Arts in Brussels featured his work. *Scenes from an Execution*, his most popular play, was produced in the United States, France, Germany, Belgium and Israel. And Vienna saw the premiere of *He Stumbled* in 1999.

Notes

1 Wrestling School (n.d.).
2 Barker (1993).
3 E.g. Rabey (1989) and Lamb (1997); *Alternatives théâtrales* 57, 1998 and *Gambit* 41, 1984 are special issues devoted to Howard Barker.
4 Arranged by the RSC in the early nineties.
5 Cf. Shaughnessy (1989). According to the Wrestling School's home page, the company has presented Barker's texts in productions, workshops, and public readings to over 56,000 people.
6 Barker (1993: 112).
7 *Ibid.*, 120.
8 "I suppose I really think that if art is to carry any power and conviction, it cannot reiterate what I regard as exhausted forms." (Barker 1986: 336)
9 The issue is analysed by Peter Paul Schnierer (1994: 95–105 and 121–157).
10 See Lamb (1997), which contains an extensive analysis of the play.

11 Barker (1988b: 2, emphasis in the text). Further references to this edition will be included in the text.
12 Barker (1988a: 2, emphasis in the text). Further references to this edition will be included in the text.
13 See also Zimmermann (1999).
14 Greek *kata* (down) *streffein* (turn). Aristotle never used the term in relation to tragedy.
15 For the historian, 'catastrophe' signifies the overthrow of an order, a balance of different forces. 'Catastrophism' as a model of explaining history understands historical change not as evolution but as disruption and discontinuity of power systems (*OED*, sv. 'catastrophe' [3] and 'catastrophism').
16 Barker (1993: 167, 172).
17 *Ibid.*, 166.
18 *Ibid.*, 144.
19 *Ibid.*, 112–113.
20 *Ibid.*, 52.
21 Reprinted *ibid.*, 43.
22 Zimmermann (1995: 13).
23 Barker (1984:24–25).
24 Barker (1993: 23).
25 Horkheimer & Adorno (1969: 246–247), Foucault (1975).
26 Barker (1985: 4).
27 Barker (1993: 97).
28 *Ibid.*, 72.
29 Zimmermann (2001).
30 Barker (1993: 113).
31 In this as in numerous other respects Barker's theatre resembles that of Brecht, even if he does not admit it.
32 Barker (1993: 147).
33 When Barker rejects pity, he is opposing the Christian appropriation of Aristotle.
34 Barker (1993: 113).
35 *Ibid.*, 171.
36 *Ibid.*, 166, emphasis in the text.
37 Lamb (1997) extensively discusses the importance of postmodern philosophy for Howard Barker's conception of the theatre.
38 I do not share Günther Klotz's opinion in "Howard Barker. Paradigm of Postmodernism" (1991).
39 Lacan (1977) and (1979).
40 For the importance of poetic language in Barker's conception of drama see Lamb (1997: the chapter "Seduction of Language") and Reitz (1997: 255).
41 Michel Foucault warned of this in his archaeology of the discourse of sexuality, cf. Foucault (1976).
42 *Scenes from an Execution* won the Sony Award for the best Radio Play of 1984 and became his most widely produced play of the nineties – much to the author's discomfort, as he no longer shares its position and presented a new version in his production of 1999.
43 Barker (1990: 28). Further references to this edition will be included in the text.
44 See Sakellaridou (1998) for an analysis of the importance of the visual, the *tableau* in Barker's recent plays, especially in *Judith*. The protagonist of *No End*

of Blame (1981) is also an artist and Holbein figures among the dramatis personae of *Brutopia*.
45 Cf. Barker (1992).
46 Charles Lamb analyses the play from the aspect of seduction, cf. Lamb (1997).
47 Barker (1994: 6). Further references to this edition will be included in the text.
48 In another passage Dancer informs the housekeeper, Jane, "This is not History. This is the opposite of History" (33).
49 Albeit, the Party emissary, talks of "constructing on the ruins of the past a new society" (45).
50 Billington (1994).
51 Barker (2001: 218). Further references to this edition of the play will be included in the text.
52 Cf. Theweleit (1977/1978).
53 Interview in Tabert (1998: 18).
54 Rebellato (1999).

Bibliography

Alternatives théâtrales 57, 1998 [special issue on Howard Barker].
Barker, Howard: "To me History is always Contemporary", *Radio Times*, 13 September 1984.
–: *The Power of the Dog*, London, 1985.
–: "Oppression, Resistance, and the Writer's Testament", *New Theatre Quarterly* 2, 1986, 336–344.
–: *The Bite of the Night*, London, 1988a.
–: *The Last Supper*, London, 1988b.
–: *The European & Judith*, London, 1990.
–: "The Truth behind Goya's Grin", *The Guardian International*, 8 July 1992.
–: *Arguments for a Theatre*, Second edition, London, 1993.
–: *Hated Nightfall & Wounds to the Face*, London, 1994.
–: *Collected Plays 5*, London, 2001.
Billington, Michael: Review of *Hated Nightfall*, *The Guardian*, 14 March 1994.
Foucault, Michel: *Surveiller et punir*, Paris, 1975.
–: *La Volonté de savoir*, Paris, 1976.
Gambit. International Theatre Review 41, 1984 [special issue on Howard Barker].
Horkheimer, Max & Theodor W. Adorno: *Die Dialektik der Aufklärung*, Frankfurt, 1969.
Kane, Sarah: *Complete Plays*, London, 2001.
Klotz, Günther: "Howard Barker. Paradigm of Postmodernism", *New Theatre Quarterly* 5, no. 7, 1991, 20–26.
Lacan, Jacques: *Ecrits*. Trans. Alan Sheridan, London, 1977.
–: *The Four Fundamental Concepts of Psychoanalysis*. Trans. Alan Sheridan, Harmondsworth, 1979.
Lamb, Charles: *Howard Barker's Theatre of Seduction*, Amsterdam, 1997.
Rabey, David Ian: *Howard Barker. Politics and Desire*, London, 1989.
Rebellato, Dan: "Sarah Kane. An Appreciation", *New Theatre Quarterly* 59, 1999, 280–281.

Reitz, Bernhard: "*Granite Crucibles*. The Theatre of Howard Barker". – In Uwe Böker & Hans Sauer (Eds.): *Anglistentag 1996, Dresden. Proceedings*, Trier, 1997, pp. 251–258.

Sakellaridou, Elisabeth: "La Qualité pictorale des pièces récentes", *Alternatives théâtrales* 57, 1998, 69–73.

Schnierer, Peter Paul: *Rekonventionalisierung im englischen Drama. 1980–1990*, Tübingen, 1994.

Shaughnessy, Robert: "Howard Barker, the Wrestling School, and the Cult of the Author", *New Theatre Quarterly* 5, no. 19, 1989, 264–271.

Tabert, Nils (Ed.): *Playspotting. Die Londoner Theaterszene der 90er*, Hamburg, 1998.

Theweleit, Klaus: *Männerphantasien*, 2 vols., Frankfurt, 1977/1978.

Wrestling School: "Howard Barker", http://home.aol.com/wrestles/barker.htm, date of access: 7 November 2001.

Heiner Zimmermann: "Die Wiedergeburt des Theaters aus dem Geist der Katastrophe", *Hard Times* 53, 1995, 8–15.

–: "Howard Barker's Appropriation of Classical Tragedy", – In Savas Patsalidis & Elizabeth Sakellaridou (Eds.): *(Dis)Placing Classical Greek Theatre*, Thessaloniki, 1999, pp. 359–375.

–: "Howard Barker's Brecht or Brecht as Whipping Boy". – In Bernhard Reitz & Heiko Stahl (Eds.): *What Revels are in Hand? Assessments of Contemporary Drama in English in Honour of Wolfgang Lippke*, CDE Studies 8, Trier, 2001, pp. 221–227.

Contributors' Addresses

Mark Berninger, Johannes-Gutenberg-Universität Mainz, Seminar für Englische Philologie, Abteilung Anglistik, Jakob-Welder-Weg 18, 55099 Mainz (Germany).

Raimund Borgmeier, Justus-Liebig-Universität Giessen, Institut für Anglistik und Amerikanistik, Otto-Behagel-Str. 10, 35394 Giessen (Germany).

Christopher Innes, York University, Department of English, 47000 Keele Street, North York, Ontario M3J 1P3 (Canada).

Mary Luckhurst, University of York, Department of English, Heslington, York Y010 5DD (United Kingdom).

Klaus-Peter Müller, Universität Stuttgart, Institut für Literaturwissenschaft, Neuere Englische Literatur, Keplergasse 17, 70174 Stuttgart (Germany).

Michael Raab, Fregestraße 22, 04105 Leipzig (Germany).

Bernhard Reitz, Johannes-Gutenberg-Universität Mainz, Seminar für Englische Philologie, Abteilung Anglistik, Jakob-Welder-Weg 18, 55099 Mainz (Germany).

Graham Saunders, 'Bleak House', 10 Hagley Villas, Balsall Heath, Birmingham, West Midlands B12 8DF (United Kingdom).

Aleks Sierz, 29 Arlingford Road, London SW2 2SR (United Kingdom).

Heiko Stahl, Johannes-Gutenberg-Universität Mainz, Seminar für Englische Philologie, Abteilung Anglistik, Jakob-Welder-Weg 18, 55099 Mainz (Germany).

Heiner Zimmermann, Ruprecht-Karls-Universität Heidelberg, Anglistisches Seminar, Kettengasse 12, 69117 Heidelberg (Germany).

